Bill Clinton's
Pre-presidential Career

Recent Titles in
Bibliographies and Indexes in American History

Judaica Americana: A Bibliography of Publications to 1900
Robert Singerman, compiler

Shield of Republic/Sword of Empire: A Bibliography of United States Military
Affairs, 1783–1846
John C. Fredriksen, compiler

Biographical Index to American Science: The Seventeenth Century to 1920
Clark A. Elliott, compiler

The Natural Sciences and American Scientists in the Revolutionary Era: A Bibliography
Katalin Harkányi, compiler

Changing Wilderness Values, 1930–1990: An Annotated Bibliography
Joan S. Elbers, compiler

The American Indian Ghost Dance, 1870 and 1890: An Annotated Bibliography
Shelley Anne Osterreich, compiler

The Immigration History Research Center: A Guide to Collections
Suzanna Moody and Joel Wurl, compilers and editors

Sports Ethics in America: A Bibliography, 1970–1990
Donald G. Jones with Elaine L. Daly

Horace Greeley: A Bio-Bibliography
Suzanne Schulze

Roosevelt Research: Collections for the Study of Theodore, Franklin and
Eleanor
DeeGee Lester

The 1960s: An Annotated Bibliography of Social and Political Movements
in the United States
Rebecca Jackson

The Haymarket Affair: An Annotated Bibliography
Robert W. Glenn, compiler

Bill Clinton's Pre-presidential Career

An Annotated Bibliography

Compiled by
Allan Metz

Bibliographies and Indexes in American History, Number 27

Greenwood Press
Westport, Connecticut • London

Library of Congress Cataloging-in-Publication Data

Metz, Allan.
    Bill Clinton's pre-presidential career : an annotated bibliography
/ compiled by Allan Metz.
        p.   cm.—(Bibliographies and indexes in American history,
ISSN 0742–6828 ; no. 27)
    Includes index.
    ISBN 0–313–29285–X (alk. paper)
    1. Clinton, Bill, 1946– —Bibliography. I. Title. II. Series.
Z8176.55.M48   1994
[E886.M]
016.973929—dc20   94–3017

British Library Cataloguing in Publication Data is available.

Copyright © 1994 by Allan Metz

Library of Congress Catalog Card Number: 94–3017
ISBN: 0–313–29285–X
ISSN: 0742–6828

First published in 1994

Greenwood Press, 88 Post Road West, Westport, CT 06881
An imprint of Greenwood Publishing Group, Inc.

Printed in the United States of America

The paper used in this book complies with the
Permanent Paper Standard issued by the National
Information Standards Organization (Z39.48–1984).

10 9 8 7 6 5 4 3 2 1

Dedicated to President Bill Clinton

Contents

Bill Clinton's
Pre-presidential Career

Introduction

Part 1 of this bibliography covers the political
career of Bill Clinton from 1974 to October 3, 1991.
The former date corresponds to Clinton's unsuccessful
bid to win a seat in the U.S. House of Representa-
tives while the latter was the date Clinton
officially announced that he was a candidate for
president. The organization of Part 1 is as follows:
Writings By and Printed Speeches of Bill Clinton;
Early Political Career in Arkansas, 1974-1978
(including the unsuccessful 1974 campaign for
representative and his term as Arkansas attorney
general, 1976-1978); First Term as Governor,
1978-1980 (including the Ft. Chaffee Cuban refugee
crisis, which contributed to his upset loss in the
1980 gubernatorial election to Republican Frank
White); Out of Office, 1980-1982 (including analyses
of the 1980 Clinton loss and Clinton's political
comeback in 1982); Second Term as Governor, 1982-1984
(including an educational reform program); Third Term
as Governor, 1984-1986 (including the Grand Gulf
nuclear power plant controversy); Fourth Term as
Governor, 1986-1990 (including speculation in 1987 on
his possible entry as a presidential candidate and
his nominating speech for Michael Dukakis at the 1988
Democratic National Convention); and Fifth Term as
Governor, 1990-1992, abbreviated due to Clinton's
victory in the 1992 presidential election. A major
focus of Clinton's writings as well as analyses of
his governorship in Arkansas is on the subject of
educational reform, especially the controversial
provision of mandatory testing for teachers. As for
the chronological scope of this section, while the
period covered is up to October 3, 1991 (when

Clinton announced that he was running for president),
assessments of his Arkansas record as governor
following this date also are covered.² For legal
cases during Clinton's term as Arkansas attorney
general (1976-1978), Lexis is recommended. An
indispensable source for newspaper accounts about
Clinton in Arkansas and later on the national level
are the Arkansas Gazette (which ceased publication in
October 1991 and has detailed annual indexes), the
Arkansas Democrat, and the product of a merger
between these two newspapers--the Arkansas
Democrat-Gazette, beginning October 19, 1991.

Part Two covers the 1992 Clinton presidential
campaign (October 4, 1991-November 3, 1992) and is
arranged in these sections: Newspapers (including a
subsection on entries for the Arkansas Times which
became a weekly newspaper beginning in May 1992. It
was previously a monthly magazine so articles in this
format are annotated separately), Specialized
Political Journals, Conservative Political Magazines,
Financial/Economic Oriented Magazines, Articles on
Early Democratic Presidential Candidates, and
Annotated Entries. This last section consists
primarily of magazine and journal articles with some
exceptions. Entries 269, 271 and 272 are for books
and are located at the beginning of the 1992 entries,
before articles dated 1992. The only newspaper
entries in this section are found in entries 387 and
392-395 because they constituted a special New York
Times series on "Clinton as Governor" and thus
warranted separate treatment.

Part Three is on the transition period
(November 4, 1992-January 19, 1992).³ Its
arrangement is similar to that of Part 2 as follows:
Newspapers (again including a subsection on the
Arkansas Times since Clinton is from Arkansas),
Specialized Political Journals, Conservative
Political Magazines, and Financial/Economic Oriented
Magazines. This last section includes a subsection
on the Economist and is followed by sections on the
Nation's Cities Weekly and National Catholic
Reporter. This variation in format (when compared to
Part 2) is due to the different nature of the subject
matter--campaign vs. transition. Articles on the
campaign tended to be more substantive while those
written during the transition by nature were more
speculative in anticipation of the new
administration. The transition pieces were more
repetitive, reflecting a lesser amount of news
compared to the campaign. Articles for these
periodicals were annotated separately in Part 2.
The final section of Part 3 is Annotated Entries,

which, like Part 2, consists primarily of magazine
and journal articles. Pertinent books published in
1993 are found in entries 1042 and 1044-1049 located
before entries for articles dated 1993. The book has
been arranged as much as possible in chronological
order, although occasionally the inclusion of
sections and collective annotations (a listing of
citations followed by a corresponding annotation) has
not always made this possible. Despite these few
necessary exceptions, however, the book has
maintained its guiding principle of chronological
order. In turn, entries for the same date are
arranged alphabetically. Entry access is facilitated
by detailed author and subject indexes. Additional
information on President Clinton may be attained from
Journal Graphics, Inc. TV/Radio transcripts service,
which includes indexes entitled "Clinton, Bill."

It is hoped that the citations contained in
this bibliography will provide insights into the
current administration based on President Clinton's
previous political history as he endeavors to change
the nation's direction, reinvent government, and lead
the United States into the next century by dealing
with the great economic and political challenges he
and the nation faces.[4] I would like to acknowledge
the staffs and librarians of the following libraries
for their reference assistance: University of
Arkansas libraries, Elizabeth McKee and Andrea
Cantrell in particular; Library of Congress,
especially the Periodicals Division; University of
Illinois (at Urbana-Champaign) libraries; Southwest
Missouri State University library; Springfield-Greene
County Public Library and its Brentwood branch; F.W.
Olin Library of Drury College, particularly Craig
Smith and Katherine Miller; and Peter Browning, also
from Drury College. Special thanks to Cynthia Harris
of Greenwood Press for her encouragement and support
of this project.

--November 1993--

Notes

1. In addition to the annotated citations on
teacher testing contained in the bibliography, see
"Arkansas Overhauling Its Education System," New York
Times, November 20, 1983, 62; "Too Much Zeal"
(Editorial), December 17, 1983, 382-383; Ellie
McGrath, "No More Dragging Up the Rear: Arkansas Bows
to Pressures to Put Schools to the Test," Time,
December 26, 1983, 77; Vicky Lytle, "The Nation's
Zaniest Test?: Blame It On the Governor," NEA Today
2, (April 1984): 3; Jim Gallagher, "State Makes Waves
With Teacher Test: Arkansas Skills Exam Angers Many

Veterans," Chicago Tribune, February 5, 1984, sec. 1, p. 4; "Boycott Fails as Educators Take Three Rs Test," Los Angeles Times, March 2, 1985, 27; Storer Rowley, "Teachers Forgo Boycott, Take Competency Test in Arkansas," Chicago Tribune, March 24, 1985, sec. 1, p. 3; Storer Rowley, "Teachers' Test Leak Probed," Chicago Tribune, March 25, 1985, A3; "Copies Sold Of Skills Test for Teachers," St. Louis Post-Dispatch, March 26, 1985, A11; "Give All Teachers Competency Tests? Pro and Con: Interview With Governor Bill Clinton, Democrat of Arkansas/Interview With Albert Shanker," U.S. News & World Report, May 6, 1985, 49; "William Bennett, Bill Clinton" (interview), Meet the Press 87, (September 6, 1987): 1-12.

2. For additional assessments of Clinton's Arkansas record, see "Bill Clinton's Homey Charm" (column), Economist, August 3, 1991, 30; Morton Kondracke, "Slick Willy: Bill Clinton, Postliberal Man (cover story), New Republic, 21, 1991, 18, 20-21; Marci McDonald, "The Battle of Arkansas," Maclean's, March 9, 1992: 24-25; Alexander Cockburn, "'Like a Soft Peanut'" (column), Nation, March 23, 1992, 366-367; Goldie Blumenstyk, "Amid Some Grumbling, Clinton Wins Praise For His Reforms of Arkansas Education," Chronicle of Higher Education 38, 34 (April 29, 1992): A23, A26-A27; Bruce Wallace, "Down Home in Clinton's Dixie," Maclean's, July 20, 1992, 26-30; Don L. Boroughs, "Why Arkansas Ranks So High," U.S. News & World Report, September 14, 1992, 66; Christopher Hitchens, "Minority Report (A Visit to Arkansas)" (column), Nation, October 5, 1992, 350; Richard Behar, "Arkansas Pecking Order," Time, October 26, 1992, 52-54; Marshall Frady, "Death in Arkansas: Annals of Law and Politics," New Yorker, February 22, 1993, 105-118, 120-126, 128-133; "The Limits of Success: East Arkansas," Economist, March 6, 1993, 29; Blant Hurt, "Mrs. Clinton's Czarist Past" (column), Wall Street Journal, March 19, 1993, A10; Robert Scheer, "Trouble Still in Forrest City: Clinton's Programs in Arkansas," Nation, March 22, 1993, 370-372, 374.

3. For post-election analyses of the 1992 presidential election, see Allan Metz, "The 1992 U.S. Presidential Election: An Annotated Bibliography," Reference Services Review 21, 4(1993): 37-52, 66.

4. As outlined in Bill Clinton and Al Gore, Putting People First: How We Can All Change America (New York: Times Books, 1992).

1

1974 to Clinton's Announcement for the Presidency, October 3, 1991

WRITINGS BY AND PRINTED SPEECHES OF BILL CLINTON

1   Clinton, Bill. "To the Alienated Americans: A Governor Speaks." Christian Science Monitor, August 27, 1980, 22.   Excerpts from Clinton's speech to the 1980 Democratic convention.   The U.S. was undergoing a "painful time of transition."   It was less competitive and had suffered economic woes like inflation, unemployment, and deficits.   Roosevelt was reelected in 1936 because people believed that he had a vision for the country.   Clinton hoped that the 1980 election would be analogous to 1936.   Democrats called for "economic revitalization" of the country, which would require redefining relations between the federal government, big business, and labor in addition to a renewal of industry and the creation of jobs.   The U.S. economic recovery also required a wise energy and environmental policy.   Clinton wanted to win back alienated middle and upper middle class citizens estranged from the political process, whose inclusion was vital to America's future.

2   Clinton, Bill. "Foreword." In The Governors of Arkansas: Essays in Political Biography, Timothy Paul Donovan and B. Gatewood Jr., eds. Fayetteville: University of Arkansas Press, 1981, ix-x.   While Arkansas' true history was constituted by the efforts of its citizens, the "fortunes of the state have rested with particular responsibility in the hands of those thirty-nine individuals elected by the people to be their governors.   This book tells their collective story."   Clinton also addressed some dilemmas his predecessors faced: "When is it time to

speak loudly and lead, and when is it time to be
silent and listen? When is it necessary to be
unyielding and when is compromise the most productive
course?" This "Foreword" was dated August 19, 1980.

3 Clinton, Bill. "Problems Facing Cities." City &
Town (North Little Rock, Arkansas) 38, 9(October
1982): 5. Letter from Clinton to the Arkansas
Municipal League during his gubernatorial reelection
bid. While some of the problems faced by Arkansas
cities were unique, most were shared by other cities
nationally. In the 1970s, cities had budget problems
due to inflation, which compelled mayors to postpone
capital improvements and large scale maintenance.
Instead, monies were designated for the delivery of
services. For Arkansas cities in the 1980s, streets,
sewers, and water works needed to be dealt with.
Home rule and interlocal cooperation were possible
means to ameliorate such problems.

4 Clinton, Bill. "Excerpts from Speech by Governor
Bill Clinton at the 48th Annual Convention," City &
Town 39, 1(January/February 1983): 6-9. Speech
delivered to the Arkansas Municipal League soon after
Clinton's 1982 election victory. Clinton dealt with
issues important to municipalities such as the state
budget, municipal services, and the spiraling cost of
corrections. Clinton noted that, as attorney
general, he played a major role in passing laws which
required repeat offenders to serve longer sentences
than first-time offenders before being eligible for
parole. Clinton hoped to make the Arkansas
Department of Corrections more self-supporting.
Clinton closed by noting that he needed the support
of the Municipal League to govern effectively.

5 Clinton, Bill. "Arkansas: Challenges and
Opportunities." Inside Arkansas 19, 1/2(Spring/Summer
1983): 4-6. Arkansas faced many challenges and so it
deserved a "government that solves problems and
seizes opportunities, [and]...will fight for the
people's interests and... give them a chance to fight
for themselves." The state needed to generate
greater income by creating more and higher paying
jobs, which was a top priority. The Arkansas
Industrial Development Commission and the promotion
of education could achieve this goal. Accompanied by
two complementary items, one containing brief
biographical information on Clinton and, the other, a
listing and explanation of new laws promoting
economic development.

6 Clinton, Bill. "Arkansas Exports: New Markets, New Methods." Inside Arkansas 20, 3/4 (Fall/Winter 1984): 20-21. Arkansas exports doubled between 1977 and 1984. An important task for state government was developing export potential through innovative promotion of products internationally. A key toward achieving this goal was through coordinated efforts within Arkansas and among neighboring states via the Mid-South Trade Council. State-sponsored overseas export programs should complement national programs. Clinton called for cooperation among states to increase trade and reduce the nation's trade deficit.

7 Clinton, Bill and Hillary Clinton. "Foreword." In Liza Ashley (as told to Carolyn Huber). Thirty Years at the Mansion: Recipes and Recollections. Little Rock: August House, 1985. Photos.

8 Clinton, Bill and Hillary Clinton. "Foreword." In Liza Ashley (as told to Carolyn Huber). Thirty Years at the Mansion: Recipes and Recollections. 2nd ed. Little Rock: August House, 1993. Photos. Bill and Hillary Clinton wrote a complimentary foreword for Liza Ashley, long-time food production manager at the governor's mansion in Little Rock.

9 Clinton, Bill and Richard D. Lamm. "Democrats' Future: Priorities, Discipline." Christian Science Monitor, January 15, 1985, 16. Lamm, then governor of Colorado, wrote this opinion piece with Clinton in response to the Democrats' loss in the 1984 presidential election.

10 Clinton, Bill. "Arkansas' Export Commitment." Business America 8, 2 (January 21, 1985): 20-21. Excerpted version of an article originally published in Inside Arkansas. (See entry 6).

11 Clinton, Bill. "Foreword." In Jerry E. Hinshaw. Call the Roll: The First One Hundred Fifty Years of the Arkansas Legislature. Little Rock, Arkansas: Rose Publishing Company, 1986, pp. vi-vii. Photo. In the foreword (dated September 9, 1985), Clinton characterized this book as a "significant contribution to the Arkansas Sesquicentennial celebration" and to Arkansas political history. Clinton thanked Hinshaw, a state representative to the Arkansas legislature, "for a job well done." In the book itself, Hinshaw discussed Clinton as governor from 1978 to 1986 on pp. 118-124. Includes a bibliography and index.

12   Clinton, Bill. "Interstate 150" (letter). <u>Wall Street Journal</u>, August 20, 1986, 15.   Clinton responded to a <u>Journal</u> story on the Arkansas and Texas sesquincentennial celebrations.   The purpose of the Arkansas event was not to outdo Texas.   Rather, it was to encourage Arkansans to commemorate their past, to learn more about contemporary Arkansas, and to contemplate its future direction.

13   Clinton, Bill. "Who Will Manage the School?" <u>In Time for Results: The Governors' 1991 Report on Education</u>. Washington, D.C.: National Governors' Association (NGA), Center for Policy Research and Analysis, August 1986, 10-11.   Clinton served as co-chairman for this report and chaired the NGA's Task Force on Leadership and Management.   He wrote the "Chairman's Summary" for the task force, whose theme was educational leadership.

14   Clinton, Bill. "Without Strong Leaders, Schools Fail." <u>USA Today</u>, August 28, 1986, A8.   Clinton continued with the theme of leadership in education as a "guest columnist."   Clinton's basic premise was that: "Strong leaders create strong schools." Administrators could promote school reform by requiring higher standards and creating conditions so that changes may occur.   Clinton outlined three challenges for education: match state training and certification requirements to the skills school administrators require for effectiveness, offer incentives and technical help to districts to foster "school cite management and school renewal," and formulate a system for an accurate evaluation of principals and reward principals and schools for their effective performance.

15   Clinton, Bill. "Who Will Manage the Schools?" <u>Phi Delta Kappan</u> 68, 4(November 1986): 208-210.   On the role of the principal in American schools.

16   Clinton, Bill and others. "Jobs, Growth & Competitiveness." <u>Making America Work: Productive People, Productive Policies</u>. Washington, D.C.: National Governors' Association, 1987.   Clinton wrote a "Chairman's Overview," (pp. vi-ix) calling for welfare and education reform, public service, and making the American labor force more competitive in the world market.   "'America won't work if Americans can't work, or learn, or believe in...tomorrow.'"

17   Clinton, Bill. "Making America Work Again." <u>Association Management</u> 39, 1(January 1987): 44, 46.

Published by the American Society of Association
Executives, to which Clinton belongs. America can
work for all its citizens only if ways can be found
"for Americans to be able to work and to have work."
Compounding America's loss of its competitive edge in
international trade were five obstacles to work
nationally: welfare dependency, teen pregnancy, adult
illiteracy, school dropouts, and substance abuse.
Clinton urged the overcoming of these barriers.

18 Clinton, Bill. State of the State Speech:
Governor Bill Clinton, January 13, 1987. Little Rock:
Office of the Governor, 1987. Clinton called on
Arkansans to continue the progress made in economic
development and education. Arkansas had moved
"forward, toward better schools and better jobs,
because of our willingness to change, to progress,
and to pay the price of doing it."

19 Clinton, Bill. Making Arkansas Work: Good
Beginnings, Good Schools, Good Jobs, State of the
State Address, Monday, January 19, 1987. "Good
beginnings" included the establishment of a state
health care program concentrating on infants and
pregnant women, strengthening child support
enforcement, and developing programs for early
childhood education. Under the rubric of "Good
schools" were such provisions as funding to complete
implementation of public school standards, create a
school drop-out prevention program, coordinate
substance abuse prevention programs in public
schools, integrate programs for the incorporation of
volunteers in public school districts, make
improvements in vocational/technical education, focus
and coordinate state and local skills training
programs for workers in Arkansas, and expand programs
to offer adult Arkansans the chance to attain the
fundamental education skills they need. Under the
category of "Good jobs," provisions included
implementation of welfare reform, establish industry
support and development, and encourage the
development and growth of small business.

20 Clinton, William. "The Common Agenda: Liberating
Undreamed-of Talent." Journal of State Government
(The Council of State Governments) 60, 2(March-April
1987): 61-63. The U.S. required a significantly more
productive economy and education system. Schools had
to be restructured and educational leadership had to
meet the challenges produced by change.

21 Clinton, Bill. "The Common Agenda: Liberating

Undreamed-of Talent." In Restructuring Education, Highlights of a Conference. Melissa Berman, ed. Washington, D.C.: August 1987. ED 296 081. See citation 20 for annotation.

22 Clinton, Bill, Robert E. Johnston, Walter W. Nixon III and Sam Bratton. "FERC, State Regulators, and Public Utilities: A Tilted Balance?" Natural Resources & Environment 2, 4(Spring 1987): 11-14, 43-46. There were two fundamental issues which utility regulators and the judiciary had to deal with: striking the correct balance between federal and state regulation and that between the interests of shareholders and ratepayers. While these were not new issues, they did have an added sense of urgency. The Federal Energy Regulatory Commission (FERC) had maintained policies which shifted the balance against state utility regulation and consumers. In a similar vein, the federal judiciary not only had approved of more federal preemption of state regulation, but also had encouraged FERC to guarantee profits to investors at the ratepayers' expense. This is a legal technical article.

23 Clinton, Bill. "Strengthening Our Nation: The Delicate Balance Between Equality and Excellence." AACJC Journal 57, 6(June-July 1987): 12-16. Speech delivered on April 25, 1987 to the AACJC (American Association of Community and Junior Colleges) Annual Convention in Dallas, Texas. Clinton outlined what he believed were two basic problems the U.S. faced--economic and people problems. The former included insufficient economic policies, trade and government deficits, Third World debt, and high interest rates. Insufficient "people policies" included inadequate education and training, which hindered America's ability to compete internationally. Clinton identified five barriers which prevented people from reaching their potential: adult illiteracy, teenage pregnancy, school dropouts, drug abuse, and welfare dependency. Community colleges represented the point where economic and people policies merged. Concerning the future of community colleges, Clinton listed four keys: better funding; even more flexibility in educational curricula and training programs; a willingness to innovate, achieving a balance between quality and equality; and encouraging the federal government to assume a leadership role with business in changing the whole American education and training system. Clinton also indicated his support for the Reagan administration's Jobs 2000 Project, which merged the

unemployment system with job training.

24 Clinton, Bill. Speaking of Leadership. Denver:
Education Commission of the States (ECS), July 1987.
ED 305 745. This report underlined Clinton's belief
that leadership constituted a distinctive and
necessary aspect of educational reform and elaborated
on much of Clinton's thought concerning leadership.

25 Clinton, Bill. "Undergraduate Education in an
Increasingly Complex World." Phi Kappa Phi Journal
67, 3(Summer 1987): 43-44. The U.S. historically has
counted on education "to meet the challenges of
social and economic change." The American
educational system faces two major economic and
social changes--international competition and student
demography. In this context, Clinton made the
following recommendations to state and educational
leaders concerning students: better preparation for
college, improve overall rates of college attendance
and graduation, and utilization of assessment for
greater accountability to enhance student and school
performance. To achieve these goals, Clinton called
for a "new form of collaboration between state...,
education..., and community leaders...."

26 Clinton, Bill. "Bill Clinton, Governor of
Arkansas." In Securing Our Future: The Report of the
National Forum for Youth at Risk. Washington, D.C.,
1988, 7, 10-12. ED 305 207. Excerpts from major
speeches delivered at this Forum. In an introductory
statement, Clinton noted that one of the main
difficulties confronting the U.S. was an increasing
number of young students at risk of school failure.
To deal with this issue, as 1986-87 chair of the
Education Commission of the States (ECS), Clinton
convened a National Forum on Youth At Risk,
co-sponsored by ECS and the Interstate Migrant
Education Council, in Washington, D.C. on December
10-12, 1987. This report summarizes the
deliberations of the conference, emphasizing that it
was essential for America's economic security to
attain educational excellence. Regarding Clinton's
remarks, youth at risk may be America's major
educational and social issue. Not enough national
attention had been given to at-risk students. All
states needed a focused assertive strategy to involve
parents in the future of their at-risk children.
Clinton cited as an example the HIPPY (Home
Instruction Program for Preschool Youngsters)
project, which was adapted from Israel.

27 Clinton, Bill. "Foreword." In Marvin E. DeBoer. Dreams of Power & the Power of Dreams: The Inaugural Addresses of the Governors of Arkansas. Fayetteville: University of Arkansas Press, 1988. In his brief foreword, Clinton noted what this compilation represents. "The great importance of the unification of past policies and principles of our state's leaders lies not only in its ability to provide an even greater understanding of our state's proud past, but also in its ability to reflect the dreams and hopes of all Arkansans for a better tomorrow." Each chapter begins with a brief biography of the governors prior to their inaugural speeches. The first, second, and third inaugural addresses of Governor Clinton are contained in this volume.

28 Clinton, Bill. "The Mission of Colleges of Education." In The Professional Imperative: Educational Excellence for All. David S. Martin, ed. Selected papers from the 1987 Annual Meeting of the American Association of Colleges for Teacher Education, 1988. ED 291 729. Speech given by Clinton as Chairman of the Education Commission of the States. Clinton called for cooperation and coordination among all education groups, political leaders, and the private sector. He expressed great hope for the part that colleges of teacher education could play in overcoming educational challenges. A willingness to change was the key. In this context, Clinton called for restructuring the curriculum and teaching leadership skills. The work done in colleges of education would be instrumental in helping meet the economic challenges faced by the U.S. into the next century.

29 Clinton, Bill. Moving Arkansas Forward into the 21st Century: Legislative Program for the 77th General Assembly. Little Rock, 1988. Clinton based his program on the following points. Arkansas' future depended on investment in its people and economic development. The federal government was not going to make such an investment. An increase in taxes was necessary for investment in Arkansas in the areas of education--public education and higher education (including accountability and efficiency, and vocational training); human resources (preventative health care for mothers and infants, adolescents, family preservation, and other health care issues); communities (economic development, environmental issues); and law enforcement.

30 Clinton, Bill. "Reforming Welfare." Proceedings,

Institute of Politics, 1987-88. Cambridge, Mass.:
John F. Kennedy School of Government, Harvard
University, 1988. The inaugural program of the
Center for Health and Human Resources Policy of the
John F. Kennedy School of Government was a panel
discussion, "The Politics of Welfare Reform," held on
November 5, 1987, co-sponsored by the Institute of
Politics. Among the panelists were, besides Clinton,
Delaware Governor Mike Castle, Blanche Bernstein,
author of The Politics of Welfare Reform: The New
York Experience, and Harvard Professor Nathan Glazer.
Clinton's remarks consisted of edited excerpts from
that panel round table. The welfare debate has
centered on the means to get more recipients of
welfare into jobs and simultaneously to assist
at-risk children. The National Governors'
Association's Welfare Reform Task Force made the
following recommendations: mandate that all welfare
recipients sign a state contract indicating the
responsibilities incurred in return for the money
they received; require all recipients with a child
over three years old, for the money allocated, to be
a participant in a program of education, training and
work; and, the state's responsibilities were to carry
out these provisions. Clinton also noted differences
between the federal government and Congress over
various issues vis-à-vis welfare reform.

31 Clinton, Bill. "Unnecessary Losses: How to Avoid
Them." Public Management 70, 1(January 1988): 3-6.
Clinton made a special presentation to an annual
conference of state and local officials held in
Montreal in 1987. The Reagan administration dealt
with economic problems in an inconclusive manner.
The U.S. became the largest debtor nation in the
world. There was a proportionally higher percentage
of the budget spent on defense, entitlements, and
interest on the debt while there was a decrease in
"'discretionary nondefense spending'" (investment in
infrastructure, the environment, and education).
More investment in discretionary nondefense spending
was necessary if the economy was to improve and
prosper. State and local government, in coordination
with the business sector, was in the best position to
promote investment in people since the federal
government had essentially abdicated its
responsibility in this regard by shifting greater
fiscal duties on state and local government.

32 Clinton, Bill. "Teaching to Rebuild the Nation."
AAHE (American Association of Higher Education)

<u>Bulletin</u> 40, 9(May 1988): 3-7. Also available as ED
296 686. Text of the keynote address delivered by
Clinton on March 9, 1988 to the AAHE National
Conference on Higher Education. Higher education
could help reverse America's economic decline, which
was the result, in part, of lower real wages and
median incomes. Clinton emphasized the close
relationship between education and economic
well-being. From this perspective, Clinton made a
number of recommendations regarding the
"college-going" and high school dropout rates, the
need of functionally illiterate workers for
educational assistance, follow-up studies on the
Grant Commission report, greater involvement of
higher education in public education, investments of
research and development in higher education to
promote economic development, and new research to
deal with the problems of the underclass.

33   Clinton, Bill. "America Is Buckling and Leaking."
<u>New York Times</u>, June 24, 1988, A31. "America is
falling apart, literally." Federal budget cuts and
changes in the federal tax law in the 1980s hastened
a decline in infrastructure spending. Infrastructure
would continue to deteriorate without adequate
funding and was "just barely adequate to support our
current level of economic activity." The pace of
infrastructure improvement and investment fell far
short. Decreasing infrastructure investment
eventually would undermine the fruits of private
capital investment. "Disinvestment in public works
is as serious a national problem as the budget and
trade deficits." The nation's economic structure
should be guided by three major principles: increased
expenditures, more local control over infrastructure
expenditures, and greater financing of public works
from those who benefit. These steps were important
because America's future could be compromised.

34   Clinton, Bill. "Prefer the Future to the Present:
American Education, American Competitiveness." <u>Vital
Speeches of the Day</u> 54, 16(July 1, 1988): 560-563.
Clinton presented this address to the Kansas
Democratic State Committee Annual Meeting in Wichita
on February 13, 1988. Clinton discussed the
importance of the 1988 election. He also criticized
Reaganomics and believed that the U.S.'s long-range
economic security was jeopardized due, in part, to a
decrease in real income. It was important to improve
the economy by reducing the deficit, gaining more
economic cooperation in terms of trade from Germany
and Japan, and enhancing economic growth in Latin

America. Compared to other industrial nations, the
U.S. did a poor job of investing in its citizens'
health, education and training, which should be the
Democrats' focus in the 1988 election. For the
Democrats to regain office and for economic recovery,
two basic notions needed to be accepted. One, was
the "idea of community--we are all in this together"
and two, a price still had to be paid for the future.

35 Clinton, Bill. "'America Is Falling Apart,
Literally.'" Nation's Cities Weekly, July 11, 1988,
15. Reprinted from the New York Times, June 24,
1988, A31. (See entry 33).

36 Clinton, Bill and Hillary Rodham Clinton. In
Victor A. Fleming. Real Lawyers Do Change Their
Briefs. Little Rock: Rose Publishing Company, 1989.
The Clintons wrote a foreword for this
humorous/satirical look at lawyers.

37 Clinton, Bill. "The State's Role: Leadership &
Partnership." Adult Learning 1, 1(September 1989):
15-17. In this article, Clinton discussed education
for those in the labor force, noting that continuing
education is essential for the U.S. to be
economically competitive. He noted the educational
partnership in Arkansas between adult educators,
community organizations, economic development teams,
and the private sector. State cooperation with
private business established an "appropriate balance
between long-term investments in basic education and
short-term, market-oriented training and retraining."
States must provide adult educators with the
necessary support to educate the work force, as: "Our
adult educators are at the heart of the states'
efforts to educate and retrain our work force."

38 Clinton, Bill. "Priority Issues for the States as
Educational Reform Continues." Stanford Law & Policy
Review 1, 1(Fall 1989): 5-16. While noting the
efforts made throughout the U.S., including Arkansas,
concerning educational reform, Clinton urged that
improvements in education had to continue in the
following six ways: promotion of school restructuring
to facilitate creative ideas among teachers and
principals to improve education; school choice for
parents and students; expand the number of good
teachers via better compensation and less
restrictions on who can teach (i.e. those who are
qualified and not limited to individuals who take
education courses); expand preschool education
programs; increase the number of students enrolled in

higher education; and expand programs in adult
literacy. This is an academic-oriented article with
46 notes. Clinton also had the distinction of being
the first author for this publication's first issue.

39   Clinton, Bill. "Foreword." In Phillip C.
Schlechty. Schools for the Twentieth-First Century:
Leadership Imperatives for Educational Reform. 1st
ed. San Francisco: Jossey-Bass, 1990, xi-xiii.
Schlechty described and explained the current
situation of education in the U.S. from the "unique
perspective" of a sociologist and offered advice on
"producing positive change" in American education for
the future. Schlechty had worked in Arkansas and
throughout the nation. There was much to agree with
the author regarding school reform and "even when we
disagree with Schlechty, he causes us to think in new
ways about the task before us." This foreword was
dated December 1989.

40   Clinton, Bill. "The Poorly Trained Are Going to
Get Murdered." Fortune 121, 7(March 26, 1990): 149.
Workers with only a high school diploma are "going to
get murdered" economically in the 1990s. Over 50% of
the jobs being created require an education beyond
high school and there was a closer correspondence
between income and education than ever before.
Clinton recommended as a solution "comprehensive
educational institutions" which would fulfill the
role of community college, vocational school,
specific industry training center, and adult
literacy center simultaneously such as Westark
Community College in Fort Smith, Arkansas. The U.S.
was founded on the principle that states would serve
as "laboratories of democracy" so that they could
learn from and borrow each others' innovative ideas
to solving problems. This creative borrowing had not
yet occurred and this situation had to change.

41   Clinton, Bill. "The Changing View From the
Statehouse: An Interview with Governor Bill Clinton."
Change 22, 7(March/April 1990): 71-73. Interview by
Frank Newman (then president of the Education
Commission of the States, a position Clinton held in
1987) on Clinton's background, philosophy of
government, and views on higher education.

42   Clinton, Bill. "Repairing the Family." New
Perspectives Quarterly 7, 4(Fall 1990): 12-15. A
brief introduction notes that since the Reagan
administration abdicated federal responsibility for a
national education policy, state and local

governments had to devise educational strategies of
their own. Clinton was described along with Henry
Cisneros (who also contributed an article) as two of
America's "most future-oriented politicians." Ways
to meet the challenge of educational reform and
challenges faced by public schools were addressed.
This piece was based on a conversation Clinton had
with New Perspectives Quarterly. Clinton's main
point was that the family was the key to public
education and cited the "HIPPY" (Home Instruction
Program for Preschool Youngsters) project in
Arkansas. In return for this government assistance,
both parents and students had to take responsibility
for education. (This article was also reprinted, with
a few minor changes, as "Education and Repairing the
Family," New Perspectives Quarterly 10, 1(Winter
1993):50-51).

43 Clinton, Bill and Michael Castle. "The States and
Welfare Reform." Intergovernmental Perspective 17,
2(Spring 1991): 15-17. Welfare reform was enacted in
October 1988 with the Family Support Act (FSA), which
allowed states to help the poor care for their
children. The legislation enhanced the ability of
states to determine paternity and collect child
support, combined new services to enable welfare
recipients to attain and retain jobs, established a
requirement that recipients participate in such
activities, and provided child care and Medicaid
benefits for one year after a recipient receives a
job. States needed to devise creative ways to get
the greatest results from limited budgets. FSA
offered states a chance to continue to experiment
with new innovative approaches.

44 Clinton, Bill. "Apprenticeship American Style."
Vocational Education Journal 66, 7(October 1991):
22-23. In the 1980s, the income and earnings
potential of low-skilled young workers in the U.S.
declined sharply, as documented in the 1988 Grant
Commission Report. The U.S. lacked a true
"school-to-work system." Clinton proposed an
"American version of European apprenticeships," which
combined vocational and academic high school
education, offered students relevant work experience,
and continued training following graduation. The
benefits of such an apprenticeship program would be:
to increase the pool of skilled workers, close the
labor earnings gap, and provide an incentive for
students to remain in school and avoid a life of
crime, drugs and pregnancy. The National Education
Goals included raising the high school graduate rate

from 72 to 90% by the year 2000.

45   Clinton, Bill. "A Strategy For Foreign Policy:
Assistance to Russia." Vital Speeches of the Day 58,
14(May 1, 1992): 421-425. Transcript of a major
speech on foreign policy addressed to the Foreign
Policy Association in New York on April 1, 1992.
While the focus of the speech was on Russia, Clinton
also referred to other areas of foreign policy such
as Haiti, China, the Middle East, Japan, and Germany.

46   Clinton, Bill. "Election '92: The Democratic
Agenda." Africa Report 37, 5(September/October 1992):
19-20. A new approach in U.S. foreign policy was
needed to foster democracy's consolidation, which was
important for Africa as in other areas of the world.
Clinton also advocated a new approach to foreign aid,
a greater U.N. peace-keeping mandate such as in
Somalia, and a firm position on South Africa until
democracy is established.

47   Clinton, Bill. "Judiciary Suffers Racial, Sexual
Lack of Balance." National Law Journal 15, 9(November
2, 1992): 15-16. Clinton's views on the American
legal system. Clinton reviewed the judicial and
legal positions of the Reagan and Bush years and how
he would change the trends in those administrations
if he were elected (by encouraging a more diverse
judiciary).

48   Clinton, Bill. "A Special Message To
H/CD[Housing/Community Development] Officials."
Journal of Housing 49, 6(November/December 1992):
286-289. Photo. On housing and community development
matters. Clinton expressed appreciation for the
National Association of Housing and Redevelopment and
called for affordable homes, secure neighborhoods,
and community and economic development.

EARLY POLITICAL CAREER IN ARKANSAS: 1974
CONGRESSIONAL BID AND ATTORNEY GENERAL, 1976-1978

49   "Arkansas Professor Wins." New York Times, June
12, 1974,32. UPI byline of June 11. Brief article
noting that Bill Clinton, then a law professor at the
University of Arkansas, won a clear-cut victory over
State Senator Gene Rainwater in the Democratic runoff
election for the Third Congressional District. The
victor was to face Representative John Paul
Hammerschmidt (at that time Arkansas' only Republican
member of Congress) in the November general election.

In the vote tally (with 655 of 694 precincts reporting), Clinton received 37,364 votes as opposed to Rainwater's 16,804.

50 "Professor Wins Runoff in Arkansas." <u>Washington Post</u>, June 12, 1974, A7. Clinton won an easy victory over state Sen. Gene Rainwater in the Democratic primary runoff. In November, Clinton would face four-term Republican Representative John Paul Hammerschmidt, 52, who was first elected in 1966. Early returns indicated that Clinton won about 75% of the vote. The Watergate scandal could help Clinton in the November election. The conservative Hammerschmidt had supported President Nixon and declared that "'the American people are tired of Watergate.'" Hammerschmidt, a good campaigner, appealed to the historically conservative but independent western Arkansas district.

51 Reed, Roy. "Inflation Issue Stressed in Arkansas Race." <u>New York Times</u>, September 5, 1974, 26. Insightful profile of Clinton's first run for national office. As a young challenger, Clinton faced an uphill battle to unseat Rep. Hammerschmidt. With Nixon's resignation prior to the election, Clinton's hopes for victory were diminished. In the campaign, Clinton focused on these issues--inflation, the negligence of congressmen like Hammerschmidt, and Nixon. This article constituted part of a series measuring the impact of the Nixon resignation on the electoral prospects of Republican members of Congress. The article perhaps constituted the first extensive national press coverage Clinton received.

52 McPherson, Myra. "Anti-Aged Bias Termed Insidious And Undefinable Despite the Laws." <u>Washington Post</u>, September 27, 1977, A3. Testimony before the Civil Rights Commission on discrimination against the elderly. Attorney General Clinton was a witness, who "stated that community health clinics often do not serve the elderly."

53 Fisher, George. <u>Fisher</u>. Little Rock, Arkansas: Rose Publishing Co., 1978. The subtitle describes this book: "300 local and national editorial cartoons since 1973 plus 100 caricatures as published in the <u>Arkansas Gazette</u>." Published in the year Clinton was first elected as governor. Clinton was a favorite subject, as well as in subsequent years, for Fisher. Due to Clinton's youth, the political cartoonist usually depicted the new governor as a baby with a large mop of hair riding in a baby carriage.

54   King, Wayne. "Rapidly Growing Arkansas Turns to
Liberal Politicians." New York Times, May 14, 1978,
26.   While Arkansas remained among the country's
poorest states, the "Sun Belt transformation" was
underway and clearly reflected in its growing economy
and the quality of its new group of politicians,
including Clinton who was the "populist-liberal"
frontrunner for governor.   Significant article since
it was one of the first to discuss Clinton and also
place the young politician within the context of
political trends in the "new south."

55   Raines, Howell. "New Faces in Southern Politics:
Women, Young and 'Outsiders.'" New York Times, July
3, 1978, 1, 8.   In this analysis of southern
politics, "the 31-year-old whiz kid of
Arkansas politics" was accorded considerable
coverage.   Clinton's education, youth, progressive
agenda, and wife were all used against him
unsuccessfully by his four senior conservative
opponents in June's Democratic gubernatorial primary.
Clinton, however, interpreted his primary victory not
"'in traditional ideological terms.'"   Instead, he
noted a tendency of southern voters to look to
candidates who reflected the region's growing
aspirations and more tolerant attitudes and who would
transform political life in the south.   Clinton
viewed the vote he received as a "'vindication of
what my wife and I have done and what we hope to do
for the state.'"   Clinton believed he was successful
because Arkansans no longer feared change and aspired
to improve Arkansas.

56   Press, Robert M. "Another 'New Breed' Governor on
Way in Dixie: 'Politician to Watch' Running in
Arkansas." Christian Science Monitor, September 13,
1978, 12.   Predicted Clinton would become the newest
member among progressive southern governors.
Clinton, a "popular young state attorney general,"
had a weak G.O.P. opponent, Lynn Lowe, director of
the Arkansas Republican Party.   There were already
forecasts of Clinton's emergence on the national
Democratic scene, including those of Jack Bass,
coauthor of The Transformation of Southern Politics,
and then Democratic Party Chairman John C. White, who
was very impressed by how Clinton ran George
McGovern's 1972 presidential campaign in Texas.   Even
political opponents, like John Paul Hammerschmidt,
stated that Clinton could have a great future in
politics.   He already had headed Jimmy Carter's
Arkansas presidential campaign.   Clinton recognized
that Arkansans were generally "'very conservative.'"

He did not support stringent gun control and his
campaign literature did not refer to his support of
the Equal Rights Amendment or his campaign efforts
for George McGovern in 1972. To Clinton, politics
was "'exhilarating,'" but he admitted that a lack of
delegating responsibility to others was one of his
weak points. Hammerschmidt criticized Clinton for
viewing government as a "'cure-all'" and his
political ambition. Press closed with speculation on
Clinton's political future.

57 Youngdahl, James E. "New Populist on the Scene."
Mother Jones 3, 9 (November 1978): 10. One of the
earliest articles about Clinton in a national
publication. Clinton was a "maverick" attorney
general "worth watching," who would be an easy winner
in the 1978 Arkansas gubernatorial election. As
attorney general, Clinton opposed utility rate
increases, supported consumer protection, and was
"innovative in anti-trust and criminal justice
programs. But despite a history of labor support,
Clinton has a reputation as a shrewd
politician--during his Carter campaign management, he
vigorously supported right-to-work laws." Youngdahl
wondered if Clinton's populism would survive as his
political career advanced.

FIRST TERM AS GOVERNOR, 1978-1980

58 Alpern, David M. "Fresh Faces of '78." Newsweek,
November 20, 1978, 53. Clinton was an "aggressive
consumer advocate," who sought environmental
protection, lower utility rates, and managed to
defeat an Arkansas equivalent of California's
Proposition 13. The significance of this and other
overviews which included Clinton is that they provide
information and assessments of him in his early
political career, just as he was entering the
national scene via his election as governor in 1978.

59 "New Faces Edge into the National Spotlight:
Impact '78." U.S. News & World Report, November 20,
1978, 32-33. Photo. Among political newcomers in
1978 was Clinton, variously described as a "moderate
liberal elected in conservative Arkansas," a
"political comet" and a "man in a hurry," who
"practices liberal-populist politics."

60 "New Arkansas Governor More than 'Pretty Face.'"
New Orleans Times Picayune, December 11, 1978, sec.
3, p. 4. Photo. While labelled by opponents as

"'just a pretty face,'" Clinton is in fact difficult
to categorize. His background was noted: a former
Senate Foreign Relations Committee employee, a
Vietnam War protester, headed George McGovern's Texas
presidential campaign in 1972 and Jimmy Carter's in
Arkansas in 1976, ran an effective U.S. House
campaign in 1974 but lost to an established
incumbent, a "utility-battling attorney general,"
and married to Hillary Rodham. The article also
discussed his political future, his view of the
governorship, and how he would like his
administration to be remembered. Regarding two key
issues, while he preferred racial integration in the
schools and the rest of society, he disagreed with
"'busing and breaking up neighborhoods.'" On women's
issues, he did not think that the Arkansas
legislature was ready to ratify the Equal Rights
Amendment. Thus, he would not push the amendment,
although he supported it "'in principle.'"

61 Roberts, Steven V. "New Breed of Arkansas
Officials Taking Race Out Politics." New York Times,
December 14, 1978, A26. The "new breed" of officials
included State Attorney General Elect Steve Clark,
Secretary of State Elect Paul Revere, and newly
elected governor Bill Clinton. Race was no longer a
factor in Arkansas as it had been. Key issues were
improvements in education, more roads, and
higher-wage jobs. Among all Arkansas politicians
(including senators Dale Bumpers and David Pryor),
Clinton was perhaps the "most impressive." Clinton
learned much about politics in his 1974 unsuccessful
congressional bid and he quickly gained a reputation
as a hard working attorney general. In the
Democratic primary for governor, Clinton won 60% of
the vote against four opponents, who tried to use his
independent wife and educational background against
him, but this strategy backfired. Clinton wished to
continue the economic progress the state had made and
improve the quality of life. While budgets were
tight, Clinton pledged to increase teacher salaries,
promote new industry, and preserve Arkansas'
environment. Clinton's greatest problem may have
been raising too high expectations.

62 "Faubus Returns to Arkansas for Clinton's
Inauguration." ("Notes On People" section).
Washington Post, January 11, 1979, C14. Brief report
noting that Clinton (described as a liberal Democrat)
made a special effort to invite the conservative
Orval Faubus to his inauguration.

63   Raines, Howell. "5 New Southern Governors Seek
Bold Changes Despite the Risks." New York Times,
February 25, 1979, 1, 42. Describes and analyzes the
efforts of five then newly elected southern
governors--Tennessee's Lamar Alexander, Alabama's
Forrest H. James, Florida's Bob Graham, South
Carolina's Richard W. Riley, and Clinton. Going
against the Proposition 13 trend, Clinton requested
new highway taxes and a $132 million investment for
Arkansas schools. Clinton believed that Arkansans
were weary of being ranked at or near the bottom in
social and economic national rankings. There was a
growing belief that the best way to deal with the
problems of the south was at the state level (and not
by pursuing a congressional career) by enhancing the
power of governors or using more effectively existing
gubernatorial powers.

64   "Budget Balancing: The Governors Argue."
Washington Post, February 28, 1979, A23. The
question of how to balance the federal budget was the
topic at the National Governors' Association meeting.
This article consists of excerpts from an ABC-TV News
tape. The speakers were Richard Snelling
(R-Vermont), Edmund G. Brown Jr. (D-California),
Bruce Babbitt (D-Arizona), and Clinton, whose
remarks included: "...the federal government's got to
be able to deficit-spend to manage the economy and
get us out of recession or to avoid recession. The
problem is, for 10 solid years now, in addition to
that, the people of this country...have accepted more
services than they are willing to pay for, or than
the Congress was willing to ask to pay for. And that
goes beyond any attempt to manage the economy.'"

65   White, Jean M. "Friendly Get-Together For Catfish
and Ribs." Washington Post, February 28, 1979, B3.
Photo. Light society-page style piece noting
Clinton's attendance at a fish fry held before a
White House dinner for governors. Clinton was a
"shrewd, engaging politician and Democratic Party
comer." Accompanied by a photo, which included
Clinton and Hodding Carter, who was then the State
Department's official spokesperson.

66   "50 Faces for America's Future." Time, August 6,
1979, 38. Photo. Clinton was among 50 individuals
chosen as America's future leaders. Notes Clinton's
accomplishments in improving education and care for
the elderly. Speculated that Clinton eventually
would run for Congress.

67   Press, Robert M. "South's New Governors are Shaking Traditions." <u>Christian Science Monitor</u>, December 4, 1979, 3. Photos.   On five southern governors and one governor-elect--Alabama's Fob James (D), Tennessee's Lamar Alexander (R), Mississippi's Governor-Elect William Winter (D), South Carolina's Richard Riley (D), Florida's Robert Graham (D), and Clinton.   This group of politicians was more "progressive" than "liberal."   Clinton had increased road repairs via tax hikes and had gotten approval for some governmental reorganization.

68   "200 Cubans Flee Arkansas Camp." <u>New York Times</u>, May 27, 1980, B6.

69   "Better Security For Camp Asked As Refugees Flee: All Caught, But Arkansas Governor Sends Appeal." <u>New York Times</u>, May 28, 1980, A14.

70   "Cuban Riot at Camp in Arkansas; Police, Refugees and Civilian Hurt." <u>New York Times</u>, June 2, 1980, A1, D15.

71   Thomas, Jo. "Troops are Ordered to Arkansas Camp After Refugee Riot." <u>New York Times</u>, June 3, 1980, A1, B11.

72   "Arkansans Protest Decision By President on Refugees." <u>New York Times</u>, August 3, 1980, 17.

73   "Military Is Held to Err In Not Quelling Cuban Riot." <u>New York Times</u>, August 28, 1980, A12.

74   "From the Media: Arkansas Appeal on Refugees." <u>Christian Science Monitor</u>, September 3, 1980, 24. (Reprint of editorial from <u>Pine Bluff Commercial</u>, Pine Bluff, Arkansas).

75   "First Refugees From Other Sites Start Arriving at Arkansas Camp." <u>New York Times</u>, September 26, 1980, A12.

President Jimmy Carter made a controversial decision in utilizing Ft. Chaffee, Arkansas as the permanent relocation center for Cuban refugees housed in other states.   About 117,000 refugees had come on the illegal "freedom flotilla" Cuban boatlift, up to 19,000 of whom had been housed at Fort Chaffee. Governor Clinton, as well as Arkansas senators Dale Bumpers and David Pryor, were on record to criticize Carter's decision.   This event was one of the decisive factors in Clinton's November 1980 defeat.

76 "Most Likely to Succeed." <u>Parade: The Sunday
Newspaper Magazine</u>, <u>Washington Post</u>, October 12,
1980, 19. On a tour promoting his book <u>Changing of
the Guard</u>, <u>Washington Post</u> journalist David Broder
was asked who he thought among young politicians
would most likely become president. Broder responded
with the names of Bill Clinton and Republican Jack
Kemp, predicting that by the 1988 election, these two
political stars could be running against each other
for president.

77 "Arkansas: The Wunderkind." <u>Newsweek</u>, October 20,
1980, 37. As part of its coverage of the 1980
gubernatorial races, <u>Newsweek</u> presented a brief
report on the Clinton-White race. Clinton was
"handsome" and "bright," with the "blue-chip
credentials" to be a "certifiable Democratic
wunderkind." His Republican opponent, Frank White,
was a banker with little government background.
Clinton forged a progressive record in his first term
as governor, increasing funding for education,
improving rural health, and encouraging gasoline
conservation. White criticized Clinton for how he
handled the Fort Chaffee Cuban refugee riots, his
support for President Carter, and what White viewed
as Clinton's unwise spending of federal monies.
<u>Newsweek</u> was following the conventional political
wisdom that Clinton would win, especially if he
wished to be in a position to later challenge the
Senate seat held by David Pryor in the 1984
Democratic primary. This "conventional wisdom,"
however, proved to be wrong since Clinton lost in an
upset victory by White.

78 Jones, Clayton and George B. Merry. "Governors'
Races: Most States Will Still Be In Democratic
Hands." <u>Christian Science Monitor</u>, October 27, 1980,
4. Highlights of governors' races in Arkansas and
other states. Noted that incumbent Clinton was
favored over G.O.P. candidate Frank D. White for two
reasons: Arkansas' Democratic tradition and the
state's record for practically automatic reelection
of a second gubernatorial two-year term. While in
retrospect this assessment was wrong, it also did
indicate Clinton's vulnerability over a tax increase,
small teacher raises, an unsuccessful firewood
project for the elderly, and permitting President
Carter to hold Cuban refugees at Fort Chaffee.
Clinton's primary opponent received a surprising 31%.

79 Mitford, Jessica. "Appointment in Arkansas." <u>New
West</u> 5, 22(November 3, 1980): 53-62. Lengthy

investigative report on prisoner James Dean Walker,
who fled Arkansas, which sought his extradition from
California. Clinton wanted this action taken so his
reelection bid would not be impaired. If Clinton
were to withdraw extradition, then he would have been
perceived as soft on crime since Walker was accused
of killing a police officer. For his part, then
California Governor Jerry Brown was cultivating
Clinton's political support in his planned run for
the presidency. If the extradition were granted,
Walker would become "just another political casualty,
caught in a squeeze between these two...liberal
governors and their respective ambitions."

OUT OF OFFICE (INCLUDING REASONS FOR 1980 GUBERNATORIAL DEFEAT AND 1982 POLITICAL COMEBACK)

80   Broder, David S. "An Arkansas Parable."
Washington Post, November 26, 1980, A17.   Excellent
column on the reasons for Bill Clinton's
gubernatorial defeat in 1980, which sidetracked a
promising political career. Clinton had emerged as
the preferred candidate of the nation's governors to
chair the National Governors' Association and he
performed a mediating role between the Carter and
Kennedy factions at the 1980 Democratic Convention.
There was a consensus in Arkansas (which Clinton
shared) that what befell Clinton was a combination of
"political misfortune, misjudgment and neglect,"
together with a sense of voter frustration, resulting
in a defeat which also could serve as a "parable" for
the defeat of Democrats at the national level.
During Clinton's term, drought, inflation and high
interest rates hurt the Arkansas economy, and other
events beyond the governor's control occurred: a
titan missile exploded and a riot occurred among
Cuban refugees at Fort Chaffee. Clinton proceeded to
follow a course he believed the voters had elected
him to do: to demonstrate "the benefits of
government" by pursuing medical, consumer, and
environmental issues, thereby challenging the medical
profession as well as the telephone and timber
industries. Also, a $17.00 increase in the auto
license fee did not sit well with voters as did not,
ironically, his successful speech at the Democratic
Convention and speculation on his political future
nationally while Arkansans were hurting economically.

81   Clymer, Adam. "15 Governors Want Shift by
Democrats: At Political Meeting, They Pledge to
Direct the National Party to Focus More on States."

New York Times, December 9, 1980, B18. Photo.
Clinton was mentioned prominently as a potential
candidate for the chairmanship of the Democratic
National Committee to replace outgoing chairman John
C. White. This speculation followed Clinton's then
recent loss to Frank White.

82 Greenberg, Paul. "A Tale of Two Speeches (Or)
Hail and Farewell." Arkansas Times 7, 7(March 1981):
18-19. Discusses Clinton's farewell speech and the
inaugural address of Frank White. Clinton's speech
was like his administration--an "uneven performance
that began with great promise and ended as a fizzle."
While highway and health programs constituted Clinton
accomplishments, the governor's policy on the Cuban
refugee crisis at Fort Chaffee was criticized as
"self-deception." Greenberg also referred to the
"shoddy compromises, the secret meetings, the various
scandals" of the Clinton administration. Since
Clinton likely would reemerge on the political scene,
his farewell address was more like a "So Long
Address." Arkansas "may have had enough glamour
[Clinton] for a time--and be ready for some dull,
careful management" under White.

83 Greenberg, Paul. ("Arkansas Politics" column).
"The Wunderkind and Consultmanship." Arkansas Times
7, 9(May 1981): 16, 18. Criticism of Clinton's first
term as governor. Despite Clinton's 1980 defeat, the
he was never really out of politics. Washington Post
columnist David Broder even speculated that Clinton
could be a future president. Greenberg, however,
criticized Clinton for explaining his defeat in terms
of electoral mechanics and not on substance. The
Clinton administration exemplified public
disenchantment with the Democratic Party nationwide.
Like the Carter administration, Clinton lacked
vision. There were many words and policies but no
underlining theme. The negative tone of this and
other columns is not surprising since Greenberg has
been a perennial Clinton critic.

84 Madigan, Charles. "Cuban Issue Becomes Key to
Arkansas Vote." Chicago Tribune, July 17, 1981, 1, 4.
Governor Frank White effectively utilized the rioting
by Cuban refugees at Fort Chaffee as an issue against
Clinton in the 1980 gubernatorial race. Clinton was
friendly to the Carter administration, which sent
thousands of Cuban refugees to Fort Chaffee. White's
message was that Clinton did not stand up to the
federal government, that Carter was able to dictate
conditions to Clinton, and that White would not allow

himself to be subjected to such a situation. This
issue paradoxically backfired on White since he would
have to defuse the Cuban issue to get reelected for
some 800 Cubans remained in Arkansas. Despite
reassurances from the Reagan administration, the
Cubans remained in Arkansas because of opposition in
other states and communities to the transfer of these
refugees from Arkansas.

85 Stuart, Reginald. "Criticism Mounts on G.O.P.
Governor: White Assailed on Leadership Issue He Used
Against Predecessor." New York Times, December 6,
1981, 33. Assessment of Governor Frank White, who
had defeated Clinton in 1980, about half-way in his
administration. Reference is made to Clinton early
in the article. White picked up the general
perception in 1980 that Clinton was out-of-sync
politically with the Arkansan electorate. White then
charged that Clinton lacked the leadership the state
needed--permitting the federal government to use Fort
Chaffee to temporarily hold Cuban refugees. White
had criticized Clinton for not challenging this
decision by the Carter administration and also for
having raised automobile license fees. Ironically,
White's leadership also came into question. There
was, however, a consensus in Arkansas that it might
be difficult to defeat White in 1982.

86 Johnston, Phyllis Fenton. Bill Clinton's Public
Policy for Arkansas: 1979-1980. Little Rock: August
House Publishers, 1982. Photos. Unique book-length
study of Clinton's first gubernatorial term based on
six policy areas emphasized by Clinton--education,
human services, energy, public health, highways, and
economic development. The last two chapters deal
with "crisis management" and Clinton's governing
style and its impact on public policy. Includes
bibliography and index.

87 Dickenson, James R. and David S. Broder.
"Political Notes: Changing All Those Changes."
Washington Post, February 28, 1982, A12. Column
which included a short section on Bill and Hillary
Clinton. Clinton was running for governor again. He
had been "touted as a rising young
Democrat--presidential material," even prior to his
loss in 1980. He was belatedly taking the advice of
those who observed that his image was not in tune
with conservative Arkansas by adopting a new shorter
hair style, and replacing his earlier young aides
with middle-aged men. Also, Hillary Rodham planned
to relinquish her law practice to campaign fulltime

and ceased using her maiden name.

88 Hamner, Buddy. "Gubernatorial Candidates Interviewed." City & Town 38, 4(May 1982): 4-7. Excerpts from responses to questions on municipal and urban policy (including Reagan's New Federalism plan) by gubernatorial candidates, including Clinton, Frank White, Joe Purcell, and Jim Guy Tucker.

89 Balz, Dan. "Wunderkind Seeks 2nd Chance." Washington Post, May 23, 1982, A2. Preview of the 1982 Arkansas Democratic primary for governor, whose key issue was "Clinton's past performance." Clinton's Democratic primary challengers were Joe Purcell and Jim Guy Tucker.

90 Clymer, Adam. "Ex-Officeholders Seek New Fortunes in Primaries." New York Times, May 24, 1982, A14. Photo. Includes discussion of the political comebacks of a number of politicians such as, besides Clinton, Michael Dukakis of Massachusetts. Gives reasons for Clinton's 1980 gubernatorial loss, beyond raising automobile license fees. Clinton had a fair chance of getting over 50% of the Democratic primary vote, thereby avoiding a runoff with his closest rivals, Jim Guy Tucker and Joe Purcell.

91 Clymer, Adam. "Wooing Voters With Bean and Barbecue." New York Times, May 26, 1982, C3. About the thirty-forth annual Mount Nebo Chicken Fry, held in Dardanelle, Arkansas, before the Democratic primary. Also notes similar events in other states. Among the candidates in attendance was former governor Bill Clinton, who held Governor Frank White responsible for higher electric rates. Clinton also asked voters at this event for a second chance.

92 Richards, Clay F. "Former Arkansas Governor Faces Runoff." Washington Post, May 26, 1982, A6. Results of the Arkansas primary. With 92% of precincts reporting, Clinton received 42%, Purcell 29%, and Tucker 24%. As background, also noted three key factors in Clinton's 1980 gubernatorial defeat: Arkansans reacted negatively to his political ambitions, to stories about crimes committed by Cuban refugees confined in crowded conditions in Fort Chaffee, and an increase in automobile license fees.

93 "Runoff Pending in Arkansas; 4 Kentucky Incumbents Win." New York Times, May 26, 1982, A24. Most of the article focuses on Clinton and Arkansas. Notes Clinton's victory in the Arkansas primary,

although a June 8 runoff was necessary since he did
not gain a majority of the vote. With 89.7% of
precincts reporting, Clinton had 41.8%, Purcell
28.7%, and Tucker 23.3%. Clinton declared that he
welcomed the runoff so that there could be a focus on
the issues. His initial political success and
"boyish, friendly manner" led to political
speculation that he would run for president some day.
However, when Clinton lost in 1980, he became only
the second single-term governor in Arkansas in the
twentieth century.

94 "Two Democrats in Arkansas Face a Tough Runoff
June 8." New York Times, May 27, 1982, A22. Previews
the June 8, 1982, runoff between Clinton and low-key
Lieutenant Governor Joe Purcell. This election would
bring Clinton one step closer to regaining the
governorship he had lost in 1980.

95 "Anomalies Mark Primary Campaign for Governor in
Arkansas." New York Times, June 8, 1982, A16.
Describes Bill Clinton's Democratic opponent, Joe
Purcell, as a "taciturn politician" with a halting
public speaking manner who still could jeopardize the
former governor's comeback. While Clinton led in the
polls, on the eve of the runoff it appeared that
Purcell had the political momentum. An irony of the
campaign was that Clinton's understanding of the
issues, his appearance, and outstanding speaking
ability were held to be a detriment while Purcell's
quiet manner and lack of polished speech symbolized a
"triumph of authenticity over charisma." Clinton
argued, and Republican Governor White tacitly
acknowledged, that Purcell's growing support came
from Republicans who wanted to see Purcell win and
face White in the governor's race since they
perceived Clinton as a more formidable opponent.

96 Clymer, Adam. "Former Arkansas Governor Wins
Chance to Run Again." New York Times, June 9, 1982,
B17. Photo. Reports on Clinton's victory in the
Democratic gubernatorial runoff primary. While many
other races were discussed in this article, Clinton
gained the headline. With 95% of precincts
reporting, Clinton received 54% of the vote and
Purcell 46%.

97 "Bad Day for Big Names: Stumbling in the
Primaries." Time, June 21, 1982, 38. Reports on the
results of nation-wide primaries in California, New
Jersey, Ohio, Iowa, and Arkansas. Regarding Clinton,
notes that in 1980 he was already being viewed as

having a bright political future on the national
scene, but also had gained a reputation in Arkansas
as an "effete snob." Thus, he was defeated two years
earlier by Republican Frank White, who depicted
himself as more down-to-earth. In 1982, Clinton
campaigned as a politician who was not above
listening to the electorate.

98   Greenberg, Paul. "Godzilla Versus The Hollow
Man." ("Arkansas Politics" column). Arkansas Times 8,
12 (August 1982): 19-20. Greenberg writes about the
inevitable gubernatorial rematch between Frank White
and Bill Clinton, criticizing both in the process.

99   "Governors: Return of Two Favorite Sons; Southern
Star Rising Again." Time, September 20, 1982, 11.
Adlai E. Stevenson III and Clinton were profiled. In
1980, there was no more promising young Democrat than
Clinton. After his impressive speech at the 1980
Democratic Convention, it seemed only a matter of
time before he would enter national politics. By
November 1980, however, Clinton had became an
"instant has-been" in "one of the truly stunning
upsets of 1980." Clinton lost to Republican Frank
White mostly because the Democrat had alienated
Arkansans with his national political ambitions. The
1982 race is a rematch of 1980, but the key issues
were of a personal nature--if voters would give
Clinton a second chance after his acknowledgement of
past political errors. Clinton changed by altering
his populist image to reflect traditional Arkansas
values. Arkansas is a heavily Democratic state, so
Clinton was favored despite White's description of
him as "'a tax-and-spend man.'" If Clinton were to
win, "it could seem less a comeback than a canny
mid-course correction in the path of a young, bright
political star."

100   Bredemeier, Kenneth. "A Chastened Rising Star
Seeks Comeback in Razorback Politics." Washington
Post, October 28, 1982, A16. Good analysis of the
1982 Arkansas gubernatorial campaign. The question
for voters was whether they wanted "the Rising Star,
former Democratic governor Bill Clinton, to soar
again, or plummet into political oblivion." Polls
indicated a close race. Bredemeier noted that just
two years earlier Clinton had been the "wunderkind of
Razorback politics," with a growing national
reputation as being "on a fast track to the White
House." Arkansans, however, wanted to send Clinton a
message, believing that he focused too much on the
national scene and not enough on Arkansas. In this

campaign, Clinton was "chastened and apologetic."
Acknowledging that he lost touch with voters, Clinton
sought to change his image and listen more. Both
candidates attacked the other's record.

101   Rawls, Wendell, Jr. "Arkansas Gubernatorial
Candidates in Close Race." New York Times, October
28, 1982, B10. Report on the Arkansas governor's
race. The campaign generally was seen as the most
negative in recent Arkansas history, giving voters a
choice of whom they least disliked. Neither Clinton
nor Frank White were that popular and both had
negatives in their political records. A major factor
in Clinton's 1980 gubernatorial defeat was the
public's negative perception of his national
political aspirations. He spent much of the campaign
being apologetic over his first term. Clinton also
emphasized that the governorship was the post he
always wanted and intended to keep "'for a long
time.'" White criticized Clinton for having a
"'liberal'" wife and not being firm enough on crime.
A key to the election would be which candidate
received the most votes from their traditional
supporters--newly arrived retirees who settled in the
northern part of the state heavily backed White in
1980 and blacks from the Mississippi Delta region of
eastern Arkansas supported Clinton.

SECOND TERM AS GOVERNOR, 1982-1984

102 Andersen, Kurt. "Fresh Faces in the Mansions."
Time, November 15, 1982, 30, 32. Photo. Includes a
good brief review of Clinton's victory and
significant past events which led to it.

103   "3 Governors Are Inaugurated." New York Times,
January 12, 1983, A12. Brief article noting the
inauguration of three governors--Democrats Richard D.
Lamm of Colorado, Joe Frank Harris of Georgia, and
Clinton. By defeating White, Clinton regained the
governorship he had lost in 1980. Clinton said his
first priority would be to reduce unemployment and
put people back to work.

104   White, Mel. "A Campaign Journal--Part One, The
Rematch: In Which the Properly Chastened Challenger
Again Seeks Public Favor." Arkansas Times 9,
6(February 1983): 22-24, 26-28, 30, 32. Random
observations in diary/journal form during the 1982
Arkansas gubernatorial rematch election between
Governor Frank White and Clinton. An impressionistic

account which conveys the flavor of campaigning.
Part I covers the period from June to September 1982.

105   White, Mel. "A Campaign Journal--Part Two, The
Rematch: In Which a Political Palindrome Reaches Its
Foregone Conclusion." Arkansas Times 9, 7(March
1983): 74-79. Part II covers the 1982 Arkansas
election campaign from early October to election day,
including Clinton's position on capital punishment,
which he traced back to his term as Arkansas attorney
general. By October, it was clear he would win.

106   "Clinton Pledges Advocacy By Jackson Bank
Department." Arkansas Banker 67, 3(June 1983): 15.
About Clinton's address to the Arkansas Bankers
Association, in which he indicated that the state
Bank Department would serve as an advocate for banks,
and not just be a watchdog and a regulator. Clinton
also talked about education and appealed to the
Arkansas banking industry to ensure that workers
receive retraining for new technology.

107   Reed, Roy. "Arkansas Recalls a New Yorker in
Little Rock." New York Times, July 11, 1983, 1, 10.
Photo. The opening at the University of Arkansas at
Little Rock of the official papers of former Arkansas
Republican Governor Winthrop Rockefeller (a
transplant from New York) in July 1983 provided the
opportunity for a consideration of his legacy for
Arkansas. Rockefeller, who served as governor from
1967 to 1971, provided an impetus for spending in
public education which only later had subsided and
which Clinton was trying to revive. Clinton was one
of four speakers for this event--Senators Dale
Bumpers and David H. Pryor and ex-Governor Frank
White. Clinton stated that he, Pryor and Bumpers
would not have been able to hold office in Arkansas
if Rockefeller had not "'opened up the political
process.'" The article was accompanied by an AP
photograph with the caption: "Gov. Bill Clinton of
Arkansas viewing Winthrop Rockefeller display."

108   Franklin, Tim. "Mayor 'Ducks Political Fight' in
Little Rock." Chicago Tribune, August 29, 1983, 1,
11. Declaring that he wished to avoid any local
controversy in Arkansas, Chicago Mayor Harold
Washington acceded to local black leaders' demands
not to attend a reception in his honor at the Clinton
governor's mansion in Little Rock. Two local black
leaders, restaurant owner Robert "Say" McIntosh and
State Representative Grover Richardson, charged
Clinton and a number of black business leaders with

being insensitive to the situation of poor blacks.
(At the time, McIntosh was contemplating running
against Clinton in the 1984 gubernatorial election).
McIntosh asserted that while Clinton won over 90% of
the black vote in the 1982 election, he had not
appointed blacks to important positions in state
government. Clinton defended his stance regarding
minorities. This article presents a unique Chicago
perspective on Arkansas politics.

109 Shields, Mark. "Testing Time for the Teachers."
Washington Post, December 23, 1983, A15. Shields
supported Clinton on mandatory competency testing for
teachers. This issue could have an impact on the
1984 presidential election (since the Democratic
nominee Walter Mondale was the NEA's endorsed
candidate) and the future of public education.

110 Schmidt, William E. "Teachers Up in Arms Over
Arkansas's Skills Test." New York Times, January 17,
1984, A16. On teacher opposition to competency
testing. The National Education Association (NEA)
and its affiliate, the Arkansas Education Association
(AEA), maintained that the governor used the testing
provision as a political issue to overcome objections
to the tax increase passed to support educational
reform. Clinton maintained that the public was
willing to pay more for education, but teacher
accountability was also important. Despite teacher
objections to the plan, most Arkansans supported
Clinton. According to an unnamed local newspaper
editor: "'The teacher testing bill was Bill Clinton's
Grenada,'" a reference to President Reagan's popular
invasion of that Caribbean island in October 1983.

111 "Arkansas Pledges Grand Gulf Battle." New
Orleans Times Picayune, January 21, 1984, 23.
Clinton promised "all-out" opposition to a plan by
Mississippi and Louisiana utility companies that
would compel ratepayers in Arkansas to help pay for
the Grand Gulf (Mississippi) and Waterford
(Louisiana) nuclear power plants. He claimed that it
was his "'issue all along,'" noting that he first
raised the question about Grand Gulf in 1977 as
attorney general. At that time, Clinton said he was
informed that Arkansas ratepayers were not liable to
help finance the plants due to Arkansas' development
of lower-cost coal and nuclear energy. But Louisiana
and Mississippi backed out of the agreement and then
required payments from the utility Arkansas Power &
Light Co. (For an update on Grand Gulf, see Doug
Smith, "The Entergy Merger and Arkansas Ratepayers,"

<u>Arkansas Times</u>, June 15, 1992, 10).

112 Kilpatrick, James J. "Paying Up for Teachers Who
Measure Up." <u>Los Angeles Times</u>, February 5, 1984,
IV-5. Kilpatrick supported Clinton on requiring
competency testing for teachers, describing the
conflict between Clinton and the teachers unions as a
"splendid little row." Clinton was a "moderately
liberal Democrat," who accurately gauged public
opinion on this issue.

113 "Governor Confident on Grand Gulf." <u>New Orleans
Times Picayune</u>, March 8, 1984, sec. 2, p. 5. Clinton
expressed optimism that Arkansas could get out from
under a federal ruling regarding construction of the
Grand Gulf nuclear plant located in Port Gibson,
Mississippi. (The February 2, 1984 court ruling was
that Arkansas Power & Light Co. had to pay 36% of the
cost for the three billion dollar plant).

114 Baldridge, Joan and Kay Gaines. "Arkansas
Education: A First Class Program." <u>Inside Arkansas</u>
20, 1(Spring 1984): 16-17. A well-trained and
educated work force was an important component for
promoting economic development and growth in
Arkansas. The article provided details of
educational reform introduced by the Clinton
administration, including student and teacher testing
and programs in vocational and higher education.

115 "Arkansas Readies Police For Extremists in
Hills." <u>St. Louis Post-Dispatch</u>, July 8, 1984, 8D.
UPI story about heavily armed extremists skilled in
guerrilla warfare, located in the hills of northern
Arkansas. Clinton wanted to provide police with
bulletproof vests to deal with such groups. He also
indicated that he would consult with the governors of
Missouri, Texas and Oklahoma regarding any
information they may have had on these groups as a
result of the killings of two police officers in
Arkansas. Clinton stated that extremists had stored
illegal weapons. One extremist group--the Cross, the
Sword and the Arm of the Lord (CSA)--and other
similar groups formed to protest tax increases.

116 Cunningham, Lynn. "'Gulfbusters' of Arkansas at
War With Miss. N-Plant." <u>New Orleans Time Picayune</u>,
September 9, 1984, A1, A18. Photo. Discusses
Clinton's opposition to the Grand Gulf nuclear plant,
which was supposed to supply power to Louisiana,
Mississippi, and Arkansas (via the Arkansas Power &
Light Co.). Clinton, in the forefront of the

campaign against Grand Gulf, was an "archenemy" of the plant. This issue developed into a "public crusade" in Arkansas largely due to Clinton, who became an expert on the subject (since he was a "quick study") and increased the public's awareness of it with his ability to explain issues. Clinton made Grand Gulf a major issue in his reelection campaign for a third term. Cunningham, a _Times Picayune_ staff writer, provides a regional perspective on this issue from a neighboring state.

117 Hamner, Buddy. "Clinton and Freeman Interviewed by Executive Committee." _City & Town_ 40, 9(October 1984): 4-5. Photos. Gubernatorial candidates Clinton and Republican Woody Freeman were interviewed by the Arkansas Municipal League in September 1984. Among the issues discussed were infrastructure programs, being accessible, and law enforcement equipment.

THIRD TERM AS GOVERNOR, 1984-1986

118 "Champions of the People." _Esquire_ 102, 6(December 1984): 450. _Esquire_'s 1984 "Register" of prominent Americans who could be the country's future leaders. The introduction to these paragraph-size profiles ironically included this disclaimer: "We do not claim to have a future President here...." Little did _Esquire_ realize back in 1984 that one of their profiles was of "William" Clinton and Hillary Rodham Clinton. Of related interest are others profiled in this register, who would be appointed cabinet members and selected as vice president in the Clinton administration: Henry G. Cisneros, Albert Gore Jr., Federico Peña, and Robert B. Reich and a nominee who was withdrawn from consideration, Lani Guinier, as well as North Dakota Senator Kent Conrad.

119 Rogers, R.J. "Clinton's Package Is No Great Shakes." _Arkansas Business_ 2, 6(March 18-March 31, 1985): 10-11. Questioned the benefits of the Clinton economic legislative package for economic development and maintained that the Clinton administration did not have a "comprehensive public policy." It also was argued that the Clinton plan did not create enough jobs nor would it offset the costs incurred by the Grand Gulf project.

120 "Bennett: Go to Cheaper Colleges." _New Orleans Times Picayune_, April 1, 1985, A5. AP story on an edition of ABC's "This Week With David Brinkley," which focused on education. Guests were Education

Secretary William Bennett, National Education
Association (NEA) president Mary Hatwood Futrell,
American Federation of Teachers' (AFT) president
Albert Shanker, and Clinton, whose state had just
administered teacher competency tests. Clinton noted
that over 25,000 teachers took the test, despite
calls for a boycott. Futrell, though, described the
tests as "'morally unjust.'" Clinton also discussed
new rules for home testing, which was a reality in
Arkansas and required yearly testing of home
students. The governor explained that parents
involved in home testing were not required to take
tests (as required of public school teachers) because
the parents were not paid by taxpayers.

121 Cawthon, Raad. "Clinton's Star Back on the Rise
After Taking a Dip." Atlanta Journal-Atlanta
Constitution, May 19, 1985, A27. Provided
considerable background on Clinton's political career
and discussed Clinton's efforts at educational reform
and his promotion of economic development for
Arkansas. By 1985, speculation on Clinton's
political future resurfaced regarding possible runs
for the senate and the presidency in 1988.
Concerning the Democratic Party's future, Clinton
declared it needed discipline and a focus on
economics and that special interest group demands had
to be controlled. Insightful article by an Atlanta
Journal-Atlanta Constitution staff writer.

122 Sanoff, Alvin P. "Who'll be America's Stars of
Tomorrow?" U.S. News & World Report, May 20, 1985,
62-63. Photo. Survey of prospective future leaders.
Noted Clinton "won acclaim by focusing on issues of
wide appeal," like education and economic
development. Clinton's political future also noted.

123 "Economic Growth Predicted By Governor and
Aides." Arkansas Banker 69, 3(June 1985): 16-17.
Clinton and administration officials presented the
message to the 95th annual convention of the Arkansas
Bankers Association that Arkansas was about to reach
a new level of economic and industrial development.
Clinton observed that Arkansas' history as a state
had been marked by a struggle against poverty. The
time soon would come when people could remain in
Arkansas because there would be adequate employment
opportunities. Clinton hoped the state would be
competitive with other states in terms of economic
growth rates and a lower unemployment rate.
Education and encouraging economic development were
keys to achieving these goals, Clinton said, and he

enlisted the support of the Arkansas Bankers Association to pass his economic plan.

124 Gutis, Philip S. "Arkansas Balks at Extradition in New York Case." <u>New York Times</u>, June 9, 1985, 48.

125 "Arkansas to Extradite Teen-Ager." <u>New York Times</u>, June 16, 1985, 26.

126 "Drug Suspect Surrenders Here." <u>New York Times</u>, June 21, 1985, B4.

About the Catherine Nicole Cowan case, whose extradition to New York on a drug trafficking charge originally had been blocked by Clinton on the grounds that since she was a first-time offender, she should not be subject to a full sentence. Queens District Attorney, John J. Santucci, agreed to drop the drug possession charge if she pleaded guilty to a lesser charge, to which she would be liable for a shorter sentence. She had been charged with assisting another Choate-Rosemary Hall (a preparatory school) student to smuggle cocaine from Venezuela.

127 Hansen, Jane O. "Southern Governors Laud Harris, Educational Reforms at Conference." <u>Atlanta Constitution</u>, June 24, 1985, A3. Georgia Governor Joe Frank Harris was praised by fellow southern governors for his educational programs at the annual meeting of the Southern Regional Education Board, which also was attended by Clinton. He noted that Arkansas for the first time experienced a larger number of students applying for college teacher-preparation programs due, in part, to higher teacher salaries. But the provision of testing teachers for competency had drawn the most attention in Arkansas, which Clinton acknowledged had become a contentious issue. Clinton defended this policy by emphasizing the importance of raising standards.

128 Walker, Tom. "Ark. Governor Blasts Reagan Farm Policies." <u>Atlanta Constitution</u>, June 28, 1985, D4. Clinton, chairman of the Southern Growth Policies Board (SGPB), stated in Atlanta that Reagan farm policies had accelerated the decline of small farmers. Clinton said this within the context of the frustrations of state government attempting to cope with federal government economic policies. Clinton was part of a panel of southern governors who attended the thirteenth annual meeting of the SGPB, a research organization promoting southern growth, located in the North Carolina Research Triangle.

Other governors on the panel included Georgia's Joe
Frank Harris, Virginia's Charles Robb, and
ex-Mississippi governor William Winter.

129 Lyons, Gene. ("Unsolicited Opinions" column).
"Some Sour Musical Notes." Arkansas Times 11, 11(July
1985): 85. Clinton should not run against Dale
Bumpers for Senate in 1986, but rather should seek
reelection as governor. While Clinton could possibly
defeat Bumpers, it was important for Clinton to
provide strong leadership as governor by following
through on his educational reforms and economic
development plans. And if Clinton could deliver on
these plans, then he had a "fine chance to earn
nearly universal acclaim as Arkansas's best governor
ever." If Clinton, however, were to challenge
Bumpers, then he would appear opportunistic and just
running out of personal ambition, especially if he
criticized Bumpers from the right. Bumpers had a
large constituency and it was best to stay with him.

130 Press, Robert M. "Arkansas' Clinton on Democrats
in the South, Region's Growth." Christian Science
Monitor, July 15, 1985, 8. The Monitor interviewed
Clinton in Atlanta, where he assumed the chair of the
Southern Growth Policies Board, an organization
promoted by state government in the south to enhance
the region's economic conditions. Clinton's efforts
in passing major educational and economic reform
legislation were noted. Among the observations
Clinton made in the interview were the following: for
Democrats to win more elections, they should not just
copy Republican policies, but should require greater
"'accountability'" in national social problems; while
the Reagan administration's transfer of authority to
states enhanced the role of governors, cuts in the
federal budget had resulted in more poverty,
particularly in the south; and, in the region, and
nationwide, infrastructure was declining. The south,
however, should not sacrifice the environment to
economic growth, Clinton cautioned. This article
demonstrated that by the mid-1980s, Clinton was
already establishing himself as a national figure.

131 "Low Rankings, High Ambitions." Economist,
September 14, 1985, 34-35. Assessment of the Clinton
record in Arkansas in the mid-1980s from a British
perspective, noting his national ambitions as well as
efforts to improve Arkansas by attracting industry
and investment and improving education and training.
In this endeavor, Governor Clinton called for a
"'decade of dedication'" from Arkansans.

132   Means, Marianne. "Clinton of Arkansas May Have
It In 1988." <u>St. Louis Post-Dispatch</u>, October 18,
1985, 3B.   On the presidential prospects of then
lesser known Democrats like Clinton and Missouri
Representative Dick Gephardt, who believed that a
southern centrist politician had the best chance to
regain the White House.   Of these two potential
candidates, Clinton, then 39, would be a "more
promising candidate," able to alter his image as
times changed.   Clinton was to chair the National
Governors' Association in 1986 and participated in
the group named Democrats for the '80s, a political
action committee, led by Democratic activist Pamela
Harriman, to assist Democratic moderates.   In
discussing Clinton's background, Means noted his
participation as a student in the antiwar movement,
that his 1980 defeat was due both to Carter's loss in
Arkansas and negative voter perception of Clinton,
and the constructive part he played as a mediator
between the Carter and Kennedy camps at the 1980
Democratic convention.   Since regaining the
governorship, Clinton attracted business to Arkansas
and promoted educational reform.   It remained
unclear, however, whether his enthusiasm and ideas
could make him into a national figure.   But in
politics anything was possible.

133   Trimble, Mike. "Bill Clinton's Campaign To
Become One of Us." <u>Arkansas Times</u> 12, 3(November
1985): 68-71, 90-91. Illus.   Trimble begins with the
reasons for Clinton's 1980 defeat, discounting the
conventional political wisdom that Clinton lost in
1980 due to the Cuban refugee situation at Fort
Chaffee and the increase in auto registration and
title fees.   Instead, Clinton lost this election
because many Arkansans did not perceive the governor
favorably.   Trimble then assessed Clinton's record as
governor, concluding that while Clinton may never be
Arkansas' "favorite son," he could at least be
accepted as a respected political leader.

134   "The Statehouses: Action and Innovation, A New
Breed of Governor Upstages Washington." Brummett,
John. "An Arkansas Phoenix Finds an Issue." <u>Newsweek</u>,
March 24, 1986, 32.   Short profiles of five governors
(besides Clinton, Massachusett's Michael Dukakis, New
Jersey's Thomas Kean, Arizona's Bruce Babbitt, and
Tennessee's Lamar Alexander), who were rated the most
effective among their peers, according to a
<u>Newsweek</u>/Gallup poll.   A short favorable sketch of
Clinton was written by John Brummett.   Clinton's
popularity was due to one key issue--competency

testing of teachers despite union opposition.
Clinton believed that the role of governors was to
ensure educational and economic opportunities for
their citizens.

135 Wyman, Hastings, Jr. "A Southern Governor Warily
Eyes the National Stage." Wall Street Journal, March
26, 1986, 30. Clinton's 1978 gubernatorial victory
constituted a "symbol of change" in the south.
Having learned the lesson for his 1980 defeat by
attempting to "lead without listening," Clinton was
in a strong political position state-wide, focusing
on two key issues, education and employment. He thus
had the political foundation to seek national office,
although Clinton was downplaying that possibility.
He had a record in Arkansas which could appeal to
more pragmatic Democrats nationwide. And while
Clinton may not have had a "great record" in
Arkansas, it was better than that of other governors
like Georgia's Jimmy Carter.

136 LaFranchi, Howard. "Arkansas: Not Exactly
Texas." Christian Science Monitor, March 31, 1986, 4.
About Arkansas' celebration of its sesquicentennial
(1836-1986), which was overshadowed by the one in
Texas. Much of the article discusses Clinton's
reflections on this event and its meaning.

137 Herbers, John. "Arkansas Tries to Regain Its
Footing." New York Times, April 27, 1986, IV-5. The
economy was the key issue in the 1986 election year.
This was particularly true for Arkansas, which had
not completely recovered from the 1982 recession.
Jobs were the central concern in Arkansas and Clinton
acknowledged that his state's future was uncertain.
Another important issue was competency tests for
teachers, first administered in 1985. Former
Governor Orval Faubus contested Clinton in the
Democratic gubernatorial primary and charged that the
tests were degrading to teachers. Most of Clinton's
time was occupied with promoting "self-help
enterprises," though he conceded that Arkansas was
struggling to gain national parity economically.

138 "Faubus Runs Again for Governor of Arkansas."
New York Times, May 25, 1986, A26. The two leading
candidates for the Arkansas Democratic nomination for
governor represented opposite poles in southern
politics. Clinton had moderated his "early
liberalism." Faubus, 76, had been a dominant figure
in the state when he was governor (including an
attempt in 1957 to prevent black students from

integrating Central High School in Little Rock).   In
the Democratic primary campaign, Faubus accused
Clinton of serving the interests of the wealthy and
the utility companies in relation to the Arkansas
Power & Light Company and the Grand Gulf nuclear
power facility.   The Grand Gulf issue and Arkansas'
continued recession were problems for Clinton,
although he was expected to win.   Clinton wished to
make the primary a referendum on his education
reform, which included strict standards for school
accreditation and he argued that all his adversaries
would have allowed the reform program to die.

139   Mashek, John W. "Ten Rising Stars of American
Politics." U.S. News & World Report, May 26, 1986,
19-21. Photo.   Survey of America's "most promising
politicians," including Clinton, described as a
"comeback winner."   Provides a brief summary of his
political career and speculation on Clinton as a
potential vice-presidential candidate in 1988.

140   "Clinton Is Victor Over Faubus." New York Times,
May 28, 1986, B5.   AP story on Clinton's win in the
Arkansas Democratic Primary for governor.   Clinton
won comfortably over Faubus (who was attempting to
make a political comeback) by a margin of 60 to 34%,
with 91% of the precincts reporting.   Faubus declared
that this would be his last race.

141   "Faubus Angry After Arkansas Loss." New York
Times, May 29, 1986, 14. Photo.   Faubus, labelling
himself a "'has-been,'" pledged grudging support to
Clinton in the Democratic primary for governor,
although he said Clinton represented the
"'superrich'" and not the average citizen.   With 99%
of precincts reporting, Clinton won 61% to Faubus'
33%.   A third candidate, W. Dean Goldsby, the first
black to seek this nomination, finished with only 6%.

142   Ficklen, Ellen. "Arkansas Governor Bill Clinton
is an Activist for School Reform." American School
Board Journal 173, 7(July 1986): 24-25. Photo.
Favorable article to Clinton.   A photo caption
describes him as "a reform-minded governor who has
charisma and clout" and noted his wife Hillary's
contribution to educational reform in Arkansas.
Ficklen summarizes Clinton's background and,
particularly, his efforts regarding educational
reform in Arkansas, especially competency testing for
teachers, despite opposition from the National
Education Association (NEA) and the Arkansas
Education Association (AEA).   Clinton, however,

defended this test and hoped that this provision
(teacher testing) was not just a passing fad.

143 Ficklen, Ellen. "School People Give Clinton's
Reforms Mixed Reviews." American School Board Journal
173, 7(July 1986): 26. Ficklen presented other
opinions of Clinton's school reforms. The executive
director of the American School Boards Association
(ASBA), J.K. Williams, stated that Clinton made his
mark in Arkansas education and that this, overall,
was good by setting standards for schools and
increasing funding for education. On the other hand,
Williams pointed to some potential longer-term
problems. Due to the increased involvement of both
the governor and the legislature in education, local
school boards had lost some of their power. The
biggest complaint was teacher testing. The AEA and
its president, Ed Bullington, firmly opposed testing
while the ASBA did not take an official position.

144 Brown, Francis C., III. "Arkansas and Texas Both
Hold Parties; Read All About It." Wall Street
Journal, July 25, 1986, sec. 1, p. 11. Report on the
Arkansas and Texas sesquincentennial celebrations.
In April 1986, Clinton and other state officials
opened the Arkansas celebration in Dallas, whose
purpose was to attract Texas tourists to Arkansas.
However, political foes like Orval Faubus charged
that Clinton held the kick-off dinner outside of
Arkansas to promote his national political
aspirations. Brown noted that despite the larger
celebration in Texas, Arkansas' sesquicentennial
event drew more tourists proportionally than Texas'.

145 Marquand, Robert. "Arkansas Governor and His
Spouse Both Put Education First." Christian Science
Monitor, August 25, 1986, 25-26. Favorable article
on the education reform efforts of the Clintons,
including mandatory testing for both students and
teachers. Notes Clinton's chairmanship of the
Education Commission of the States (ECS),
traditionally an influential forum for state
education leaders. Mrs. Clinton, who led the
Arkansas educational reform movement, believed that
education constituted an "inherent value."

146 Herbers, John. "Governors Preparing to Challenge
President Over Welfare Revision." New York Times,
August 27, 1986, A16. On the response of the
National Governors' Association (NGA) to Reagan
welfare revision, which would shift more of a burden
on states for the provision of welfare. The NGA

wanted to devise its own solutions. Its efforts were
motivated by the same factors which compelled it to
seek education restructuring--concerns over economic
decline. In his acceptance speech as new NGA
president, Clinton noted that since the mid-1970s,
the U.S. had lost its competitive edge in the world
economy. This international dimension compounded
preexisting domestic problems (such as more
single-family homes, children in poverty, illiterate
adults who were unemployable, people on welfare,
teenage pregnancy, and school dropouts). To devise
an overall plan for reducing welfare dependency,
Clinton appointed committees to study new ways to
reduce illiteracy, teen pregnancy and substance abuse
and encourage job training, economic development, and
stronger families.

147 Hayden, Ellen Tollison. "Education as a State
Priority: Five Governors' Views." NASSP (National
Association of Secondary School Principals) Bulletin
70, 491(September 1986): 11-19. In Fall 1985, the
NASSP Bulletin interviewed five governors on the
significance of education as a state issue. The
governors interviewed were Tennessee's Lamar
Alexander, Utah's Norman Bangerter, South Carolina's
Richard Riley, Texas' Mark White, and Clinton, whose
responses dealt with education and its relation to
economic development, funding, higher pay and
standards for teachers, and state regulation.

148 Jaschik, Scott. "A Governor Pours Millions More
Into Education." Chronicle of Higher Education 33,
1(September 3, 1986): 25. In mobilizing political
and public support for greater funding of higher
education, Clinton emphasized the close relationship
between education and economic development. In turn,
universities and colleges needed to be held
accountable for how they spent additional funds so
taxpayers could be assured that their tax dollars
were spent wisely and efficiently. While more
responsibility for higher education was shifted from
the federal government to the states, there was less
federal funding under Reagan. Thus, state government
had to provide leadership for higher education.

149 Rosser, Dennis. "NBC/LEO to Hear Gov. Clinton
and Randall Robinson." Nation's Cities Weekly 9,
41(October 13, 1986): 5. Preview of Clinton's
appearance before the National Black Caucus of Local
Elected Officials (NBC/LEO) during the Congress of
Cities. Noted that Clinton also was chair of the
Southern Growth Policies Board, which had assumed "an

aggressive role for state and local governments of
the region in stimulating economic growth and
supporting investment in education and training."

150 Wagnon, Ted. "Brokers Talk Politics, But Covet
Bond Fees." Arkansas Business 3, 23(October
13-October 26, 1986): 4-5. About the controversial
Arkansas Development Finance Authority (ADFA).

**FOURTH TERM AS GOVERNOR, 1986-1990 (INCLUDING
POSSIBLE RUN FOR PRESIDENT IN 1988 AND JULY 1988
NOMINATING SPEECH FOR MICHAEL DUKAKIS)**

151 "Southern Politicians to Watch." Atlanta
Journal/Atlanta Constitution, November 9, 1986, A14.
Ten brief profiles of southern political figures who
emerged from the 1986 elections as "national
prospects." Clinton is described as a "populist with
the human touch." Provides background on Clinton.
His reelection in 1986 demonstrated that most
Arkansans were persuaded by his argument that
increased economic development depended on a better
educational system. Among others profiled were Henry
Cisneros, then mayor of San Antonio, Representative
John Lewis of Georgia, and senators Sam Nunn
(Georgia), Bob Graham (Florida), Charles Robb
(Virginia), and Lloyd Bentsen (Texas).

152 Hansen, Jane O. "School Tour Gives Leaders an
Education." Atlanta Journal/Atlanta Constitution,
November 15, 1986, D3. Photo. About Clinton's visit
to Atlanta's Rich's Academy, a magnet and alternative
school, which focused on helping potential high
school dropouts who faced issues like drug abuse,
teenage pregnancy and unemployment. The visit was
part of a two-day program for over 100 state and
national leaders, who met in Atlanta for a Education
Commission of the States conference. Clinton, chair
of the national educational policy group, said that a
top priority for the organization was the problem of
dropouts. He advocated developing programs at the
preschool level for at risk students to prevent
future dropouts. Clinton also noted that another
important issue was the need for programs to enhance
the work of principals and superintendents.

153 "Four Governors' Approaches to the Problem."
Atlanta Constitution, November 20, 1986, A12. In
conjunction with a feature article (in which Clinton
is noted) on poor blacks in the rural south, four
governors (besides Clinton, Georgia's Joe Frank

Harris, South Carolina's Richard Riley, and
Mississippi's William Allain) offered possible
solutions. Clinton pointed to the need for
constructing an "economic infrastructure in the rural
South" and attempted to change the views of companies
that did not want to locate in areas with large black
populations by demonstrating the viability, cost
effectiveness, and productivity of companies
employing a large black work force. Clinton also
noted the success of training programs to prepare the
local work force for such jobs.

154 Shipp, Bill. "Clinton is a Comer, But He May Not
Arrive by '88." Atlanta Journal-Constitution,
November 21, 1986, A27. Bill Clinton was a "gifted
political evangelist. Some might say demagogue." He
also was "one of the Democratic Party's brightest
Southern stars." While Clinton was one of the
founders of the Democratic Leadership Council, as of
late-1986 he had only played a marginal role in it,
unlike more active members like Sam Nunn, Charles
Robb, and Bruce Babbitt who were mentioned as
presidential hopefuls. Clinton presented his views
on several topics including the 1988 presidential
campaign (when the electorate would look for a leader
like John F. Kennedy as in 1960 following
Eisenhower), the 1986 elections and the Reagan
program, and the economic downturn produced by the
trade deficit and loss of jobs and markets to other
countries. The electorate wanted a new leader and a
new direction on the national level, Clinton
believed. If based solely on personality, Clinton
could win the White House, according to Shipp, who
added that Clinton may have waited too long to run
for president. Shipp, though, closed prophetically:
"But, in the end, if he decides against seeking the
nomination in 1988, it may not matter. Time is on
the side of this bright young governor."

155 Woodhouse, Linda R. "Clinton: Governors Don't
Want to End City Programs." Nation's Cities Weekly 9,
48(December 8, 1986): 20. Report on Clinton's
participation in a National League of Cities
conference, which included his presentation to its
Board of Directors on November 29, 1986. The main
theme was welfare reform and a Reagan administration
proposal for a state-federal exchange of welfare for
city programs. Clinton rejected this idea,
maintaining that many states did not have enough
funds to finance city programs. Then-mayor (and now
Secretary of HUD) Henry Cisneros represented the
Board and thanked Clinton for addressing it. Clinton

also spoke to the National Black Caucus of Local
Elected Officials (NBC/CEO). At this event, while
Clinton acknowledged that the Reagan administration
had been able to lower inflation and interest rates,
it had not dealt with the huge federal and trade
deficits nor with other problems like high urban
unemployment, a failing educational system, and other
social ills which prevented America from successfully
competing with other countries in the global economy.
Clinton also made a general appeal to all Americans
to work together to solve the difficult problems
facing the U.S.

156   Fisher, George. Fisher's Comic Relief: Editorial
Cartoons of Arkansas in the '80's. Fayetteville:
University of Arkansas Press, 1987. In the Preface,
Fisher observed that Clinton was the major figure of
the 1980s in Arkansas and succinctly described the
Clinton Arkansas experience. The contents of the
book is on a year-by-year chapter basis. A sample of
those chapters, which began with excellent summaries,
specifically mentioning Clinton included: "1980,
Republican Frank White unseats Governor Bill
Clinton;" "1982, Clinton regains seat;" "1983,
Clinton initiates new school standards program;"
"1986, Clinton defeats Faubus, White in their
comeback try;" and "1987, Bumpers backs out of
presidential race and Clinton is attracted to it."

157   Starr, John Robert. Yellow Dogs and Dark Horses:
Thirty Years on the Campaign Beat. Little Rock:
August House Publishers, 1987. A 30-year political
history of Arkansas, including an account of
Clinton's political career in Arkansas, which is
essentially negative since Starr is a well-known
Clinton critic. Starr was fond of labelling
politicians, including, Clinton--Bill "Defend the
Indefensible" Clinton. Various aspects of Clinton's
political career were covered in this book such as
the Cuban refugee crisis, educational reform,
Clinton's first three terms as governor, Clinton's
political races (for the U.S. Congress, attorney
general, and governor), and the Grand Gulf issue.
Includes index.

158   Herbers, John. "Governors Urge Tying Welfare
Benefits to Jobs." New York Times, February 18, 1987,
A15. Clinton, as chair of the National Governors'
Association (NGA), called President Reagan's plan for
changing the welfare system insufficient. Instead,
Clinton touted a plan formulated by the NGA, which
would require a majority of welfare recipients to

work. Clinton made this proposal at the National
Press Club.

159 Mashek, John W. "Ark.'s Clinton Still Studying
'88 Campaign." Atlanta Constitution, April 15, 1987,
A15. Clinton declared he was considering the
possibility of running for president and that he was
encouraged to do so nationwide. Arkansas political
observers thought Clinton would make a bid. On the
other hand, Clinton could face political problems in
Arkansas if he did run because of a then just
completed difficult session with the Arkansas
legislature and potential resentment for making such
a bid, having just won reelection as governor.

160 Lyons, Gene. ("Unsolicited Opinions" column).
"Who Cares Where Clinton Goes on the Weekend?"
Arkansas Times 13, 9(May 1987): 96. Lyons expressed
his disappointment with Clinton's record as governor.
After the Cuban refugee and auto license fee
controversies, Clinton appeared to have gone out of
his way to avoid offending any vested interests. In
this television age, Clinton was best at "public
performance," which might be the greatest asset he
could bring to the presidency. Presidential politics
involved images and symbols, which Clinton was good
at. Having thus established his position vis-à-vis
Clinton, Lyons addressed the title of his column--
public officials had a right to their privacy. Lyons
criticized Arkansas Gazette political columnist John
Brummett, who scrutinized Clinton very closely, which
only served to foster the "cult of personality" that
transforms political figures into celebrities and
encourages the trivial over substance.

161 Schmidt, William E. "Presidential Race Beckoning
Arkansas Governor." New York Times, May 31, 1987,
sec. 1, p. 28. Speculation on a possible bid by Bill
Clinton for the Democratic presidential nomination
following the withdrawal of Gary Hart from the race.
Clinton supporters both within and outside of
Arkansas felt the time was right for such a bid.
However, with state budget cutbacks and resultant
inadequate funding for prisons, welfare, and higher
education, Clinton was under growing criticism for
his many trips exploring presidential possibilities.
Some political observers in Arkansas observed that
Clinton seemed restless, even bored, in part, because
the next logical progression in his career would have
been the Senate. But the two Senate seats were in
the firm control of Dale Bumpers and David Pryor.
Schmidt wondered how far Clinton could go if he chose

to run since another "progressive Southerner,"
Senator Albert Gore, Jr. of Tennessee, was already in
the race and a late start by Clinton could put him at
a disadvantage in fundraising.

162   Lyons, Gene. ("Unsolicited Opinions" column).
"The Volvo Wagon As Getaway Car." Arkansas Times 13,
10(June 1987): 128.   The "most depressing educational
development of 1987" was the state Education
Department announcement that it planned to strengthen
teacher certification requirements with a mandate for
teachers to take a uniform number of "edu-babble
courses."   Lyons claimed that the Clinton
administration had "people in it who know better,
among them the governor and his wife."   But Clinton
did not wish to take on the educational lobby over
teacher requirements, especially as Clinton was about
to run for president.   This was an example of
self-interest by deferring reform efforts as a means
to preserve the educational bureaucracy.

163   "Arkansas Governor Advises Mayors Group." St.
Louis Post Dispatch, June 18, 1987, E1.   Clinton,
considered a possible contender for the 1988
Democratic presidential nomination, addressed big
city mayors at the annual U.S. Conference of Mayors
meeting.   Clinton advised the mayors that rather than
seek any specific commitments of aid from
presidential candidates, they should instead call for
consultations with whoever becomes president.
Clinton, who followed presentations by eight
presidential hopefuls, indicated he would decide soon
whether to run himself.   If he did, Clinton believed
that the key issue would be to demonstrate to the
country's rich and poor that their needs were
interconnected and that educational and social reform
helped both.   The remainder of the article was about
Senator Paul Simon (D) of Illinois, who addressed the
meeting as a presidential contender.

164   Toner, Robin. "Clinton is Poised to Enter '88
Race: Arkansas Governor Would Be 8th Democrat in
Campaign and Third From South." New York Times, July
2, 1987, A28.   On political speculation that Clinton
would run for president.   His press secretary, Betsy
Wright, believed that Clinton was so inclined, but
noted that a final decision had not yet been reached.
Clinton often debated whether he could run for
president and still be an effective governor.

165   Mooney, Carolyn J. "States Told They Must Take
Steps to Find New Breed of Leaders for Public

Schools: Arkansas Governor Says Recent
Education-Reform Plans Did Not Adequately Address
Issue of Leadership." Chronicle of Higher Education,
July 15, 1987, 19-20. Presents highlights of
Clinton's July 1987 speech to the annual meeting of
the Educational Commission of the States and a report
Clinton prepared for the conference entitled
"Speaking of Leadership."

166 Treadwell, David. "Clinton to Forgo Race for
White House." Los Angeles Times, July 15, 1987, I-4.
Clinton announced that he would not run for
president, citing the fact that he and his wife
wished to spend more time with their daughter Chelsea
and that he did not wish to begin a new campaign
after having undergone 15 in the last 13 years.
Clinton hoped that he could seek the presidency in
the future. While many political observers were
surprised by Clinton's announcement, most believed
that his absence would not make much of a difference
in an already a crowded Democratic field.

167 Baxter, Tom. "Clinton Puts Family Over
Presidency: Ark. Governor Rejects Race as Too
Demanding." Atlanta Constitution, July 16, 1987, A17.
Photo. Clinton cited as reasons for not running for
president concern about being away from his daughter
and a wish to have a normal family life. Until the
announcement, it was thought Clinton would run. He
did express an interest in making a future
presidential bid. When Gary Hart dropped out of the
presidential race, Clinton reconsidered running, but
family considerations eventually won out. This was
one of the major factors why other politicians like
Bill Bradley decided against seeking higher office.
Clinton thought he could win since being governor
provided insights into such crucial issues as
economic development and education. Clinton earlier
had thought that 1988 may have been his last
opportunity to run for president since if a Democrat
won in 1988 and was reelected in 1992, 1996 would
have been the next available year. Clinton hoped the
1988 campaign would involve a series of debates which
would lessen the need for extensive intense
individual campaigning. He noted, however, that,
despite the toll on family life, there were
politicians who were willing to pay that price.

168 Marshek, John W. "With Clinton Out, Gore's Staff
Expects More Southern Support." Atlanta Constitution,
July 16, 1987, A18. Clinton's decision not to run
for president enhanced the outside presidential hopes

of Tennessee Senator Albert Gore Jr. Still clouding
the political picture for Gore was the possible
candidacy of another southern politician, Georgia
Senator Sam Nunn. Gore staff officials said
Clinton's decision provided an opportunity for Gore
to raise more money in Arkansas and other southern
states. Charles Robb, former Democratic governor
from Virginia, expressed surprise at the Clinton
decision and would continue his efforts to encourage
a Nunn candidacy.

169 Dionne, E.J., Jr. "Clinton Traces His Decision
Not to Run for President to Family Obligations." New
York Times, August 16, 1987, 40. Based on an
interview Dionne conducted with Bill and Hillary
Clinton in July 1987. Clinton's decision not to run
for president was based on weighing personal versus
professional considerations, reflecting the dilemmas
faced by many working couples of their generation.
Eventually, the former prevailed, mainly out of a
concern to pay sufficient attention to their daughter
Chelsea, who was seven years-old at that time. Mrs.
Clinton pointed out, had Clinton decided to run, that
one of the key issues in the campaign would have
focused on children, but this would conflict with not
paying as much attention to their own daughter due to
the rigorous demands of campaigning. Clinton's
concern about long absences was reinforced by his
difficult childhood--his father was killed in an car
accident before he was born and his stepfather died
when he was 21. His announcement against running
surprised some of his supporters because, as Clinton
noted, he may never again achieve the national
recognition he had received as president of the
National Governors' Association. Clinton denied that
the new press scrutiny on candidates' personal lives
(like Gary Hart received) was a factor in his
decision against running, although he acknowledged
that all politicians think about it. Clinton summed
up his decision not to run for president in this way:
"'It hurt so bad...to walk away from it.'"

170 Kern, David F. "Paging Dr. Elders, Paging Dr.
Elders: Gov. Bill Clinton Needs You To Lead the
Health Department." Arkansas Business 4, 25(December
7-December 20, 1987): 12-14. Excellent profile of
Joycelyn Elders, who Clinton appointed to head
Arkansas' Health Department. Includes valuable
information on her background. This article's
significance was even more enhanced since Dr. Elders
is the current U.S. Surgeon General.

171 Blair, Diane D. <u>Arkansas Politics & Government:</u>
<u>Do the People Rule?</u> Lincoln: University of Nebraska
Press, 1988. Clinton has played a prominent role in
Arkansas politics. Blair discusses Clinton in
relation to the following topics--blacks; education;
as governor; the National Governors' Association; the
1974 congressional bid, the 1978 attorney generals
race; the 1980, 1982, 1984 and 1986 gubernatorial
elections; presidential prospects; and as a speaker.
The book also includes quotations from Clinton and is
well documented and contains an index. Includes
detailed bibliographic essay (chapter 15) and a
foreword by political scientist Daniel J. Elazar.

172 "Clinton, Bill." In <u>Current Biography Yearbook,</u>
<u>1988</u>. Charles Moritz, ed. New York: H.W. Wilson Co.,
1988, 1989. Basic biographical information on
Clinton until approximately August 1988.

173 Neuharth, Allen H., with Ken Paulson and Phil
Pruitt. <u>Profiles of Power: How the Governors Run Our</u>
<u>50 States</u>. Washington, D.C.: <u>USA Today</u> Books, Gannett
Co. Inc., 1988. Based on interviews conducted in
1987 with all 50 governors. Biographical information
was current as of June 30, 1988. Clinton was cited
in the introduction and issue sections on education
and welfare, including the Good Beginnings program,
which provided poor women and their children with
comprehensive health care. The section on Arkansas
included "Impressions" of Clinton, compiled only a
few weeks following the governor's decision not to
enter the 1988 presidential election. This decision
surprised <u>USA Today</u> as well as many Democrats for
Clinton had been a "man in a hurry." He appeared to
have presidential qualities--intelligence,
assertiveness, and a good personality--and he
demonstrated leadership in education at both a state
and national level. "'88 was not to be Bill
Clinton's year in the spotlight. But don't bet that
he's not already getting in tune for '92 or '96." In
the interview with Clinton, topics discussed included
teacher competency testing and educational reform,
Arkansans' self-image and the country's view of
Arkansas, the "business climate," and race relations
in the state. The "Clinton Profile" consisted of
highlights and basic information on Clinton's life
and political career. Regarding the future, Clinton
answered that: "'For what it's worth, I'd like to be
president.'" And his priorities were listed as
education, job creation, and welfare reform.

174 Osborne, David. <u>Laboratories of Democracy</u>.

Boston: Harvard Business School Press, 1988. On the
innovative ways Clinton and five other governors ran
their states. Chapter three, "Arkansas: The
Education Model," (pp. 82-110) analyzed Clinton's
education and economic development efforts. Clinton
also wrote the forward to the book, in which he
expressed pleasure at the discussion of his efforts
and described the book as "splendid." The Arkansas
chapter consisted of historical background, Clinton's
first term, his educational reform program, adult and
vocational education, and economic development.
Osborne described the governor as a "classic
new-paradigm liberal," a phrase which could be summed
up by an observation Clinton made: "'We may want the
government off our backs,...but we need it by our
sides.'"

175 Hardy, Thomas. "For Gov. Clinton, A Road Not
Taken This Election Year." (Column). Chicago Tribune,
January 3, 1988, sec. 4, p. 3. Clinton was a
"progressive Democrat with aspirations for national
office," who was not running in 1988 because he
believed putting his family first over politics was
best. Considering the field of announced candidates
and his political skills, Clinton could have emerged
as a front-runner for the Democratic nomination. If
Clinton made the right decision, then he had
positioned himself for a presidential run in 1992 or
later. If not, then he risked becoming another
political phenomenon. Both he and Mario Cuomo cited
the need to remain at home to be effective governors.
Clinton would become an increasingly important factor
in 1988 as he would like to use the presidential year
and the Democratic convention to achieve the sort of
national recognition and stature Cuomo had attained
in 1984. Clinton could be a good prospective
vice-president for a Democratic nominee like Paul
Simon and this could be the path to a future White
House bid.

176 Boul, David. "Ark. Prefers Bumpers to Clinton
for Vice President." Atlanta Journal/Atlanta
Constitution, January 31, 1988, A25. According to
The Southern Primary Poll, sponsored by the Atlanta
Journal-Constitution, 51% of those Arkansans polled
favored Senator Dale Bumpers for vice president
versus 29% who preferred Clinton. They were both
considered as possible national candidates.

177 Osborne, David. "And in Little Rock, Trenton,
and Richmond." Washington Monthly 20, 1(February
1988): 19-21. Accompanied Osborne's feature story on

ex-Arizona Governor Bruce Babbitt. Both adapted from Osborne's book Laboratories of Democracy.

178   Pertman, Adam. "Clinton Hints a Preference for Dukakis." Boston Globe, February 15, 1988, 9. Clinton thought Massachusetts Governor Michael Dukakis would make the best Democratic presidential candidate in 1988 and said he may later be involved in his campaign. In evaluating the field of presidential Democratic candidates, Clinton expressed regret at not making his own bid and noted that the Democratic field offered only parts of policies necessary to win back voter support for the party. Clinton was most enthusiastic about Dukakis, but felt constrained to make a formal endorsement due to pressure from southern party officials to support Tennessee's Senator Albert Gore Jr.

179   Graves, Beth Arnold. ("Southern Lights" section). "Hillary Clinton, Troubleshooter." Southern Magazine 2, 6(March 1988): 103. Photo. Graves noted that attorney Hillary Rodham Clinton was famous for her great interest in social issues (particularly children) and she earned a reputation as a "sharp-eyed troubleshooter" as chair of the Arkansas Education Standards Committee between 1983 and 1985. Governor Bill Clinton took some political heat for the controversial provision of teacher testing as part of educational reform. In contrast, according to Graves, "Hillary came out smelling like a rose."

180   "The Yuppie Governors of Dixie." U.S. News & World Report, March 28, 1988, 24. Brief profiles of three southern governors with a "can-do" attitude--Charles "Buddy" Roemer III of Louisiana, Ray Mabus of Mississippi, and Clinton, who "at 41,...[was] the old hand of the new Southern-leadership game," improving his state through such measures as educational reform. The resulting significant improvement in student performance earned him a national recognition. While receiving less coverage in this article than his other two southern counterparts, this article is important in that it places Clinton within the context of the efforts of other southern governors.

181 Sack, Kevin. "Arkansas Governor Gets the Honor of Nominating Dukakis." Atlanta Journal and Constitution, July 3, 1988, A12. Clinton was an "eloquent Southerner with close ties" to Dukakis, whose campaign announced that the Arkansan would give the nominating speech. Both politicians praised each

other. This friendship developed from their
involvement in the National Governors' Association
and the Democratic Governors' Association, both of
which had been chaired by Clinton.

182 Carman, John. (Datebook section). "Rambling Bill
Takes the Stand." San Francisco Chronicle, July 21,
1988. Carman, Chronicle television critic, panned
Clinton's long nominating speech.

183 Weinstein, Henry. "Clinton Talk Lauds Virtues of
Dukakis: Restores Focus on 'Apostle of Hope.'" Los
Angeles Times, July 21, 1988, sec. 1, p. 4. Clinton
had a key role at the 1988 Democratic convention,
making the presidential nominating speech for Michael
Dukakis. Clinton faced several challenges, including
returning the spotlight on Dukakis after Jesse
Jackson's moving speech the previous night. Instead
of speaking extemporaneously, Clinton closely
followed the prepared text and did not "exactly
electrify" the audience. In doing so, however,
Clinton may have set the tone for the convention--a
reasoned rational case for electing Michael Dukakis
by lauding Dukakis' character, vision and leadership
ability. Clinton is a practical southern politician,
who could make a compelling speech even while
discussing the details of government. Weinstein also
noted the opinions of others on Clinton, including
David Osborne, author of Laboratories of Democracy,
and political consultant William Schneider.

184 Christensen, Mike. "Clinton Finds Spotlight Can
Cast a Harsh Glare." Atlanta Constitution, July 22,
1988, C4. Clinton discovered that addressing a
national political convention was a two-edged sword.
It could enhance a politician's future or harm it.
Political commentators quoted in this article, Tom
Cronin and Stephen Hess, downplayed the negative
impact of the speech on Clinton.

185 Kurkjian, Stephen and Curtis Wilkie. "Ark.
Governor Winces Over a Failed Nominating Speech."
Boston Globe, July 22, 1988, 5. Instead of being a
shining moment in his career, Clinton's nominating
speech for Dukakis turned out be an embarrassment and
the subject of ridicule. It was described as being
too lengthy, devoid of memorable quotes, and
compounded by technical problems and an inattentive
audience. Clinton attempted to downplay the speech's
long-range impact. The article also noted that some
Dukakis campaign officials criticized Clinton for not
having endorsed Dukakis in the Arkansas Democratic

primary on Super Tuesday.

186 "Bill Clinton Goes on Carson: Speech Gets a Lot
of Laughs." <u>San Francisco Chronicle</u>, July 29, 1988,
13. About Clinton's appearance on the Tonight Show
with Johnny Carson following the governor's
nominating speech for Dukakis, which was criticized
as being too long and uninspiring. Both Clinton and
Carson joked about the speech. Clinton explained
that while his speech had been panned in the media,
his constituents continued to back him. He described
his speech as a "'good idea that didn't work.'"

187 McMath, Anne. <u>First Ladies of Arkansas: Women of
Their Times</u>. Little Rock, Arkansas: August House
Publishers, 1989, esp. pp. 249-256. Photos. Includes
extensive chapter on "Hillary Rodham Clinton," which
also contains many references to Bill Clinton. This
is both a factual and sympathetic account of the
Arkansas First Lady. (Page 258 of the index includes
entries for "Clinton, Bill" and "Clinton, Hillary
Rodham").

188 Blumenstyk, Goldie. "Governor of Arkansas Faces
Tough Battle With Legislature in Crusade to Raise
Taxes for Renewal of Higher Education." <u>Chronicle of
Higher Education</u> 35, 20(January 25, 1989): A21-A22.
On Clinton's efforts to improve higher education in
Arkansas and opposition to them from the legislature.
Clinton believed it was crucial for the state's
future to have a better educated work force.
Clinton's $192 million package included programs for
education, health, and economic development. Also
notes Clinton's national aspirations.

189 Applebome, Peter. "3 Governors in the South Seek
to Lift Their States." <u>New York Times</u>, February 12,
1989, 26. Photo. About the common struggle and
similarities among three young progressive southern
governors attempting to improve their respective
states, epitomizing the "New South." The governors
profiled were Mississippi's Ray Mabus, Louisiana's
Buddy Roemer, and Clinton.

190 Gay, Faith. "Power in the Delta." <u>Southern
Exposure</u> 17, 4(Winter 1989): 56-59. About voting
rights for blacks in Arkansas. Jeffers v. Clinton
was a voting rights case initiated by 17 blacks who
maintained that the state purposely divided black
neighborhoods into several legislative districts in
1981 to lessen their voting power and opportunities
of being elected to the legislature. This case

reflected the sharp racial and economic fissures in
Arkansas politics. Involved the district (located in
the predominantly black Mississippi delta region of
Arkansas) of State Senator Paul Benham, Jr. in which
blacks were underrepresented. The plaintiffs in
Jeffers v. Clinton wanted the provisions of the
amended Voting Rights Act to apply to Arkansas.
However, Olly Neal, the plaintiffs' lawyer, asserted
that two of the members of the Arkansas Board of
Apportionment, Clinton and Secretary of State Steve
Clark, would oppose redistricting for political
reasons (so not to put Benham out of office).

191 Brown, Raisin. "Thirty-Four Years at the
Governor's Mansion." Ebony 44, 9 (July 1989): 52, 54,
56. Photos. Story about Liza Ashley, food production
manager, at the governor's mansion in Little Rock.
Article notes her book of remembrances and recipes
entitled Thirty Years at the Mansion.

192 Decker, Cathleen. "Arkansas Governor Schooled on
South L.A. Life." Los Angeles Times, September 30,
1989, II-1. Photo. Clinton visited south Los Angeles
to gather information in conjunction with his
educational activities. Clinton was co-chair of an
education summit held in Charlottesville, Virginia,
by President Bush and other governors. Clinton was
selected to draft national education goals. Clinton
also had a political motivation for the L.A. visit
since he then was a potential presidential candidate.
Clinton's low-key visit included a tour of south
central Los Angeles. Conversations with children
there revealed stories of crime and random violence,
reflecting national discussion about improving
schools and related city problems of gangs and drugs.

193 Leveritt, Mara. "Hillary on Her Own Terms."
Arkansas Times 16, 2 (October 1989): 32-35, 102.
Insightful article about then Arkansas First Lady
Hillary Rodham Clinton and her relationship with Bill
Clinton as advisor and the "consummate political
spouse." Includes background information on Hillary
Clinton such as her participation, with Bill Clinton,
in the 1972 McGovern campaign in Texas and the
impeachment case against President Richard M. Nixon.
Leveritt also discussed her role as chair of the
Arkansas Education Standards Committee, to which she
was appointed in 1983 by the governor. Accompanied
by opinions on Hillary Clinton from prominent
Arkansans, including former Clinton chief of staff
Betsy Wright and political scientist Diane Blair. An
informative sympathetic portrayal.

194   Dillin, John. "Gov. Clinton: Country's Future at Stake." <u>Christian Science Monitor</u>, February 28, 1990, 7.   Interview with Clinton, who believed that education was a top priority because the nation's future depended on it for economic growth and prosperity.   Clinton also advocated a 90% graduation rate for public schools because that was the international standard.   Clinton wanted schools, teachers, and principles to have more responsibility so they could have greater flexibility in their work.

195   Dillin, John. "Governors Back Education Goals: National Governors' Association." <u>Christian Science Monitor</u>, February 28, 1990, 7. Photo.   Discusses Clinton in his role as co-chair of the National Governors' Association (NGA) Task Force on Education and his views on education.   All sectors of society should contribute to education.   The federal government ought to play a "'limited, but very significant'" role in education (Head Start, funding of research and development, and funding of college loans, grants, and work-training programs). Regarding allocation of funds, 90% still would be provided at the state and local level.   The corporate sector and higher education would assist in school reform.   The major focus, however, would be on the schools and educators.   Accompanied by an article entitled "Education Goals of America's Governors," adopted February 25, 1990, by the NGA.

196   Broder, David S. "A Close Governor's Race in Arkansas? Longtime Incumbent Clinton to Face Ex-Democrat in Fall Showdown." <u>Washington Post</u>, May 31, 1990, A10.   Outlook for the Arkansas gubernatorial race between incumbent Clinton and Sheffield Nelson, an ex-Democrat and Clinton state appointee.   The Republican gubernatorial primary drew attention because it matched two Republicans who had just the year before switched party affiliation. Nelson defeated Representative Tommy F. Robinson 55 to 45% in the Republican primary.   President Bush welcomed Robinson's entry into the G.O.P. and he was encouraged by national leaders to run for governor. But Nelson was favored by Arkansas Republican leaders.   On the Democratic side, Clinton won the primary by a vote of 54 to 39%, thereby just avoiding a runoff.   While Clinton said he was "'not surprised,'" both state Republican and Democratic politicians believed the closeness of a near runoff indicated that voters were growing weary of him.

197   Kaplan, Dave. "Arkansas, Ex-Democrats Provide
Action In GOP Gubernatorial Race." <u>Congressional</u>
<u>Quarterly Weekly Report</u> 48, 22(June 2, 1990): 1743.
Discusses interest in Arkansas Republican
gubernatorial primary race between Republican
Representative Tommy F. Robinson and ex-utility
executive Sheffield Nelson, who won. Clinton won on
the Democratic side, but by a narrower margin than
expected. This closer margin fostered speculation
that Arkansans may have grown tired of Clinton's long
tenure. Clinton's major opponent in the Democratic
primary, Tom McRae, criticized Clinton and tried to
tap into voter discontent with the incumbent.
Clinton responded by shoring up his electoral
support. A number of his constituents, however,
wanted to vote in the GOP primary against Robinson,
who Clinton supporters thought could pose a greater
threat to the governor than the lower-key Nelson.

198   "A Candid Interview: Governor Bill Clinton."
<u>Arkansas Times</u> 16, 11(July 1990): 4 unnumbered pages
between pp. 66 and 67. While this is a political
advertisement paid by the Committee to Re-Elect
Governor Clinton, some important information can
still be gleaned, keeping in mind this fact. The
introduction and interview itself share the theme
that the governor had established the groundwork for
important issues (such as education and economic
development) in his past terms as governor and that
they would be achieved in another term.

199   "Clintonland." <u>Economist</u>, July 14, 1990, 29.
Photo. Prospects for the 1990 Arkansas gubernatorial
race. Prediction that Clinton would win, but "not by
much" since he only won 54% of the vote in the
Democratic primary. This primary was overshadowed by
the spirited Republican primary won by Sheffield
Nelson. Predicted that Nelson would criticize
Clinton based on the latter's record and for
increasing taxes. (Nelson viewed the governor's
educational reform as a sham). Nelson also would
portray him as a "Dukakis liberal," while Clinton
likes to be seen as a moderate. Finally, Nelson
would assert that Clinton cared more about fostering
his national ambitions rather than be governor of
Arkansas. Most Arkansans, however, were proud to
have a governor with presidential potential as would
members of the Democratic Leadership Council, who
preferred a "non-liberal southern presidential
candidate." A fellow DLC member, Georgia Senator Sam
Nunn, however, made Clinton the brunt of a joke,
claiming that Clinton, in paraphrase, was the "first

American politician to have been a bright young rising star in three successive decades."

200   Farney, Dennis. "Clinton of Arkansas, Ex-Boy Wonder Still Hoping To Be President, Is Battling to Remain Governor." <u>Wall Street Journal</u>, September 27, 1990, A20. Describes Clinton's challenging reelection bid against Sheffield Nelson. This election could either renew Clinton's political career or end it. Clinton expressed his desire "'to serve another term and run'" for president. Another term would afford Clinton a chance to see the achievement of his reforms and revive his national image. Nelson was a harsh critic who described the incumbent as a politician who had worn out his welcome and asserted that Clinton was only seeking reelection to maintain his presidential aspirations. This election would demonstrate that Clinton was not "'presidential timber.'" Nelson's major theme was echoed by highway billboards reading "'Ten Years is Enough!!'" Nelson also challenged Clinton's claim of being an "'education governor.'" Nelson, who supported Edward Kennedy's bid against Jimmy Carter in 1980, was described by Clinton as a political opportunist. The election, however, really amounted to a referendum on Clinton. Clinton acknowledged he had presidential ambitions for 1996 and that he nearly declared for president in 1987.

FIFTH TERM AS GOVERNOR, 1990-1992 (INCLUDING ASSESSMENTS OF CLINTON'S ARKANSAS RECORD AS GOVERNOR)

201   Leveritt, Mara and Judith M. Gallman. "Grading the Gov: A Special Report." <u>Arkansas Times</u> 17, 3(November 1990), 34-43. Analysis of Clinton's education record as governor of Arkansas. Noting that "accountability" had been a theme of Clinton's education reform efforts, the article also contains the opinions of Arkansan educators and politicians. Leveritt also noted: "One of Clinton's greatest achievements...is that he brought such inseparable issues as prenatal health, early childhood development, teen pregnancy, and drug abuse into the overall discussion of education."

202   Brummett, John. "The Politics of Death Row." <u>Arkansas Times</u> 17, 4(December 1990): 50-56. Deals with attitudes towards capital punishment in Arkansas among politicians and the general public. (Among those interviewed were Betsy Wright, Clinton's former chief of staff and then chair of the Arkansas

Democratic Party). Clinton declined to be
interviewed because he did not want to talk about
capital punishment in a political context. Arkansas
was late in joining other southern states in
reinstituting the death penalty. A politician's
career sometimes could be jeopardized if that
politician opposed capital punishment since public
opinion generally supported it. Clinton enjoyed
solid support among blacks in Arkansas, although more
than not blacks were on death row in the state's
prison system.

203 Brummett, John. "Dusty Wisdom: Those Who Ignore
the Lessons of the Past are Condemned To Repeat It;
In Arkansas, They Also Win Elections." ("I Speak
Arkansaw" column). Arkansas Times 17, 9(May 1991):
106. Within the context of a consideration of
environmental policy in Arkansas under various
administrations, Governor Clinton's position on the
environment is noted.

204 Clift, Eleanor. "Desperately Seeking
Southerners: Will Gore or Clinton be the Democrats'
Hope?" Newsweek, May 13, 1991, 33. As potential
Democratic presidential candidates, Gore and Clinton
had advantages because to win the presidency, the
Democratic Party needed to carry the south and at
least a portion of the west. Clift compared their
relative strengths and weaknesses. Mary Matalin,
chief of staff for the Republican National Committee
(and later a major official in the Bush reelection
campaign), made an interesting comparison between the
two Democrats. She dismissed Clinton ("'What's his
base?'") while viewing Gore as a formidable opponent.
Clift also mentioned Virginia Governor Douglas Wilder
as another possible Democratic candidate for
president. It is ironic that Clinton and Gore were
considered as potential rivals for the Democratic
nomination at this time, but later became the
Democratic ticket due to their complementary
qualities.

205 Brummett, John. ("I Speak Arkansaw" column).
"Have You Ever? Founded or Not, Rumors of Sexual
Escapades Would Likely Dog Bill Clinton in a
Presidential Campaign." Arkansas Times 17, 10(June
1991): 90. In the 1990 gubernatorial race,
unsubstantiated allegations were made regarding
Clinton's personal life. Opponent Sheffield Nelson
did not think the governor would run for president
due to this issue. Brummett described innuendos like
these as "have-you-ever-questions" and speculated

that if Clinton did run for president, his refusal to
answer such questions would fuel speculation
regarding his vulnerability on it and that he would
be plagued by this issue. Brummett believed that
such questions were getting out of proportion and he
was not sure if Clinton would deal with the issue
directly if he became a presidential candidate. This
article foreshadowed the question that would plague
Clinton during the 1992 campaign. Brummett is
generally viewed as a political observer who formerly
was favorable to Clinton, but later criticized him
from the left.

206 Harbrecht, Douglas. ("Washington Outlook"
column). "Bill Clinton: Can He Make It Out of
Arkansas?" Business Week, July 8, 1991, 43.
Harbrecht wondered if a southerner like Clinton could
win the Democratic presidential nomination since the
nominating process for Democrats was dominated by
liberals and labor. Even so, it seemed that Clinton
was the only Democrat willing to run. While he did
not have a powerful political base (Arkansas), he
earned a reputation as an activist governor and made
effective speaking appearances, notwithstanding his
1988 nominating speech for Dukakis. What
distinguished Clinton from other Democratic hopefuls
was his record as a problem-solver. During his
governorship, he made educational and welfare reform
"into national models" by calling for responsibility
from those receiving government help. Clinton has a
lot of "pluck," declaring that the role of government
was not social engineering but to help people succeed
on their own. Positioning himself as a centrist,
Clinton cautioned that Democrats could not have
national appeal without going more to the political
center. Harbrecht, however, was skeptical whether a
southern Democrat could capture the nomination.

207 Allen, Charles Flynn. Governor William Jefferson
Clinton: A Biography with a Special Focus on His
Educational Contributions. Ph.D., University of
Mississippi, August 1991. The Clinton period was one
of the most important in Arkansas history for
education. Educational reform was a major component
of the Clinton years. Allen described his study as a
"comprehensive account of...[Clinton's] educational
reform movement." This study concentrated on which
factors influenced the governor to make education a
top priority both in Arkansas and nationally. The
dissertation studied Clinton's early life and Clinton
as a scholar, teacher, politician, and reformer.
Allen concludes this work with a quantitative and

qualitative assessment of the success of Clinton's
educational reform program in Arkansas. This work is
not only valuable for its content, but also for its
documentation, which provided many valuable
citations. In addition, the relative newness of this
work also enhances its value due to the added
perspective it provides.

208   Klein, Joe. ("National Interest" column).
"Arkansas Traveler: Here Comes Clinton." New York 24,
31(August 12, 1991): 12-13. Klein discussed
Clinton's tentative testing of the presidential
waters as he visited New York. Despite being from a
small state, not having any foreign policy
experience, viewed as controversial by some within
the Democratic Party for being president of the
moderate Democratic Leadership Council, and reticent
to discuss details of his personal life, Clinton's
message of being a "New Democrat" (or in David
Osborne's terminology a "'new paradigm liberal'") had
appeal as did the phrase "'reinvent government.'"
The major issue appeared to be the U.S.'s declining
standard of living and a concern over health care.
Klein reviewed Clinton's record in Arkansas regarding
educational reform, public service in exchange for
college financial assistance, and an emphasis on
personal responsibility. Clinton was well-versed on
a variety of issues. New Democrats like Clinton
could rebuild the moribund Democratic Party.

209   Clift, Eleanor. "The Clinton Experiment: Can He
Help Change the Democrats' Image?" Newsweek,
September 30, 1991, 37. Photo. Clinton's anticipated
entrance into the Democratic race gave Democrats an
opportunity "to break the liberal lock on the party."
Clinton's charisma and centrist positions had made
him the best candidate for many Democrats after the
1988 Dukakis defeat. It was questionable if he could
emerge on top in a "primary process dominated by
liberal activists." The perception of Clinton as a
moderate came from his willingness to limit
government and tie rights with responsibilities.
Yet, Clinton also believed in government activism.
As a candidate, Clinton's strengths were in his
contradictions. He was well-educated, but came from
humble beginnings, an ideal life scenario for beltway
image makers. While Clinton's record had critics, he
generally had served his state well. University of
Arkansas political scientist, Robert Savage, rated
Clinton "a 7, maybe an 8" on a scale of 1 to 10.
Clift assessed Clinton's political prospects on the
eve of his entrance into the presidential race.

Regardless of how he fared, Clinton could change
Democratic politics by closing the "chapter on the
New Deal and the Great Society."

210 Lemov, Penelope. "Art Lockhart: The End of a
Feud?" Governing 5, 1(October 1991): 17. On the
long-standing dispute between Clinton and Art
Lockhart, director of the Arkansas state prison
system. Clinton disapproved of Lockhart's management
style, which he termed autocratic, and asserted that
Lockhart did not focus enough on rehabilitation.
Lockhart believed that Clinton opposed him due to
political reasons. (Republican Governor Frank White
appointed Lockhart in 1981). Lemov predicted that
what may have been the "longest-running public feud
in Arkansas politics" appeared likely to reach an end
since an important Lockhart supporter on the state
Board of Corrections (Knox Nelson, an influential
state senator) had been defeated and thus would no
longer be on the Board, which had exclusive authority
over the position of prison director.

211 Toner, Robin. "Arkansas' Clinton Enters the '92
Race for President." New York Times Biographical
Service 22, 10(October 1991): 1036-1037. Reprinted
from New York Times, October 4, 1991, p. A10.
Clinton's formal announcement for the Democratic
presidential nomination. He criticized G.O.P.
domestic policy and vowed to restore the hopes of the
overlooked middle class, pledging to "'reinvent
government,'" infuse it with American values, and
refocus attention on neglected domestic ills. He
promised improvements in education, middle class tax
breaks, and a stronger economy, but also called for
responsibility from everyone. This reflects
Clinton's belief that the government should be more
activist and problem-solving without being wasteful.
Clinton and other Democratic hopefuls like Nebraska's
Bob Kerrey believed that Bush had weaknesses which
were overlooked due to his high poll numbers.
Clinton and Kerrey were willing to challenge
Democratic orthodoxy and traditional thinking.
Clinton's speech reflected a populist tone and he
attempted to avoid ideological labels, maintaining
that the public wanted workable policies. While the
emphasis of the speech was on the neglected middle
class, he did discuss issues like race and expressed
concern for the poor.

2

1992 Presidential Campaign, October 4, 1991-November 3, 1992

NEWSPAPERS (OCTOBER 4, 1991-NOVEMBER 3, 1992)

Arkansas Times (Weekly newspaper)

212 Brummett, John. "Bill: Thanks, Old Buddy: I'm Having a Wonderful Time While You Run for President." May 7, 1992, 5.

213 Brummett, John. "James Carville, Clinton's Human Missile, Spins and Wins With the 'Comeback Kid.'" May 7, 1992, 30.

214 Brummett, John. "The Mean Streets: Bill's Bloody Path to Victory." May 7, 1992, 1, 28-29, 32-34. Photo.

215 Smith, Doug. "A Tale of Two Scholars: The Clinton Campaign." May 7, 1992, 35.

216 Brummett, John. "Bill, Jim Guy: Which of You Runs Things Around Here?" May 14, 1992, 22-24. Photo.

217 Brummett, John. "A Big Deal For Little Rock: We're Off the Beaten Path, But Clinton Turns Us Into a National Nerve Center." May 28, 1992, 11-12.

218 Brummett, John. "With Pen in Hand: Here's Another Letter to Clinton With the Only Advice He'll Need." June 11, 1992, 5.

219 Brantley, Max. "Clinton Campaign Deficit Not Insurmountable, Aide Says." June 18, 1992, 12.

220   Brummett, John. "Bill Clinton's Big Moment: Next Week's Convention is His Showcase, But the Networks are Reducing Coverage." July 9, 1992, 10, 12.

221   Brummett, John. "Reintroducing Bill Clinton, the Rocky Balboa of Politics: Democratic Convention." July 16, 1992, 10, 12. Photo.

222   Brummett, John. "Clinton Will Win--Unless: It Will Be Mean, But the Candidate is Resilient, the Game Plan is Good." July 23, 1992, 22-23. Photos.

223   Martin, Richard. "Northwest Arkansas Water: The Real Story." August 6, 1992, 22-23.

224   Brummett, John. "The Clinton 'War Room.'" August 27, 1992, 10, 12.

225   Leveritt, Mara. "The First Lady Removes Her Gloves: The Democratic Candidate's Wife Strikes Back at a Strategy She Calls 'The Big Lie.'" August 27, 1992, 15, 20-21.

226   Brummett, John. "Economy vs. Credibility." September 10, 1992, 5.

227   Brummett, John. "The Real Arkansas: It Fits Neither of the Portrayals Dominating the Political Debate." September 17, 1992, 5.

228   Brummett, John. "White Folks For Bill: Only a Candidate of Splendid Dexterity Could Execute the Democrats' Plan." October 1, 1992, 5.

229   Brummett, John. "Abroad Press Bus No. 4 With the Clinton Caravan: It's a Wild, Maybe Triumphant Journey." October 8, 1992, 16-17. Photos.

230   Brummett, John. "Ending Welfare: Clinton Has Promised To Do Just That, But the Key Phrase is 'As We Know It.'" October 8, 1992, 5.

231   Brummett, John. "The Year That Was: The Highs and Lows of Bill Clinton's 12-Month March From Southern Governor To Presidential Front-Runner." October 15, 1992, 14-16. Photos.

232   Brummett, John. "My Life With Bill: He's Funny, Boyish and Competitive; Maybe He'll Be An O.K. President." October 29, 1992, 6.

233   Christian Science Monitor

234 Los Angeles Times

235 New York Times

236 USA Today

237 Washington Post

Extensive newspaper coverage of the Clinton campaign.

SPECIALIZED POLITICAL JOURNALS

238 Congressional Quarterly Weekly Report

239 National Journal

Provides detailed information and analysis.

CONSERVATIVE POLITICAL MAGAZINES

240 American Spectator

241 Insight on the News

242 National Review

In addition to specific annotated citations
contained in this bibliography, these publications
also covered Clinton during the campaign from a
conservative political perspective.

FINANCIAL/ECONOMIC ORIENTED MAGAZINES

243 Business Week

244 Forbes

245 Fortune

In addition to specific annotated citations
contained in this bibliography, these publications
also covered Clinton during the campaign from an
economic viewpoint.

ARTICLES ON EARLY DEMOCRATIC PRESIDENTIAL CANDIDATES

246 Fineman, Howard. "The '60s Democrats." Newsweek,
October 7, 1991, 38-39. Photos.

247   West, Woody. "Political Waters Sure Lack Fizz."
("The Last Word" column). Insight on the News,
October 7, 1991, 48.

248   Alter, Jonathan. "Voters to Press: Move Over."
("Between the Lines" column; Cover story). Newsweek,
October 14, 1991, 29.

249   Fineman, Howard. "The No Bull Campaign." (Cover
story). Newsweek, October 14, 1991, 22-27. Photo.

250   MacKenzie, Hilary. "Chasing a Dream." Maclean's,
October 14, 1991, 32.

251   "Straight Talk." Newsweek, November 4, 1991, 29.

252   "Democrats in Peril: Southern Politics."
Economist, November 16, 1991, 32-33. Photo.

253   "Show Time for 'the Six-Pack': A Reader's Guide
to the Democrats and Their Issues." Newsweek,
November 25, 1991, 21, 24.

254   Clift, Eleanor. "How To Run Against Cuomo."
Newsweek, December 9, 1991, 29. Photo.

255   "Fields For Dreamers." Maclean's, December 9,
1991, 22.

256   Gleckman, Howard. "Running Against the Bush
Economy: How the Democratic Contenders are Vying for
the Middle Class." Business Week, December 9, 1991,
60-62.

257   Will, George F. "No Happy Warriors Hear."
Newsweek, December 16, 1991, 82.

258   Fineman, Howard. "Tough Love From the Dems."
Newsweek, December 23, 1991, 32. Photo.

259   Roberts, Steven V. and David Gergen. "Ready,
Set, Propose: At the Starting Gate, Democrats Show
They are Re-Examining Their Flaws." U.S. News & World
Report, December 23, 1991, 24-27.

260   Roberts, Steven V. "Horse Race." U.S. News &
World Report, December 30, 1991, 23.

261   "In 1992, I Resolve To...: The Candidates Offer
Their New Year's Resolutions." Newsweek, January 6,
1992, 24.

262 Dowd, Ann Reilly. "What the Leading Democrats Want." Fortune, January 27, 1992, 88-89.

263 Garland, Susan B. "Harkin vs. Clinton: The Tug of War for Labor is Just Beginning." Business Week, January 27, 1992, 43.

264 Barone, Michael. "Where the Choices are Clear." U.S. News & World Report, February 10, 1992, 37.

ANNOTATED ENTRIES (INCL. ARTICLES, BOOKS, NEWSPAPERS)

265 Klein, Joe. "Beating Bush (It Could Happen)." New York 24, 43 (November 4, 1991): 36-41. Despite the conventional wisdom that George Bush would win the 1992 election, a majority of Americans felt that the country was heading in the "'wrong direction.'" Democratic presidential hopefuls like Clinton and senators Bob Kerrey and Tom Harken believed that Bush was vulnerable and could be defeated. But of all Democratic candidates, Klein believed that Clinton had the most comprehensive vision for America in a call for a "'New Covenant'" between the "'people and their government, to provide opportunity...inspire responsibility...and restore a sense of community to this great nation.'" While Clinton was still a "longshot" to defeat Bush, he and other Democratic candidates were determined enough to make the 1992 election the "first real debate about the nation's soul and purpose in a long time."

266 Ifill, Gwen. "Clinton Delivers a Mainstream Message With a Southern Accent." New York Times Biographical Service 22, 12 (December 1991): 1418-1421. Reprinted from New York Times, December 27, 1991, p. A16. About early stages of the Clinton campaign which involved securing adequate financial support and gaining name recognition. Like the centrist Democratic Leadership Council he helped establish in 1985, Clinton is seeking a middle-of-the-road stance, calling for essentially a blend of historically Democratic social issues with economic policies adopted from the Republicans. Clinton believed that the Democratic Party's future was contingent on changing its focus. He called for middle class tax cuts and individual responsibility. Clinton supporters were trying "to make a marketable virtue of his moderation." Senator Sam Nunn stated that Clinton would "'run straight and true.'" Clinton, however, remained a "governor from a small, impoverished state that has improved but not

flourished under his leadership" and who, in Clinton's words, "'spent 11 years on the receiving end of the Reagan revolution.'"

267 Kramer, Michael. ("The Political Interest" column). "At Least Someone Has a Plan." Time, December 2, 1991, 20. Clinton was the only candidate who had a reasonably coherent economic plan. He rejected both trickle-down-economics and the traditional Democratic "tax and spend" philosophy. His greatest economic concern was to make the U.S. competitive internationally so he focused on education and worker training. Clinton, unlike Bush, understood the advice Jack Kemp had given to President Bush: Americans would forgive attempts at helping the economy even if they fail, but not making any effort economically would be unacceptable.

268 Carlson, Margaret. "Bill Clinton: Front Runner By Default." Time, December 30, 1991, 19-21. Photos. Clinton was doing very well, apparently having put behind him questions about his personal life (only to have them reemerge in January and February).

269 Allen, Charles F. and Jonathan Portis. The Comeback Kid: The Life and Career of Bill Clinton. New York: Birch Lane Press, 1992. Photos. Based on Allen's research for his doctoral dissertation from the University of Mississippi. (See entry 207). Portis had followed Clinton's political career since the mid-1970s. As was the case with Allen's dissertation, a major focus here is Clinton's education record as governor. Other aspects of the Clinton years are considered plus his earlier political career in Arkansas and his presidential prospects. Sources are largely from interviews, newspapers, and magazines. Contains a detailed index.

270 Cortez, John P. "Bill Clinton." In Newsmakers: The People Behind Today's Headlines. Louise Mooney, ed. 1992 Cumulation. (Includes Indexes to 1985 through 1992). A good biographical overview of Clinton's life and political career.

271 Levin, Robert E. Bill Clinton: The Inside Story. New York: S.P.I. Books, 1992. Photos. This popularly written paperback discusses in considerable detail Clinton's political career from the mid-1970s to September 1992, devoting much attention to his Arkansas political record. Like the Allen/Portis and Moore books, it was written to correspond with the

1992 presidential campaign. Lacks notes and index.

272 Moore, Jim with Rick Ihde. <u>Clinton, Young Man in a Hurry</u>. Fort Worth, Texas: Summit Group, 1992. Photos. Unauthorized political biography of Clinton by two Arkansas journalists. To understand Clinton as a candidate, it was important to know his record (including education) as governor. The authors are generally supportive of Clinton. Drawbacks to the book include the lack of footnotes and an index.

273 "Governor Bill Clinton (D-Arkansas)." <u>Meet the Press</u> (NBC News), January 5, 1992, 1-10. Transcript of an interview with Clinton conducted by moderator Tim Russert (NBC News) and a panel of David Broder (<u>Washington Post</u>) and Lisa Myers (NBC News). Among the wide range of issues discussed were: trade with Japan, the recession, the economy, the budget deficit, Medicare, health care reform, term limits for Congress, welfare reform, and foreign policy, including the Middle East and economic aid to Russia.

274 Schorr, Daniel. ("Washington Notebook" section). "From Adultery to Adulthood." <u>New Leader</u> 75, 1 (January 13-27, 1992): 4. Clinton's personal life had been always just beneath the surface in the campaign, but came to the surface and became a big issue when the Gennifer Flowers story appeared in the tabloid newspaper the <u>Star</u>. In the CBS program, "60 Minutes," Clinton appeared with Hillary and did acknowledge previous marital difficulties, which had since been resolved. Schorr hoped that the American electorate would distinguish between private life and public performance.

275 Alter, Jonathan. "More Inspection for Mr. Beef." ("Between the Lines" column). <u>Newsweek</u>, January 20, 1992, 37. Notes a potential conflict for Clinton in his proposal to reinvent government--his "innate caution about offending people. His message is to challenge; his nature and experience tell him to please." If Clinton were to make budget cuts, he would have to ask for sacrifices (entitlement cuts).

276 Barone, Michael. "The Clinton Surge." ("Tomorrow" column). <u>U.S. News & World Report</u>, January 20, 1992, 31. Photo. Upbeat assessment of the Clinton campaign just prior to the Flowers' allegations and draft letter controversy.

277 Clift, Eleanor. "Bold Plans--And Trims on the Edges: A Look at Clinton's Record in Arkansas."

Newsweek, January 20, 1992, 36. Clinton assumed bold
positions, but then made so many concessions that his
message became blurred. He had a vision to solve
long-term problems, but his reticence to make enemies
diminished his initiatives ("politician's disease").
In many policy areas (education, taxes, crime,
environment, poverty), Clinton's rhetoric did not
match the results. Clinton had to convince "voters
he can turn around America when he hasn't been able
to do it in Arkansas."

278   Klein, Joe. "Bill Clinton: Who Is This Guy?"
(Cover story). New York 25, 3(January 20, 1992):
28-35. Photos. While a Clinton trademark had been
the "clarity and detail" of his responses to
questions, Clinton tended "to describe issues rather
than take stands on them" and, according to David
Broder, tried "'to have it both ways
on...controversial questions.'" Clinton's "signature
program" could be the national service/loan repayment
plan. Opinions on Clinton also are presented by
David Osborne, author of Reinventing Government, and
journalist John Brummett.

279   Kramer, Michael. "Why Clinton is Catching On."
("The Political Interest" column). Time, January 20,
1992, 18. Photo. Explains Clinton's appeal (just
before the Gennifer Flowers and draft controversies).
Clinton stood out from a not-so-distinguished
Democratic field of candidates. Liberals, tired of
losing, wanted a Democrat in the White House.
Clinton had domestic policy experience in Arkansas
and his linkage of responsibility with rights
appealed to voters in general. In the past, to get
nominated Democrats had to go left and then veer to
the right to compete in the general election. This
"ideological zigzag" only served to alienate the
voters and Clinton recognized this.

280   Carlson, Margaret. "Hillary Clinton: Partner as
Much as Wife." Time, January 27, 1992, 19. Photo.
Fine summation of Hillary Clinton's background and
her marriage on which she commented: "'The public can
learn enough to know whether a candidate is a decent
person without having to pick you apart so much that
there is nothing left at the end.'"

281   Church, George J. "Is Bill Clinton For Real?"
Time, January 27, 1992, 14-18. Photos. Although
proclaimed early on as the front runner, Clinton
still appeared contradictory--an innovative planner
but a poor implementor and a conciliator who

occasionally shifted his position. Yet, he seemed the most electable and that satisfied many Democrats. Much of the article discussed Clinton's background as governor and a candidate.

282 Kramer, Michael. "The Self-Making of a Front Runner." ("The Political Interest" column). Time, January 27, 1992, 20. Photo. Clinton was his own "chief strategist and tactician." Clinton discussed campaign strategy in the primaries and looked ahead to the fall campaign against Bush. Written on the eve of the Gennifer Flowers allegations.

283 Brummett, John. "Meeting Big-Time Reporters." ("I Speak Arkansaw" column). Arkansas Times 18, 6(February 1992): 112. Brummett notes contrast in favorable press coverage of Clinton nationally with more critical treatment of him in Arkansas from, for example, journalists John Robert Starr, Meredith Oakley, and Brummett himself, who described Clinton as an "inattentive, wishy-washy governor."

284 DePaulo, Lisa. "He Came From the Swamp." Washingtonian 27, 5(February 1992): 56-59, 141, 143-149. Extensive popularly written article about the career of the unconventional political consultant James Carville. One of Carville's themes was that Democratic candidates must be in tune with issues affecting the middle class (such as the cost of higher education and not with special interest group issues). Or, as a friend of Carville stated it, "...most of America isn't on K Street, but in Kmart."

285 Young, Gordon. "The Moderate Stance of Bill Clinton." World & I 7, 2(February 1992): 46-49. On Clinton's Arkansas record. Clinton had been criticized for "his tentative approach to leadership," which can be traced to his "disastrous" initial term as governor and loss in the so-called "'Cubans and Car Tags'" 1980 election. Clinton only had one major political confrontation in Arkansas, that with the Arkansas Education Association over competency testing for teachers. In his own defense, Clinton maintained that he was able to achieve more via compromise than he did with the "headstrong" manner which characterized his initial term as governor. Young, however, maintained that Clinton "successes" ran into problems and cited Project Success, a workfare program. Thus, Young characterized Clinton's record as "spotty."

286 Blumenthal, Sidney. "The Anointed: Bill Clinton,

Nominee-Elect." New Republic, February 3, 1992,
24-27. Clinton quickly became the Democratic
front-runner because most Democrats believed he had
the best chance to win largely due to his political
skills. He had been consistent in "ideological
circle-squaring," meaning that he assumed positions
on issues which appealed to both the right and the
left. He supported tougher work requirements for
welfare, but linked that requirement with education
and child care. Whether Clinton's "circle-squaring"
efforts would help him gain the nomination was still
in question at this time. He did want to make the
federal government a positive force for Americans.

287   "'I Think We're Ready.'" Newsweek, February 3,
1992, 21-23. Photo. Excerpts of an interview by
Eleanor Clift with Hillary Clinton, who discussed her
family, career, and marriage.

288   Kopkind, Andrew. "The Manufactured Candidate:
Clinton Already?" Nation, February 3, 1992, 116-118,
120. Criticism of Clinton from the left, which
questioned Clinton's Arkansas record. Clinton's
long-range economic strategy was inconclusive and he
offered "no evidence that he can reverse the decline"
of American politics. This was a "status quo
election....Clinton's success must be counted in the
devalued currency of American politics. His is a
masterpiece of manufacturing, a triumph of
positioning rather than positions...."

289   "The Candidates' Sex Lives." U.S. News & World
Report, January 27, 1992, 46.

290   Kinsley, Michael. "Private Lives: How Relevant?"
Time, January 27, 1992, 19.

291   "Bill Clinton, Hanging by Three Threads."
Economist, February 1, 1992, 30.

292   "Clinton Agonistes." (Editorial). Economist,
February 1, 1992, 16-17.

293   Alter, Jonathan. "Substance vs. Sex." Newsweek,
February 3, 1992, 18-20. Photo.

294   Borger, Gloria. "Who's Waiting in the Wings?"
U.S. News & World Report, February 3, 1992, 35.

295   Greenfield, Meg. "Electoral Strip Search."
Newsweek, February 3, 1992, 72.

296 Kramer, Michael. "Moment of Truth." <u>Time</u>, February 3, 1992, 12-14. Photo.

297 McDonald, Marci. "The Sex Factor." <u>Maclean's</u>, February 3, 1992, 60-61. Photo.

298 Morrow, Lance. "Who Cares, Anyway?" <u>Time</u>, February 3, 1992, 15.

299 Roberts, Steven V. "Defusing the Bombshell: Bill Clinton Puts His Antiscandal Strategy into Effect Amid New Charges About His Private Life." <u>U.S. News & World Report</u>, February 3, 1992, 30-31, 35. Photo.

300 "Sex and the Candidate." (Editorial). <u>New Republic</u>, February 3, 1992, 7-8.

301 Turque, Bill and Nancy Cooper. "'We're Voting for President, Not Pope.'" <u>Newsweek</u>, February 3, 1992, 23.

302 Heim, David. "Virtues and Vices: Public and Private." (Editorial). <u>Christian Century</u> 109, 5(February 5-12, 1992): 115.

303 Barone, Michael. "Where the Choices are Clear." <u>U.S. News & World Report</u>, February 10, 1992, 37.

304 Borger, Gloria and Steven V. Roberts. "Democrats' Fatal Vision." <u>U.S. News & World Report</u>, February 10, 1992, 34-35, 37. Photo.

305 Carroll, Ginny. "Surviving the Smear: One Woman's Story." <u>Newsweek</u>, February 10, 1992, 26-27.

306 Clift, Eleanor. "Character Questions." <u>Newsweek</u>, February 10, 1992, 26-27. Photo.

307 "Clinton at the Boiling Point: On Guard." <u>U.S. News & World Report</u>, February 10, 1992, 35.

308 Henry, William A., III. "Handling the Clinton Affair." <u>Time</u>, February 10, 1992, 28-29.

309 Kramer, Michael. "The Vulture Watch." ("The Political Interest" column). <u>Time</u>, February 10, 1992, 27. Photo.

310 "Notes and Comments." <u>New Yorker</u>, February 10, 1992, 25-26.

311 Zuckerman, Mortimer B. "Money for Mischief."

(Editorial). <u>U.S. News & World Report</u>, February 10,
1992, 82.

312 Collum, Danny Duncan. "The Slippery Road From
Edward R. Murrow to Tabloid TV." <u>National Catholic
Reporter</u> 28, 15(February 14, 1992): 22.

313 "The Clinton Letter." <u>Economist</u>, February 15,
1992, 27.

314 "The Beast is Always Hungry." <u>Newsweek</u>, February
17, 1992, 23.

315 "Bed and Broad." (Editorial). <u>National Review</u>,
February 17, 1992, 14-15.

316 Blumenthal, Sidney. "Bill and Ted: An
Unexcellent Adventure." <u>New Republic</u>, February 17,
1992, 13, 16.

317 "Clinton and the Vietnam Draft Question."
<u>Newsweek</u>, February 17, 1992, 22. Photo.

318 Diamond, Edwin. "Crush Course: Campaign
Journalism 101." <u>New York</u> 25, 7(February 17, 1992):
28-31.

319 Kramer, Michael. "The Vulture Watch, Chapter 2."
("The Political Interest" column). <u>Time</u>, February 17,
1992, 24.

320 Pruden, Wesley. "Scrappy Nuggets for Clinton's
Jam." <u>Insight on the News</u>, February 17, 1992, 17-18.
Illus.

321 "Sex and the Candidate II." <u>New Republic</u>,
February 17, 1992, 8.

322 Turque, Bill. "Northern Exposure." <u>Newsweek</u>,
February 17, 1992, 20-22. Photo.

323 Church, George J. "Will Someone Else Leap In?"
<u>Time</u>, February 24, 1992, 22. Photo.

324 Morrow, Lance. "The Long Shadow of Vietnam."
<u>Time</u>, February 24, 1992, 18-21. Photo.

325 Pollitt, Katha. "Clinton's Affair?" <u>Nation</u>,
February 24, 1992, 220-221.

326 Turque, Bill. "Reliving the 60's." <u>Newsweek</u>,
February 24, 1992, 22-23. Photo.

327   Pruden, Wesley. "Of Morals, Politics and the Media." Insight on the News, March 2, 1992, 17-18. Illus.

328   Blackburn, Thomas E. "Below the Belt? It's What's Between the Ears that Counts." National Catholic Reporter 28, 18(March 6, 1992): 17.

329   Eastland, Terry. "In Bed with Bill." American Spectator 25, 4(April 1992): 58-60.

330   "Press Affection, and Vivisection." Newsweek, April 6, 1992, 26.

331   Sidney, Ken. "A Question of Character." (Editorial). Christianity Today 36, 4(April 6, 1992): 16.

Articles on Clinton's draft history, personal life, and press coverage of it.

332   Fox, Tom. "Bill Clinton's Dangerous Liaison Not With Flowers." ("Inside NCR" column). National Catholic Reporter 28, 14(February 7, 1992): 2. Clinton's "dangerous liaison" was not with Gennifer Flowers, but with Arkansas death row inmate, Rickey Ray Rector. Fox wanted the media to pay more attention to Rector. Clinton made a point to be in Arkansas when Rector was executed on January 24, 1992. Clinton never gave clemency to a death row inmate. Thus, capital punishment should be an issue.

333   Cockburn, Alexander. "Sex, Clinton and Contras." ("Beat the Devil" column). Nation, February 10, 1992, 151-152. Gennifer Flowers incident and allegations of a link between Arkansas and the contras when Clinton was governor in the 1980s.

334   Dwyer, Paula. "Clinton Bashes Business--But Does He Mean It?" Business Week, February 10, 1992, 97-98. Photo. Clinton's populist anti-corporate record leading up to the New Hampshire primary contradicted his pro-business record as governor. There were also differences in Clinton's positions as candidate and his record as governor in the areas of income, tax policy, civil rights, environment, and job safety.

335   Klein, Joe. "The Bimbo Primary: Bill Clinton Confronts the Media's Heart of Darkness--and His Own." New York 25, 6(February 10, 1992): 22-26. Despite Clinton's problems regarding rumors (besides Flowers, Larry Nichols, a disgruntled state employee

who raised money for the Nicaraguan contras),
Clinton's prominence over the other Democratic
hopefuls was not that surprising since the Arkansas
governor was the best candidate based on political
talent. The New Hampshire primary, however, had
become the "Bimbo Primary," with an "uncontrollable
media." To Clinton's credit, this episode "revealed
a rather attractive--and important--aspect of his
character: grace under pressure."

336 Klein, Joe. "Missing in Action: The Democrats in
New Hampshire." ("The National Interest" column). <u>New
York</u> 25, 7(February 17, 1992): 14-15. Klein reports
a week before the New Hampshire primary, discussing
candidates Jerry Brown, Bob Kerrey, Tom Harkin, Paul
Tsongas, and Bill Clinton. Before scandals broke,
Clinton had been in a solid position. But they took
a toll on the campaign and the candidate, physically
and emotionally. The New Hampshire primary thus
became a "referendum on Bill Clinton's character."
Compounding this turn of events was the impression
Clinton gave of trying to please and finesse
everyone. Being on both sides of an issue only
served to heighten questions about his character. As
the front-runner, Clinton grew more cautious and
stopped challenging voters to demand change, although
Clinton's tendency is toward conciliation.

337 Cockburn, Alexander. "Chapters in the Recent
History of Arkansas." ("Beat the Devil" column).
<u>Nation</u> 254, 7(February 24, 1992): 222. Cockburn
claimed that by the mid-1980s, Arkansas played a key
role in the Nicaraguan contra war and the covert
arms-for-drugs supply network. It is alleged that a
plan to maintain a cover-up of Oliver North's plan
was carried out in the governor's mansion.

338 Cockburn, Alexander. "Homage to Clintonia."
("Beat the Devil" column). <u>Nation</u> 254, 7(February 24,
1992): 223. Argues that since the appearance of the
Clintons on "60 Minutes," the press had been giving
the governor "strictly kid-glove treatment" because
it wanted Clinton to gain the Democratic nomination.
Thus, the "establishment has made its pick," Cockburn
citing the <u>New Republic</u>, the <u>New York Times</u>, and the
<u>Washington Post</u>. He offered a harsh characterization
of Clinton. "Psychologically as well as politically,
he's a man with two faces."

339 Mayer, William G. "Do You Take This Man...?
Voters & Vows: The Character Issue." <u>Commonweal</u>,
February 28, 1992, 6-7. The Clinton campaign

minimized the damage generated by the Gennifer
Flowers/marital infidelity issue. However, character
remained a significant issue since personality
affects how presidents make decisions. Lyndon
Johnson was stubborn, Nixon duplicitous and
dishonest, Carter lacked leadership, and Reagan's
manner of governing hindered him at times. Clinton
was trustworthy enough to serve as president. Over
the past 30 years, the Democrats' most consistent
difficulty in national elections had been their
stance on social and cultural issues like race,
crime, religion, abortion, and patriotism. This
position alienated many blue collar voters who might
otherwise have backed Democratic economic policies.

340 Brantley, Max. "The Insider...: Hillary Redux;
Bill's Bills." Arkansas Times 18, 7(March 1992): 27.
Changes in Hillary Clinton's appearance. Clinton
still was in debt for his 1990 campaign for governor.

341 "The Democrats and Arms Control: The Questions
in 1992." Arms Control Today 22, 2(March 1992): 3-6.
Paul Tsongas and Bill Clinton on nine defense related
questions, including possible risks posed by the
demise of the Soviet Union, the Strategic Arms
Reduction Treaty (START), defense budget cuts,
reduction of nuclear proliferation, restraint of the
international trade in conventional weapons, the
Strategic Defense Initiative (SDI) and the
Antiballistic Missile (ABM), comprehensive ban on
nuclear testing, the U.N.'s role in regional
conflicts and regional arms control, and other major
arms priorities (chemical and biological weapons).

342 Magaziner, Ira and Hillary Rodham Clinton. "Will
America Choose High Skills or Low Wages?" Educational
Leadership 49, 6(March 1992): 10-14. If the U.S.
were to restore its competitive position in the
global economy, it was necessary for education and
industry to teach all workers high level skills.
Beginning in the 1980s, U.S. productivity had
declined and income distribution had worsened. The
Commission on the Skills of the American Workforce
identified a number of problems and offered
solutions. The authors called for a system by which
all employers would invest 1% of their payroll on
worker education and training. Also addressed were
the issues of school dropouts and worker retraining.

343 "Worst-Best." Arkansas Times 18, 7(March 1992):
37. Presents a "Worst-Best" of Arkansas on various
topics including the "Clinton administration," whose

"best" was the appointment of Dr. Joycelyn Elders as
director of the Arkansas Health Department. Other
references to Clinton are in categories such as "Gun
control," "Political analysis," and "Cheap eats."

344 Fineman, Howard. "Wondering Who's 'Electable.'"
Newsweek, March 2, 1992, 24-26. Photo. Compares the
"electibility" of Clinton and Tsongas based on
honesty, political strength, and consensus building.

345 Klein, Joe. "Something Happened: New Hampshire
Signals that the '92 Election May be One of Those
Historic Turning Points." New York 25, 9(March 2,
1992): 24-27. Photo. The New Hampshire primary could
foreshadow the November election as a turning point
like those of 1932 and 1968. Clinton's persistence
resulted in a solid second-place finish in New
Hampshire. Yet, the Clinton campaign was weakened by
the Flowers and draft controversies and could
ill-afford any other damaging revelations.

346 Roberts, Steven V. and Matthew Cooper. "Slick
Willie vs. Plain Paul." U.S. News & World Report,
March 2, 1992, 39-41. Photos. Clinton and Tsongas on
various issues. Both had similar views on education
and trade while differing over taxes. Also discusses
Clinton's Arkansas record.

347 Wills, Gary. "H.R. Clinton's Case." New York
Review of Books 39, 5(March 5, 1992): 3-5. Illus.
Wills discussed the writings and speeches of Hillary
Rodham Clinton, including those in these edited
works--The Rights of Children, Children's Rights, and
Beyond the Looking Glass. Wills also surmised to
what extent Bill Clinton agreed with his wife's
advocacy of "'activist' state programs in child care,
health, and education."

348 Applebome, Peter. "Bill Clinton's Uncertain
Journey." New York Times Magazine, March 8, 1992,
26-29, 36, 60, 63. Reprinted in: New York Times
Biographical Service, 23, 3(March 1992): 274-279.
Applebome writes a wide-ranging article on Clinton,
just prior to the March 1992 Super Tuesday primaries.
Applebome discusses Clinton's earlier political
career, his political record as governor of Arkansas,
and the campaign from December 1991 to March 1992.

349 Barnes, Fred. "The Clinton Gap: Why Paul Tsongas
Won New Hampshire." New Republic, March 9, 1992,
25-27. Clinton lost the New Hampshire primary
because, besides the Flowers and draft issues, he

became cautious as the so-called Democratic front-runner. Thus, without a strong message from Clinton, Tsongas was able to win. Also discussed was Bob Kerrey's ineffectual candidacy.

350 Clift, Eleanor. "Political Ambitions, Personal Choices." Newsweek, March 9, 1992, 36-37. Photos. Interview with Clinton, who still was plagued by controversies over infidelity and the draft. Among the topics discussed were work, ambition, his marriage, religious faith, and the campaign.

351 Hertzberg, Hendrik. "New Hampshire Diarist: Press Pass." New Republic, March 9, 1992, 46. Hertzberg's observations on New Hampshire, including Clinton. While the press still may have questioned the candidate's private character, they became convinced of his public character due to his ability to weather political storms.

352 Kinsley, Michael. "Colonel of Truth." ("TRB From Washington" column). New Republic, March 9, 1992, 6. Kinsley defends Clinton on the draft issue and, more specifically, the letter Clinton wrote in 1969 to Col. Eugene Holmes of the Arkansas ROTC.

353 Klein, Joe. "No Pain, No Gain: Slick Willie and Pawky Paul." ("The National Interest" column). New York 25, 10(March 9, 1992): 14-15. The primary campaign's focus was about to shift to the "Super Tuesday" southern primary states. Tsongas presented more problems to the Clinton campaign than the other candidates due to Tsongas' direct style and blunt remedies for the country's economic problems.

354 "St. Paul Meets the Comeback Kid: The Democrats." Economist, February 22, 1992, 22.

355 Alter, Jonathan. "Stepping It Up." Newsweek, March 16, 1992, 22-24. Photo.

356 Barrett, Laurence I. "Southern Fried Feuding." Time, March 16, 1992, 25, 27.

357 Dentzer, Susan. "Can Either Fix the Economy? The Ideas of Clinton and Tsongas Aren't as Different as They Claim." U.S. News & World Report, March 16, 1992, 26-27, 29.

Stories about the Clinton and Tsongas campaigns as the Democratic primary process continued.

358   "The Fine Old Contest That Could Be." Economist,
March 14, 1992, 25-26.   Outlook on a likely contest
between Bush and Clinton, who could be the best
Democratic candidate since Robert Kennedy.

359   "Moody Michigan." Economist, March 14, 1992, 26.
Prospects of the presidential contenders (including
Clinton) in the usually volatile Michigan primary.

360   Klein, Joe. "Profile in What?: Clinton's Real
Character Gap." ("The National Interest" column). New
York 25, 11(March 16, 1992): 27-28.   Despite primary
election victories, character questions continued to
plague Clinton. He discussed general themes such as
opportunity, responsibility, and community, but did
not really take a difficult and consistent stand on
issues like nuclear power and welfare reform.
Clinton needed to display political courage.

361   Kramer, Michael. "Onward to the Rust Belt."
("The Political Interest" column). Time, March 16,
1992, 29.   The Illinois primary would be a critical
contest for Clinton to show that he was not just a
regional candidate but a national one, a lesson
Clinton gained from Al Gore's experience in 1988.

362   "A Voter's Guide to the Issues." Newsweek, March
16, 1992, 30-36.   Includes brief profile of Clinton
and other Democratic candidates. Also presents
Clinton's positions on energy/environment, education,
health care, national security, economic growth, and
social policy. Assesses how Clinton might govern in
terms of vision, management, collegiality,
communication, and style.

363   "Clinton's Message." (Editorial). Economist,
March 21, 1992, 13-14.   Following the Super Tuesday
and midwest primaries, Clinton emerged as a
"plausible Democratic messenger," though doubts
remained about his character. Clinton needed to
appeal nationally beyond the south to win.

364   "Governor Bill Clinton (D-Arkansas), Candidate
for 1992 Democratic Presidential Nomination." Meet
the Press (NBC News), March 22, 1992, 1-9.   Much of
this program concentrated on the character question
and alleged shifts of position (the gas tax).   Other
topics included the Democratic primaries, the role of
Hillary Clinton in a Clinton administration, change,
Congress, defense cuts, and speculation on a vice
presidential running mate for Clinton.

365 Barone, Michael. "Old-Time Liberalism: The
Sequel." ("On Politics" column). U.S. News & World
Report, March 23, 1992, 42. Clinton's program
represents an updated version of traditional
Democratic (Hubert Humphrey) liberalism.

366 Barrett, Laurence I. and Stanley W. Cloud. "A
Clash of Visions." (Cover story). Time, March 23,
1992, 14-15. Photo. Clinton and Tsongas were leading
the Democratic Party in a new direction "away from
interest-group economics toward a new vision of
American competitiveness." A Clinton-Tsongas ticket
could pose a formidable challenge to the G.O.P.

367 Cooper, Matthew. "An Uncertain Embrace." U.S.
News & World Report, March 23, 1992, 30-33, 36.
Photos. Doubts still lingered about Clinton's
character. Cooper examined Clinton's political
career in Arkansas regarding his willingness to take
firm stands on issues. Clinton had not yet shown the
candor a president needs to make difficult choices.

368 Greenwald, John. "May the Best Plan Win." Time,
March 23, 1992, 24-25. Clinton and Tsongas on income
taxes, capital gains, competitiveness, social
spending/entitlements, and energy.

369 Kramer, Michael and John F. Stacks. "'Now That
We're Face to Face.'" Time, March 23, 1992, 16-23.
Photos. One-on-one debate between Clinton and
Tsongas over economic policy and an accompanying
smaller article on negative campaigning (pp. 18-19).

370 "A Talk With Bill Clinton: 'I Want to Generate a
Lot of Millionaires.'" Business Week, March 23, 1992,
28-29. Taxes, donations, and economic policy were
discussed in this interview.

371 Turque, Bill. "Playing Hardball." Newsweek,
March 23, 1992, 33, 35. Bush campaign plots strategy
for the November election against Clinton based on
two premises--an economic recovery and growing voter
doubt about his character.

372 Alter, Jonathan. "The Real Character Issues."
("Between the Lines" column). Time, March 30, 1992,
33. Clinton's perseverance and commitment to public
service were a good measure of his character.

373 Baer, Donald and Steven V. Roberts. "The Making
of Bill Clinton." (Cover story). U.S. News & World
Report, March 30, 1992, 28-31, 34. Was Clinton an

instrument of principled change or a shallow
candidate whose ambition dictated his positions and
actions? Exploration of Clinton's background and
political past to determine what influenced him.

374 Barone, Michael. "Entering the Cultural Combat
Zone." ("On Politics" column). U.S. News & World
Report, March 30, 1992, 39. Hillary Clinton's views
on social issues like children's rights.

375 Clift, Eleanor. "Testing Ground: The Inside
Story of How Clinton Survived the Campaign's Worst
Moments." Newsweek, March 30, 1992, 34-36. Photo.
How Clinton endured the draft and Flowers
controversies before the crucial New Hampshire
primary and the key role played by James Carville.

376 "Clinton Express?" (Editorial). Nation, March
30, 1992, 399-400. The media rejoined the Clinton
bandwagon, which had been temporarily sidetracked by
personal questions. The editorial doubted the
premise that Clinton appealed to both blacks and
whites, making him a viable candidate.

377 Drew, Elizabeth. "Letter From Washington." New
Yorker, March 30, 1992, 70-78. In her "Letter" dated
March 19, Drew assessed the 1992 presidential
campaign. Voters remained uncertain about Bush and
Clinton. Clinton's nomination would be the result of
luck and his own abilities.

378 Fineman, Howard and Ann McDaniel. "Can He Beat
Bush?" Newsweek, March 30, 1992, 24-27. Photo. The
fall campaign essentially began with Tsongas'
withdrawal from the Democratic primaries because
Clinton now had a clear path to the Democratic
nomination. Clinton's challenge was to devise a
strategy to defeat Bush. Fineman and McDaniel also
speculated as to how Clinton would deal with the
"'character'" question and if Hillary Clinton would
constitute a plus or minus for Clinton.

379 Harbrecht, Douglas and Richard S. Dunham. "The
Trouble with Bill." Business Week, March 30, 1992,
23. Photo. Despite Clinton's political assets,
misgivings about his character, alleged shifts in
positions, and missteps by his wife were liabilities.

380 Hull, Jon D. "Sweet Smell of Success." Time,
March 30, 1992, 20-25. Clinton had won the Illinois
and Michigan primaries and Tsongas withdrew from the
race. Thus, Clinton had the nomination all but

secured, unless he faltered. Clinton had yet to
prove, however, whether he could defeat Bush in the
fall election, whose outcome could depend on whether
the economy improves sufficiently for Bush to win or
whether Clinton's new coalition of blacks and the
middle class would hold. The article is accompanied
by a photo essay by P.F. Bentley entitled "Behind the
Scenes of the Clinton Campaign."

381 "'I Do Have Core Principles.'" U.S. News & World
Report, March 30, 1992, 30-31. Photo. Interview with
Clinton, including these topics: Hillary Clinton,
congressional Democrats, political ambition, and
being governor.

382 Klein, Joe. "Elvis vs. Big Daddy: Fall Preview."
New York 25, 13(March 30, 1992): 31-33. Many voters
continued to harbor doubts about Clinton. Media
speculation about Clinton's electibility and
character overshadowed the substance of his campaign.
Political conjecture was emerging over anticipated
Republican attacks against Clinton in the general
election. Clinton needed to articulate his vision
for the country.

383 Kramer, Michael. "Clinton's Foreign Policy
Jujitsu." ("The Political Interest" column). Time,
March 30, 1992, 27. Clinton was attempting to
achieve what Mario Cuomo termed "'political jujitsu'"
(appropriating your opponent's area of expertise)
vis-à-vis George Bush on foreign policy. In
anticipation of a major foreign policy address,
Kramer speculated that this was Clinton's strategy by
advocating more aid to Russia than Bush had.

384 "Taking on Bill Clinton: Quayle's First Salvo."
U.S. News & World Report, March 30, 1992, 38.
Interview with Dan Quayle on topics such as foreign
policy, Congress, Hillary Clinton, and family values.

385 Walsh, Kenneth T. "Face-Off: Bush vs. Clinton:
The Fall Campaign Will Center on Competing Risk
Assessments." U.S. News & World Report, March 30,
1992, 36-38. Predictions on Republican and
Democratic campaign strategy for the fall campaign.
Bush's strategy would be to attack Clinton's Arkansas
record, question his character, and emphasize his
lack of foreign policy experience. As for Clinton,
he would argue that Bush just reacted to problems as
they occurred, Bush was out of touch, and that Bush
conducted an "amoral, timid foreign policy."

386 "'You Didn't Reveal Your Pain: Clinton Reflects
on the Turmoil in His Childhood.'" Newsweek, March
30, 1992, 37. Photo. On early influences in
Clinton's life, including his upbringing, stepfather,
and his alleged tendency to overplease.

387 Brinkley, Joel. "Clinton Remakes Home State in
Own Image." New York Times, March 31, 1992, A1, A16.
Although many Arkansans believe their state had made
progress under Clinton's leadership, it still has a
long way to go in terms of most measurements of the
quality of life partly due to Arkansas' long-term
poverty. Some Arkansans believe that without
Clinton, the state would be even further behind in
its quality of life. Refers to Diane D. Blair's
book, Arkansas Politics and Government. Part one of
a five-part series entitled "Clinton as Governor: 12
Years at Arkansas's Helm," which continued in the
April 1-4 issues (see entries 392-95).

388 Brantley, Max. "The Insider...: The People Pay;
Telling Habit; Promises, Promises; Where There's
Smoke." ("In Our Times" column). Arkansas Times 18,
8(April 1992): 26-27. Various items on Clinton--
funding raising for him in Arkansas, the death
penalty for Rickey Ray Rector, gay rights, and Betsy
Wright, Clinton's former chief of staff.

389 Brummett, John. "The New Demopublicans." ("I
Speak Arkansaw" column). Arkansas Times 18, 8(April
1992): 90. Criticism of Tsongas and Clinton for
promoting the "neo-liberal" version of Reaganomics.

390 Hammer, Joshua. "The Miracle Worker?" GQ
(Gentlemen's Quarterly) 62, 4(April 1992): 136, 138,
140-141, 143-144, 146. Photos. Good profile of
Clinton political consultant James Carville, written
at a pivotal point in the Clinton campaign as the
Arkansas governor was recovering from negative
publicity in January and February 1992.

391 Warren, Mark. "Taking a Sound Bite Out of the
Republicans." Esquire 117, 4(April 1992): 53-54,
56-58. On Clinton campaign consultants James
Carville and James Begala. Their successful
management of the Harris Wafford senatorial campaign
in 1991 set the tone for the 1992 campaign. They
believed that obstacles within their own party were
as great as those they faced with the G.O.P. An
important part of their campaign strategy was to
attack Republicans at their weak points and stay with
a basic message such as addressing the concerns of

the "'forgotten middle class.'" They were pleased
with the New Hampshire primary outcome.

392 Ayres, B. Drummond, Jr. "Despite Improvements,
the Schools in Arkansas are Still Among Worst." New
York Times, April 1, 1992, A22. Despite many
accomplishments by Clinton in the education field
(increased expenditures, mandatory testing for
teachers, expanding curriculums, establishing new
academic standards, lowering the dropout rate, and
fostering greater college attendance), Arkansas still
remains near the bottom of most national ratings,
although Clinton's efforts have prevented Arkansas
from falling even further behind. The fact that
Clinton had made education a top priority is
reflected in Arkansas being ranked third in the
proportion of its budget allocated to education.
Regarding the Clinton record on education, Sid
Johnson, president of the Arkansas Education
Association, offered a favorable evaluation.

393 Gerth, Jeff. "Policies Under Clinton Are a Boon
to Industry." New York Times, April 2, 1992, A20.
Clinton's economic policies have made Arkansas a
state friendly to business due to tax breaks, low
wages, and a cooperative atmosphere between
government and business, resulting in higher economic
growth rates. On the other hand, industry wields a
great political influence. Arkansas has had above
average unemployment rates and a larger proportion of
households with lower incomes. But no governor has
single-handedly been able to transform a poor state
into a rich one.

394 Holmes, Steven A. "Race Relations in Arkansas
Reflect Gains for Clinton, but Raise Questions." New
York Times, April 3, 1992, A14. Clinton as governor
tried to promote racial harmony. A number of blacks
have been appointed to state government. Arkansas'
legislature, however, failed to pass a civil rights
bill in 1991, despite Clinton's support for it. The
delta southeast region has a large black population,
which generally has been unaffected by the economic
growth in other parts of Arkansas. Most black
leaders, however, agree that Clinton had done his
best, considering the obstacles he faced (a
conservative legislature resistant to change).

395 Schneider, Keith. "Clinton Relies on Voluntary
Guidelines to Protect Environment in Arkansas." New
York Times, April 4, 1992, 10. Supporters of
Clinton's environmental policy believe his approach

offered an effective balance between economic growth and environmental protection. But critics maintain that his "hands-off approach" sacrifices the environment to influential state industries. However, even environmentalists concur that Clinton is a "staunch preservationist." Clinton's policy has been to encourage voluntary industrial compliance with environmental protection through voluntary guidelines and tax incentives, similar to Bush's approach.   More time was needed to determine whether Clinton's voluntary approach to environmental compliance ultimately would prove effective.

396   Baer, Donald. "Is the Press Fair to Bill Clinton?" U.S. News & World Report, April 6, 1992, 33-34. Photo. The media appears to alternate between being too harsh on Clinton and then too soft.   A large measure of Clinton's frustration was that a number of allegations which surfaced during the campaign already had been leveled against him in Arkansas and were being revived by his local political enemies. The character question was related to other concerns people had about the Democratic candidate--some did not believe his explanations to questions raised, his trustworthiness, his personal style (charm), and the fact that Clinton believed in politics when most Americans are cynical about government. Voters also wanted to know more about Clinton's "biography."

397 Blumenthal, Sidney. "The Poll: Bill Clinton in Illinois." New Republic, April 6, 1992, 16-19. Politics is a very personal matter to Bill Clinton. There is no distinction between the person and the politician. Clinton enjoys the political process when many Americans are disillusioned with it. The personal nature of politics fits in well with Illinois politics. With his victory in the Illinois primary, Clinton was one step closer to securing the Democratic nomination and a contest with Bush.

398 Cockburn, Alexander. "Beat the Devil." Nation, April 6, 1992, 438-439. On Arkansas' alleged link, including Arkansas Development Finance Authority and Terry Reed, in the contra supply network in 1985 when military aid to the contras was banned by Congress.

399 Diamond, Edwin. "Selling Clinton." New York 25, 14(April 6, 1992): 36-38. Photos. About the Clinton media campaign for the New York primary, whose underlining theme was to control Clinton's image while defining the images of other candidates like

Jerry Brown. Frank Greer headed the Clinton media campaign in New York and nationally.

400 Fineman, Howard. "A Blood Sport: Brown's Protest Candidacy is Part of a Democratic Ritual: Devour the Presumptive Nominee." Newsweek, April 6, 1992, 24-25. Discusses Jerry Brown's challenge to Clinton prior to the New York primary. Although Clinton was still in a good position for the nomination, Brown's win over Clinton in the Connecticut primary revealed the "fragility of Clinton's candidacy."

401 Klein, Joe. "The Piñata Primary: Jerry Brown is Going to Try to Whack a Big, Tempting Target Named Bill Clinton in Next Week's Showdown." New York 24, 14(April 6, 1992): 32-35. Photo. It was ironic that while Clinton portrayed himself as an agent of change, he was perceived as an old-time politician in New York. Clinton was well aware of the difficulty in overcoming this public image--an adverse result in this primary could foreshadow problems in the fall.

402 Kondracke, Morton. "Greaseman: What Does Clinton Stand For?" New Republic, April 6, 1992, 19-22. Clinton detractors have portrayed him as a Walter Mondale Democrat, tied to special interests. Advisors James Carville and Paul Begala urged Clinton to project himself as the most "'electable'" Democrat, which may suggest that Clinton was without fundamental principles, "Bush with a twang." However, Clinton did hold certain policies and beliefs, including a belief in an active government, in revitalizing the U.S.'s ability to compete world-wide economically, in worker training, education, and "tax fairness." He also stood for racial harmony, personal responsibility, and government reform to deliver services in the best, most efficient manner. This distinguished Clinton from past Democratic liberal philosophy. Still, Kondracke wondered if Clinton had basic principles he would not sacrifice or compromise on.

403 Lief, Louise. "Clinton, Bush and the World: Dueling Foreign-Policy Offensives." U.S. News & World Report, April 6, 1992, 34. Both the Bush and Clinton campaigns realized that Bush was open to criticism on a wide array of foreign and national security issues (Russia). Despite such criticism, Bush was still perceived by the public as better suited than Clinton in dealing with foreign policy. The Bush campaign hoped to capitalize on that perception.

404   McCloud, Thom. "New York City Event is
Campaign's First Urban Forum." <u>Nation's Cities Weekly</u>
15, 14(April 6, 1992): 1, 14.   Clinton and Jerry
Brown met with 15 mayors at a meeting on urban
issues, discussing gun control, infrastructure,
employment, trade, federal mandates, recycling, and
preservation of the economy.   Event was held one week
before New York, Kansas, and Wisconsin primaries.

405   Talbott, Strobe. "Clinton and the Draft: A
Personal Testimony." <u>Time</u>, April 6, 1992, 32, 37.
Photo.   Defense of Clinton on the draft issue.

406   "Will He Do?" (Editorial). <u>New Republic</u>, April
6, 1992, 7.   Following the Clinton victories in the
Illinois and Michigan primaries, it became clear that
Clinton would be nominated.   The question remained
whether he would be a new Democrat or whether he
(like his predecessors Carter, Mondale, and Dukakis)
would cater to traditional Democratic special
interests.   Clinton's knack for reconciling contrary
positions, charming all sides without confronting
anyone, fosters distrust on the part of voters.
Clinton at times in Arkansas confronted interest
groups (like unions), but still retained their
support and got reelected.   Despite "slipperiness,"
he has demonstrated some hint of "policy spine."   If
he would show more of this quality, then he would be
a stronger candidate.   A way to keep track of Clinton
would be to follow his stances on such issues as
welfare reform, the deficit, and foreign policy.

407   "The Royal Banners Forward Go." <u>Economist</u>, April
11, 1992, 25-26.   Clinton's New York primary victory
all but secured the nomination, but doubts remained
about his honesty and integrity.   Clinton, however,
continued to win because he was a strong candidate
and had devoted considerable thought to issues and to
being president.   The generational gap between he and
Bush could attract more voters to the Democrat.

408   Allis, Sam. "Watch Yer Back: Democrats." <u>Time</u>,
April 13, 1992, 22-24. Photo.   Allis described the
raucous campaign leading up to the New York primary
between Jerry Brown and Clinton, which was a
"must-win" primary for Clinton.   A defeat would cause
Democrats to seek an alternative candidate.   The
experience Clinton gained from this primary would
serve him well in the fall campaign.

409   Church, George J. "How Clinton Ran Arkansas: He
Won More Battles Than He Lost But Rarely Upset

Special-Interest Groups in the Process." Time, April
13, 1992, 24-27. It was important to examine
Clinton's ability to govern based on his Arkansas
record. While Clinton emphasized change, he was
inclined to make compromises with business interests
and retained a regressive tax system. Some of his
priorities were controversial--job growth was a
higher priority than the environment. He achieved
educational reform, although some of the national
praise for this program had been excessive. Welfare
reform, while a well-thought out program, lacked
sufficient follow-through. Arkansas was a difficult
state to govern due to its low rankings in various
national measurements and constitutional restrictions
on executive power (and enhanced powers of the
legislature). These constraints plus lessons learned
in his first administration have enhanced Clinton
natural inclination toward conciliation and
compromise. Clinton's Arkansas record was a mix of
major accomplishments and great disappointments in
the areas of economic development, the environment,
education, welfare, taxes, and race relations.

410   Clift, Eleanor. "Running Against the Past."
Newsweek, April 13, 1992, 30. Photo. Questions
lingered about Clinton's character (marital
infidelity, draft evasion, ambition, marijuana use,
and ethical conduct). "For Clinton, his future may
depend on how well he can run against his past."

411   "Fed Up to Here." (Editorial). Nation, April 13,
1992, 471-472. While the Clinton candidacy persisted
despite adversity, the Democratic nomination had not
yet been clinched and most voters did not want this
process to be decided so early. "If Bush and Clinton
do indeed become their parties' nominees, a lot of
voters are going to feel unrepresented, and rightly
so. 1992 may yet turn out to be one of those
third-party years."

412   Klein, Joe. "Breathless." ("The National
Interest" column). New York 25, 15(April 13, 1992):
16, 18. Clinton was becoming too cautious and seemed
increasingly a "generic Democrat." What Clinton
truly believed in and really cared about constituted
the campaign's "character issue." He had "lost the
freshness, the creativity, the zest for innovative
policy discussion that marked his career" prior to
his 1991 entry into the campaign.

413   Kramer, Michael. "Two Visions, 21 Minutes
Apart." ("The Political Interest" Column). Time,

April 13, 1992, 28. Photo. Compares the foreign
policy positions of Bush and Clinton, who differed in
their approach to support democracy and reform in
Russia and human rights in China.

414   Behar, Richard. "Anatomy of a Smear." Time,
April 20, 1992, 45. Allegations from Arkansan Terry
Reed linking Clinton and Arkansas with the effort to
supply the contras in Nicaragua. These allegations
were reported by Alexander Cockburn in the Nation,
which Behar argued were false and unsubstantiated.

415   Church, George J. "Questions, Questions,
Questions." (Cover story). Time, April, 20, 1992,
38-42, 44. Photos. The now famous (or infamous)
negative cover photograph of Clinton with the caption
"Why Voters Don't Trust Clinton." While Clinton
seemed to be headed toward the Democratic nomination,
a number of voters still had doubts about his
character and beliefs, as reflected in Time/CNN
polling. Questions about Clinton included
infidelity, marijuana, the draft, playing golf at a
segregated club, conflict of interest, and alleged
shifts in policy on such issues as the Persian Gulf
War, military spending, abortion, and labor unions.

416   Clift, Eleanor. "The Open-Convention Fantasy."
Newsweek, April 20, 1992, 34. Despite Clinton's
victory in the New York primary, some congressional
Democrats still hoped for a brokered convention where
one of their own (like senators Lloyd Bentsen or Sam
Nunn) would be nominated. However, the days of
brokered conventions were over and this notion
demonstrated how out of touch some members of
Congress were with public opinion, which held
Congress in low esteem. Accompanied by a related
article entitled "Clinton and the 'Superdelegates': A
Newsweek Poll."

417   Cockburn, Alexander. "Clinton Cocaine Scares."
("Beat the Devil" column). Nation, April 20, 1992,
510-511. About unsubstantiated rumors in Arkansas
that Clinton used cocaine and was associated with
people who did. Cockburn also again tried to link
Arkansas and Clinton with involvement in the supply
of the Nicaraguan contras.

418   Cockburn, Alexander. "Dances With Chickens."
("Beat the Devil" column). Nation, April 20, 1992,
510. Mocks Clinton as he moved closer to the
Democratic nomination.

419   Cooper, Matthew, Steven V. Roberts and Donald
Baer. "Time For a Makeover; Clinton: Identity
Crisis." U.S. News & World Report, April 20, 1992,
30-31. Illus. Related the various campaign
strategies considered within the Clinton campaign
following the victory in the New York primary such as
emphasize substance like aid to Russia over the
press' focus on Clinton's personal life, address the
character question directly, discuss Clinton's
childhood and background more, and take firm stands
on issues regardless of evoking criticism from
interest groups ("show some edge").

420   Harbrecht, Douglas and Paula Dwyer. "Can the Two
Bill Clintons Make Up a Winning Team?" Business Week,
April 20, 1992, 45. Photo. Clinton still had to
convince Democrats that he would be their best
candidate. He needed to recover from the bruising
primary campaign and shift attention to a campaign
against Bush.

421   Klein, Joe. "What Clinton Must Do: The Who-I-Am
Speech." ("The National Interest" column). New York
25, 16(April 20, 1992): 16-17. Klein expressed
concern over Clinton's tendency to straddle both
sides of issues. Not enough Democrats supported him
to defeat Bush in the general fall election.

422   Kramer, Michael. "It's Not Going to Be Pretty."
("The Political Interest" column). Time, April 20,
1992, 46. The upcoming fall campaign promised to be
very negative as the Republicans planned their
strategy by targeting both Clinton and his wife and
focusing on the character and trust questions.

423   Whitman, David. "His Unconvincing Welfare
Promises." U.S. News & World Report, April 20, 1992,
42. Clinton's welfare programs (like Project
Success) in Arkansas were not as effective as he
claimed. Cited as examples were an "empty work
requirement," the "job-referral default," and the
"sanction shortfall" (lack of adequate enforcement).

424   Fallows, James. "What Can Save the Economy?"
(Review). New York Review of Books 39, 8(April 23,
1992): 17. Illus. on p. 12. A Plan for America's
Future by Bill Clinton (Clinton for President
Committee, 15 pgs., free) was included in this
review. Fallows discusses Clinton's economic plans
as explained in this pamphlet. Clinton writes with
authority on issues he had focused on as
governor--education, crime, welfare reform, and race

relations. Clinton should be judged on his record as
governor of Arkansas. Clinton's economic plan met
the "standard for political seriousness"--it took
into account the nation's economic problems and
recognized that they were not solving themselves.

425 Barnes, Fred. "Basic Instinct: Clinton and the
Interest Groups." New Republic, April 27, 1992, 12,
14. Leading up to the New York and Wisconsin
primaries on April 7, Clinton demonstrated his
tendency to please. Thus, he "pandered," but he did
not make specific promises to Democratic interest
groups, as past Democratic candidates had (like
Walter Mondale and Gary Hart in 1984).

426 Blumenthal, Sidney. "The Survivor: Clinton in
New York." New Republic, April 27, 1992, 15-20. The
New York primary campaign reflected the "collapse of
the great liberal coalition" of the Democratic Party.
In this primary, "Clinton replayed the crisis of his
early campaign," an example of which was his
ineffective admission of not having inhaled
marijuana. The primary's most important media event
for Clinton was his appearance on the Don Imus radio
talk show and the most substantive event was his
address on foreign policy (mainly on Russian aid).
While Clinton had overcome political opponents (like
Jesse Jackson, Brown, and Tsongas), he still was
trapped by his own ambiguities which were obscuring
his intelligence and commitment. Blumenthal argued
that Clinton only could "redeem" himself by leading a
"resurgent Democratic Party."

427 Cooper, Matthew. "The Hillary Factor." U.S. News
& World Report, April 27, 1992, 30-31, 34-37. Photos.
Hillary Clinton's liberal political views, role in
the campaign, professional career, and some
controversial remarks made her a key player in the
1992 election. The public holds various opinions
regarding a proper role for her in the White House,
reflecting societal opinions on gender and equality.
Mrs. Clinton's politics combined "liberal
idealism...with a big dose of political pragmatism."
There were areas in Hillary's record which the G.O.P.
could exploit in the campaign: legal writings,
Children's Defense Fund, Legal Services Corporation,
and her legal career.

428 Hitchens, Christopher. "Minority Report."
Nation, April 27, 1992, 546. Highly critical piece
on Clinton, listing 14 negatives regarding the
Arkansas governor, including his support of the death

penalty, his personal life, his support by AIPAC and of the Gulf War, sending the Arkansas National Guard to Honduras, his political ambition, and a general lack of candor in answering questions directly.

429 "New York Prime." (Editorial). Nation, April 27, 1992, 543-544. Downplays the significance of Clinton's New York primary victory. "Clinton himself is still little more than 'not George Bush.'"

430 Trudeau, Garry. "Bill's Bogus Experiment." New Republic, April 27, 1992, 14-15. Trudeau, the cartoonist of "Doonesbury," jokingly chides Clinton for his explanation of his brief past experiment with marijuana. Clinton avoided the past Democratic practice of making liberal promises leading up to the nomination and then trying to move to the right in the general election, a tendency which left Democrats open to Republican attacks.

431 Wickenden, Dorothy. "Washington Diarist." New Republic, April 27, 1992, 46. Considers media coverage of Clinton.

432 "Clinton Cruising Toward Democratic Nomination." Arkansas Educator 17, 8(April/May 1992): 1. Photos. Reports on the NEA endorsement of Bill Clinton for president made on May 1, 1992 by Keith Geiger, NEA president. Geiger pointed out the many times he previously had worked with Clinton by way of the National Governors' Association and noted Clinton's accomplishments in education as governor.

433 Johnson, Sid. "Taking the Political Plunge." Arkansas Educator 17, 8(April/May 1992): 2. Photos. Johnson, president of the Arkansas Education Association (AEA), noted Clinton's positive education record in Arkansas (with the exception of mandatory testing for teachers). The AEA endorsed Clinton for president and made the same recommendation to the NEA, which followed suit. In a related item, in a page headed "Political Action" (p. 9), Bill Clinton is endorsed for president.

434 Boo, Katherine. "The Hillary Loophole." (Cover story). Washington Monthly 24, 5(May 1992): 26-30. While political spouses like Mrs. Clinton had a right to pursue their careers, they did not have the right to peddle their influence through those careers.

435 Crump, Joseph. "Managing Clinton." Chicago 41, 5(May 1992): 74, 76-77, 118-120. Profile of

Clinton's national campaign manager, David Wilhelm,
including information about his earlier career in
politics. Wilhelm was instrumental in Clinton's big
victory in the Illinois primary due to his
familiarity with Chicago and Illinois politics and in
helping Clinton weather controversial issues like
Gennifer Flowers and the draft, which threatened to
ruin his candidacy. The Clinton campaign had six
goals, according to Wilhelm: one, establish Clinton
early as the leading candidate; two, raise as much
money early as possible to support his candidacy;
three, place second or third in the New Hampshire
primary; four, attempt to narrow the Democratic
presidential field, with hopefully Senator Bob Kerrey
dropping out since he would have given Clinton the
most competition in the southern primaries; five, win
Super Tuesday decisively; and six, in the Midwest,
win both the Illinois and Michigan primaries. This
article provides a local perspective like other
similar publications--the Texas Monthly and the Texas
Observer--to the 1992 national presidential campaign.

436 Georges, Christopher. "Substance Abuse: In
Presidential Politics, More Beef is Sometimes Less."
(Cover story). Washington Monthly 24, 5(May 1992):
21-25. It was more important for a candidate to have
a few basic political convictions than detailed
positions on a wide variety of issues without a
vision to underpin them. Having political conviction
was important, which included the ability to tell
people things they did not want to hear. Clinton
helped to form the Democratic Leadership Council,
which sought to transcend traditional liberal
solutions. Its establishment basically represented a
will to face up to organized labor, a refusal to bow
to interest group pressures, and a refusal to make
populist appeals like a middle class tax cut.
Clinton had not succeeded in maintaining these
principles due to the pressures of the political
campaign. Some issues on which Clinton was not
consistent or had watered down were deficit
reduction, health insurance, welfare reform, ending
the recession, and the middle class tax cut.

437 Ivins, Molly. "A Pol in a Lousy Year." ("Small
Favors" column). Progressive 56, 5(May 1992): 46.
Defends Clinton as a politician who built a strong
organization, which could be translated into an
ability to run an even larger organization, the
federal government. Clinton enjoyed the political
process and campaigning. Also discusses Perot.

438 Matusow, Barbara. "Pack Attack: What You Get
When Rumormongers Meet Scandal-Hungry Reporters."
Washingtonian 27, 8(May 1992): 53-57. Discussed the
issue of press coverage on presidential candidates'
personal lives, including Clinton regarding Gennifer
Flowers and past marijuana use. Precedents had been
set in the 1988 campaign concerning unsubstantiated
rumors about Dukakis and his wife Kitty. The press'
tendency to delve into the personal lives of
presidential candidates already had a chilling effect
on potential candidates, according to Dukakis.

439 Rothenberg, Stuart. "The Character Question."
World & I 7, 5(May 1992): 58-61. The 1992 Democratic
presidential campaign resembled a roller coaster, but
Bill Clinton emerged as the obvious front-runner.
Clinton announced for the presidency as a "party
outsider" who maintained that the Democrats had to
transcend traditional Democratic constituencies.
Clinton focused on the middle class, fiscal
accountability, and a solid defense policy. Clinton
would have cinched the Democratic nomination earlier
than the Illinois and Michigan primaries, but the
character and draft issues delayed this process.
Clinton's strong showing in the March 10, 1992 Super
Tuesday primaries gave him momentum for the March 17
midwestern primaries. Clinton had "survived charges
and attacks that would have demolished other
politicians." He had a firm political base and was
also strong financially and organizationally. The
nomination was clearly Clinton's to lose. Yet,
concerns persisted about Clinton's character and
political viability. This is a good balanced
political analysis of the campaign up to spring 1992.

440 Sheehy, Gail. "What Hillary Wants." Vanity Fair
55, 5(May 1992): 140-147, 212-217. Photos. Extensive
article on Hillary Clinton, including background
information on the Clintons. At this point in the
campaign, she was the most controversial figure, who
wanted to play a prominent national role. As Bill
Clinton promised: "'If I get elected president,...it
will be an unprecedented partnership.'"

441 "Better Than Halfway Home?" Economist, May 2,
1992, 28-29. Clinton attended a meeting of the
Democratic Leadership Council (DLC) held in New
Orleans, having just convincingly won the
Pennsylvania primary on April 28. While he made some
concessions to liberals during the campaign, he was
"still, at heart, the DLC's golden boy." The DLC's
perspective on the proper role of government was

determined by the experience of its southern members,
including Clinton. The remainder of the article
discusses a report on the future of the south
entitled by Clinton "Halfway Home and a Long Way to
Go," produced by the Southern Growth Policies Board,
of which Clinton was chairman in 1986.

442 Barnes, Fred. "Loser: Why Clinton Can't Win."
New Republic, May 4, 1992, 19-21. Clinton could not
win in November because he had problems in four
distinct areas--character, turnout, the South, and
foreign policy--which could not be overcome. Even
though most voters desired change, their continued
misgivings about Clinton's character would prevail.
Probably less than half the electorate would vote,
which was bad news for the Democrats who needed a
higher voter turnout to win. As for the south,
Clinton would only win Arkansas and any hopes he had
of winning more southern states were greatly
diminished by the character and draft issues, which
would not play well with conservatively-inclined
southern voters. Regarding foreign policy, voters in
November would be voting for not just president, but
also a commander-in-chief, and Bush clearly had an
advantage over Clinton in this area. Barring a White
House scandal or an economic catastrophe, Clinton was
a "goner."

443 Blumenthal, Sidney. "Losers: The Democrats
Against Clinton." New Republic, May 4, 1992, 15-19.
About the reluctance of Democrats to fully support
Clinton. There were still brokered-convention
scenarios being floated. Blumenthal noted two images
of Clinton in the campaign--that of "Slick Willie,"
as reflected on Time's negative April 20 cover, and
the other as a candidate who persevered. Clinton's
major goal was "to force the campaign for the
presidency to be, in fact, about the presidency. His
every impulse must be to close in on Bush."

444 Cockburn, Alexander. "Time's Attack on The
Nation." ("Beat the Devil" column). Nation, May 4,
1992, 582-583. Cockburn's rebuttal to Time's story
by Richard Behar, which disputed the Nation story on
the alleged connection between Arkansas and the
supply of the contras.

445 Klein, Joe. "The Oprah Track: Clinton, Perot,
and Infotainment." ("The National Interest" column).
U.S. News & World Report, May 4, 1992, 10-11.
Earlier in the campaign, Clinton had suffered great
damage to his reputation. Since then, Clinton had

been eclipsed by Perot, although Clinton was the best candidate in the traditional and new media.

446 Kramer, Michael. "The Brains Behind Clinton." Time, May 4, 1992, 45. Many of Clinton's more moderate centrist positions came from the Democratic Leadership Council (headed by Al From) and the Council's think tank, the Progressive Policy Institute (led by Will Marshall). The basic ideas of From and Marshall are presented.

447 Buel, Stephen. "The Politics of Agreements: Bill Clinton's Arkansas Reinvented His Politics." Texas Observer: A Journal of Free Voices 84, (May 8, 1992): 7-9, 17. Excellent article on Clinton, who emerged as his party's front-runner. Clinton sought to "reinvent" the Democratic Party, which would become more pragmatic and less ideologically inflexible. Following his 1980 gubernatorial defeat, Clinton forged a new politics, described by Buel as the "Politics of Agreements," based on compromise. Buel studied Clinton's record as governor, noting that Clinton practiced more confrontational politics in his first term as governor. Once elected again in 1982, he became a "more contrite incremental politician," focusing on the issues of education and economic development during his remaining terms.

448 Fineman, Howard. "Leadership? Don't Ask Us." Newsweek, May 11, 1992, 42. Fineman was critical of all three candidates (Bush, Clinton, and Perot) concerning their lukewarm response to the Los Angeles riots, which revealed the campaign as largely an "exercise in rhetoric and timidity" and one which was ignoring urban America's problems.

449 Kramer, Michael. "Two Ways to Play the Politics of Race." Time, May 18, 1992, 35-36. Photo. Republicans may use the Los Angeles riots as a "wedge" issue playing on racial fears while the Clinton campaign viewed this as a "web" issue, an attempt to foster racial harmony by focusing on cooperative cleanup efforts and issues (like community development banks, welfare reform, and national service) related to urban areas.

450 Toch, Thomas and Jerry Buckley. "The Blackboard Jumble: After the Riots, the Presidential Candidates Focus on Fixing Schools." U.S. News & World Report, May 25, 1992, 32-33, 35. Both Bush and Clinton believed that the best federal response to urban problems was in education and improving schools.

Clinton favored educational excellence over equity
and believed that federal spending alone was not the
key element in educational reform. They also held
similar positions on educational issues like
accountability, national testing, incentives, student
aid, youth apprenticeships, and preschool education.
Also discussed was educational reform in Rochester,
New York, which was having difficulties, lessons from
which Bush and Clinton could learn.

451 Lerner, Michael. "My Meeting with Bill Clinton."
(editorial). Tikkun 7, 3(May/June 1992): 7. Lerner,
the influential editor of Tikkun, related that he was
impressed following a meeting with Bill Clinton. The
Clintons read Tikkun and Lerner's concept of the
"politics of meaning" influenced the thought of both
Bill and Hillary Clinton.

452 Lydon, Christopher. "Sex, War, and Death:
Covering Clinton Became a Test of Character--For the
Press." Columbia Journalism Review 32, 1(May/June
1992): 57-60. Lydon is essentially critical of press
coverage of the 1992 campaign. The "Character Issue"
had dominated coverage of the Clinton campaign. In
an "'invisible primary'" the media had all but
declared Clinton the winner of the Democratic
nomination, weeks before the first primary in New
Hampshire. And, though reluctantly at first, the
established media followed their tabloid counterparts
in reporting stories about Clinton's personal life.
And once the Wall Street Journal published a story
about Clinton and draft, the rest of the media
followed suit. While the Gennifer Flowers and draft
issues received wide coverage, the media largely
ignored the case of Rickey Ray Rector, who was given
the death penalty in Arkansas in January 1992, and
Clinton's position on capital punishment. This is a
particularly useful article for the researcher since
Lydon cites numerous media sources like Time, New
York, and the New Republic (largely from January to
March 1992) to illustrate his points.

453 "A Presidential Wetlands Debate." National
Wetlands Newsletter 14, 3(May/June 1992): 5. Jerry
Brown, Bush, and Clinton on wetlands regulation.
Clinton's response follows. National wetlands must
be preserved for the future. Clinton supported no
net loss of wetlands and believed they should be
preserved. He denounced Bush's attempts to redefine
the meaning of wetlands so he could keep his campaign
pledge. Clinton also supported the expansion of the
Clean Water Act for regulation of activities

impacting wetlands. The Democratic candidate
declared that his administration's policy would "be
based on science, not politics."

454   "Sizing Up the 1992 Candidates." <u>American
Enterprise</u> 3, 3 (May/June 1992): 104-109. Analysis of
polling results in the form of graphs, ranging from
January to April 1992. A wide variety of polls were
represented, including Gallup, ABC News/<u>Washington
Post</u>, and <u>New York Times</u>. While it was noted that
Bush's disapproval rating had exceeded his approval
rating, Clinton's negative ratings also had increased
as voters developed more of an opinion of him.
Regarding "candidate characteristics," Bush polled
higher than Clinton on the topics of family values,
leadership, and trust while the Democrat was more
closely linked with the average American. In trial
matchups between Bush and Clinton, the former came
out favorably. Only around 50% of voters in the
early Democratic primaries expressed satisfaction
with Clinton as a candidate for president. As more
Democrats predicted that Clinton would be the
Democratic nominee, more also forecasted that Bush
would win in November. Polling results also were
presented on "party ties" and Perot.

455   Blumenthal, Sidney. "The Secret War for the
White House." <u>Vanity Fair</u> 55, 6 (June 1992): 58, 60,
62, 64, 66, 68, 70. The dominant theme of the
campaign had been the "'politics of personal
destruction,'" a phrase dubbed by Clinton. The focus
of the article is Republican efforts (and those of
Clinton's political enemies) to ruin the Clinton
candidacy on the basis of the character issue and
rumor-mongering. The opposition-research unit of the
Republican National Committee had been gathering
information on Clinton for over 10 years, dating back
to when he first ran for governor. Within this
context, Blumenthal discussed questions about
Clinton's personal conduct and the draft. The rumor
campaign against the governor originated from his
political enemies in Arkansas, especially Sheffield
Nelson, whom Clinton defeated for governor in 1990.
The Republicans wanted the character issue to stick
since this was the best way to defeat Clinton.

456   Reed, Julia. "Clinton on the Brink." <u>Vogue</u> 182,
(June 1992): 148-152, 213. Clinton is an
accomplished politician, whose career was geared to
eventually becoming president, but did this hinder
Clinton's character development? The public was
still not convinced of his trustworthiness and

integrity and the <u>New Republic</u>'s Michael Kinsley
endorsed him with the observation that "'He'll do.'"
Clinton was the best candidate among the Democrats
due to his enthusiasm for campaigning and empathy.
His political skills were not a problem, but his
tendency not to directly answer questions (on his
personal life, draft history, and marijuana use) was.
Reed also reviewed Clinton's Arkansas background. As
governor, Clinton demonstrated his mediating ability
and political prudence, though he still had a
"credibility gap" as a presidential candidate.

457 Mandelbaum, Michael. "Not So Slick: Why
Clinton's No Draft-Dodger." <u>New Republic</u>, June 1,
1992: 14, 16-17. Defense of Clinton on the draft.
An image of Clinton was created as "'Slick Willie,'
the smooth-talking, corner-cutting Southern
politician" who avoided the draft. Mandelbaum argued
that most men did so out of self-interest and not out
of principle. But Clinton also acted on principle.

458 "The Home Front: Bill Clinton." <u>Economist</u>, June
6, 1992, 24-25. Photo. Clinton's Arkansas record as
governor was one of mixed results in terms of
political reform, education, and economic growth and
development. Accompanied by another article entitled
"Clucking At Clinton," which discusses the tradeoffs
of jobs in the poultry industry with its adverse
effects on the environment in Batesville, Arkansas.

459 Hitchens, Christopher. "Minority Report."
<u>Nation</u>, June 8, 1992, 774. Criticism of Clinton's
support for the bill called the Cuban Democracy Act.

460 "Play It Again, Bill: The Campaign." <u>Economist</u>,
June 13, 1992, 27. Photo. Brief overview of the
political fortunes (and misfortunes) of Bush, Quayle,
Perot, and Clinton. The latter received mixed
reviews for his saxophone performance on Arsenio Hall
as to how it may help attract voters. Also notes
that the presentation of Clinton's economic plan was
shortly forthcoming.

461 Alter, Jonathan. "Clinton in the Twilight Zone."
("Between the Lines" column). <u>Newsweek</u>, June 15,
1992, 28. Photo. Clinton was running in third place.
People needed to know more about him because his
image had been defined mostly by negative publicity.
He had very "little political identity" and needed to
focus on a few key issues like education, employment,
and health care. Clinton had to be bolder in
proposing solutions to the nation's problems.

462 Baer, Donald. "Bill Clinton, Political Victim."
("On Politics" column). <u>U.S. News & World Report</u>,
June 15, 1992, 32. Photo. Insightful commentary on
Clinton as "political victim." While Clinton's
appearance on the Arsenio Hall program was most
remembered for his playing the saxophone, his
conversation revealed a man who had been on a
grueling quest. While Perot overshadowed him and
negative press coverage left him with a poor image,
Clinton was really a victim of his overcautiousness.
He could have taken a more decisive stand on the Los
Angeles riots, select an unconventional vice
presidential running mate, and reveal more about his
past earlier. And while Americans seem fascinated
with victims on the popular day time talk shows, they
would not elect one as president.

463 Drew, Elizabeth. "Letter From Washington." <u>New
Yorker</u>, June 15, 1992, 90-96. 1992 campaign as of
June 5. The race was uncertain due to Perot's
candidacy. George Bush was victorious over a
challenger (Pat Buchanan), who never had a realistic
chance of winning. Clinton's primary victories were
"more a matter of survival than a triumph." He won
over a "weak field," which reflected the fact that
several other possibly stronger candidates declined
to enter the race. Many Democrats already in office
were not pleased with the prospect of having Clinton
lead the ticket. Low voter participation in the
primaries signalled voter discontent, for which Perot
was the vehicle.

464 Turque, Bill. "Wiring Up the Age of
Technopolitics." <u>Newsweek</u>, June 15, 1992, 25. Uses
of communications technology in the campaign.

465 Kaus, Mickey. "The End of Equality: The Ugly
Truth About America's Future." <u>New Republic</u>, June 22,
1992, 21, 24-27. Clinton pledged to restore the
middle class via "state-of-the-art
neo-liberalism"--the U.S. was losing unskilled jobs
to cheaper overseas labor so good jobs in the U.S.
would have to be skilled jobs. The more education
and training a worker received, the higher-paying his
job. This "Skills Solution" concerned Kaus because
it could lead to a meritocracy in a "'smart-work,
high-wage'" economy; that is, greater economic
stratification based on skills, thereby threatening
social equality by leaving less educated and trained
workers behind.

466 Klein, Joe. "The Jesse Primary." ("Public Lives"

column). <u>Newsweek</u>, June 22, 1992, 37. Ross Perot's
May 30 appearance on Jesse Jackson's CNN program
"Both Sides" included a consideration of Clinton's
distancing himself from Jackson. Unlike Mondale or
Dukakis, Clinton wanted to avoid the appearance of
deal making with Jackson and wished to stay with his
original notion of running a more centrist campaign.
Klein also noted Clinton's criticism of the
controversial rap singer Sister Souljah.

467 "Millionaire-Bashing: The Campaign." <u>Economist</u>,
June 27, 1992, 28. Report on the campaign, including
Perot and Bush criticism of Clinton. Also noted
Clinton's speech before the National Association of
Manufacturers, in which he touted his newly released
economic plan. Gone was the proposed middle class
tax cut and in were proposals to increase public
investment and reduce the federal budget deficit by
half in four years. The <u>Economist</u> was very favorable
to Clinton's plans for job training, noting his
substantial background on this subject.

468 Borger, Gloria. "Setting Words to Music Over
Values." ("Outlook" column). <u>U.S. News & World
Report</u>, June 29, 1992, 8-9. Photo. Reflections on
Clinton's successful appearance on MTV. Values had
taken on an importance in the campaign and among
voters. Clinton was "contesting the anything-goes
wisdom of his left flank" of the Democratic Party.
Values served as an important means by which the
electorate could seek some degree of comfort facing
the prospect of fundamental change.

469 Kramer, Michael. "The Green-Eyed Monsters."
("The Political Interest" column). <u>Time</u>, June 29,
1992, 49. Clinton realized that to win the election,
he had to appeal to the political center. Other
Democrats, like Jesse Jackson and Mario Cuomo, were
undermining Clinton in this effort by criticizing him
for this strategy and, more specifically, for the
Arkansas governor's criticism of Sister Souljah.

470 "Running Room." (Editorial). <u>Nation</u>, June 29,
1992, 879-880. Clinton should appeal to and seek the
support of the "progressive constituency" in the
Democratic Party.

471 Barone, Michael. "'Tell Us a Story.'" ("On
Politics" column). <u>U.S. News & World Report</u>, July 6,
1992, 43. Most Americans (83%) believed that the
U.S. was on the "wrong track," which was not only a
reflection of current conditions, but also an unease

over its future direction. Thus, to reassure voters, candidates needed to tell their story/biography. All three candidates had contradictions in their pasts. Clinton's problem was a "biography and a message" that contradicted each other. Clinton shifted from McGovernite liberalism in his youth to a governor who, after his 1980 defeat, "discovered...the virtues of capital punishment, limits on abortion, conditions on welfare recipients and taking driver's licenses away from student dropouts."

472 Easterbrook, Gregg. "Green Cassandras: Has Environmentalism Blown It?" New Republic, July 6, 1992, 23-25. Easterbrook criticizes the environmental movement in general and Al Gore's environmental views found in Earth in the Balance.

473 Glastris, Paul. "High Stakes in Little Rock: How Bill Clinton's Best Program Fueled Stories About 'Slick Willie,'" U.S. News & World Report, July 6, 1992, 34-35, 37, 40-41. Illus. Clinton was still being hurt by negative publicity against him in the primaries. Journalists who investigated Clinton's record in Arkansas wrote a series of stories (all either mostly or totally false) largely revolving around the Arkansas Development Finance Authority (ADFA), a small agency whose purpose was to issue tax-exempt bonds for economic development and other projects. While these stories greatly hurt Clinton's image, ADFA ironically was a major factor in Clinton's success in producing jobs, which was a key component of his presidential campaign.

474 Gleckman, Howard. "Clintonomics, Round Two: Packed With Compromises, His Plan Reveals a Lot About the Candidate." Business Week, July 6, 1992, 26-29. Photo. Clinton gained much needed publicity with the unveiling of a detailed domestic policy package in Houston on June 22, which indicated how he would govern the country as well as his economic philosophy and consensus-building governing style. The major theme of the plan was an emphasis on both human capital and investment. Some other key elements of the plan included infrastructure, trade, taxes, health care, and social policy.

475 Greenfield, Meg. "Clinton's Danger Zone." Newsweek, July 6, 1992, 64. The Clinton campaign did not wish to repeat the decline of Dukakis' in 1988, which appeared strong following the convention but fell flat. Clinton's challenge was to brace himself against inevitable Republican attacks and unite the

Democratic Party behind his candidacy, which could be
his greatest challenge.

476 Samuelson, Robert J. "This Plan is Too Slick."
Newsweek, July 6, 1992, 39. Clinton's "national
economic strategy" (cutting the deficit in half by
1996 and equating investment in people with economic
growth) was unrealistic and "wishful thinking."

477 Shapiro, Walter. "Spelling Out the Job Specs."
Time, July 6, 1992, 30. Speculation on vice
presidential running mates for Clinton and Perot.

478 "'They'll Vote For Me Because They Want a
Leader, Not a Boss.'" Business Week, July 6, 1992,
28. Interview with Clinton on his economic plan,
which the Democrat described as "probusiness."

479 Burros, Marian. "Hillary Clinton on the Home
Front." Family Circle 105, 10(July 11, 1992): 43-44.
Photos. On the Clintons' family life.

480 "The Democrats' Hour?" Economist, July 11, 1992,
13-14. Clinton largely was able to make the
Democratic Party more centrist. Voters seemed ready
to give Clinton the benefit of the doubt for past
indiscretions, although doubts lingered due to his
less than direct disavowals.

481 "Keep It Simple, Bill." Economist, July 11,
1992, 32. On the eve of securing the Democrat
nomination, the public still lacked much enthusiasm
for Clinton. He should heed his campaign strategist,
James Carville, who was attracted to Clinton due to
his commitment to education and racial harmony. If
Clinton added a third element (a credible deficit
reduction plan) to these two other themes, then
voters would become more receptive to what the
Clinton campaign was trying to communicate.

482 Morgan, James. "An Arkansas State of Mind."
Washington Post Magazine, July 12, 1992, 13-17,
30-35. Morgan offers some important insights into
the Arkansas character which helped shape Clinton.
He describes Arkansas as an "interconnected" state
where politics is comparable to Chicago politics and
very personalized. Clinton's political career is
discussed, including comments by both supporters and
detractors on his governing style of compromise and
consensus. This is an excellent article since it
places Clinton within the Arkansas context and
analyzes well his political style.

483 Gergen, David. "Return of the Comeback Kid."
("On Politics" column). <u>U.S. News & World Report</u>,
July 13, 1992, 40. Photo. Clinton was making a
political comeback and it could be sustained based on
these factors: the continued stagnant economy, appeal
of Clinton to prochoice voters, potential for further
revelations regarding the Iran-contra affair, and the
"Clinton-Perot axis" (both Clinton and Perot were
opposed to Bush).

484 Klein, Joe. "Slipping on the Second Banana."
("Public Lives" column). <u>Newsweek</u>, July 13, 1992, 21.
Photo. Speculation on Clinton's selection of a vice
presidential running mate. The Democrats should take
a cue from the Republicans by selecting a skilled
partisan politician and not a statesman, as the
Democrats had done in previous elections--and lost.

485 Pooley, Eric. "Friends of Bill." <u>New York</u> 25,
27(July 13, 1992): 46-49. Profiles of New Yorkers
who supported Clinton in the New York primary.

486 Smith, Chris. "The Player: Rising-Star Media
Consultant Mandy Grunwald Comes Out Swinging for
Clinton." <u>New York</u> 25, 27(July 13, 1992): 50-55.
Good profile of a key Clinton campaign staff member,
Mandy Grunwald. Smith believed that Grunwald and
other Clinton media consultants still needed "to find
a way to change the public image of Clinton as a
slick politician who lacks a core set of beliefs."

487 Taylor, John. "The Blur: Can Clinton Get Himself
Back in Focus?" <u>New York</u> 25, 27(July 13, 1992):
22-27. Clinton was trying to redefine the Democratic
Party by expanding its base in an appeal to former
Democratic voters. The campaign's dynamics had swung
back to Clinton. Clinton's greatest asset was his
ability to endure political adversity.

488 Will, George F. "The Dumpling Also Rises."
<u>Newsweek</u>, July 13, 1992, 66. Attributed Clinton's
rise in the polls to the economy and political
sniping between Bush and Perot. People were thus
overlooking Clinton's economic plan.

489 Zoglin, Richard. "Minding Their Q's and A's."
<u>Time</u>, July 13, 1992, 77-78. Zoglin reviewed the
performances of Clinton, Bush, and Perot on call-in
programs like CBS This Morning and NBC's Today show.
Zoglin described Clinton's television appearances as
"both more smoothly presidential and more drably
predictable" in comparison to Bush and Perot.

490   Barnes, Fred. "Schizo: Clinton's Boomlet
Fizzles." New Republic, July 13 & 20, 1992, 11-12.
Illus. Barnes described Clinton as "torn." He
intellectually became a reform Democrat, the
candidate from the centrist Democratic Leadership
Council. But he still had emotional attachments to
the Democratic Party's liberal wing. And when he
tries to please both sides, he satisfies neither.

491   Glass, Andrew J. "An Open Letter to Bill
Clinton." New Leader 75, 9(July 13-27, 1992): 3-4.
Like Jack Kennedy did in 1960, Clinton needed "to
raise the comfort level of swing voters with the idea
of a President Clinton" and act boldly. Glass also
advised the candidate on campaign strategy and the
need to cultivate good relations with Congress.

492   McWilliams, Wilson Carey. "What Clinton Should
Do: Let Democrats Be Democrats." Commonweal, July 17,
1992, 4-5. The Democratic Party should return to its
roots by appealing to its core constituencies and
loyal party supporters. Clinton's call for rights
and responsibilities evoked the legacy of John F.
Kennedy. It was up to Democrats to fulfill that
legacy. McWilliams also speculated on Clinton's
choices for vice president and discussed Perot.

493   "The Left-Out Left." Economist, July 18, 1992,
30. Disputes "claim of the Clintonised Democratic
Party to represent every social and economic strain
in America to the left of George Bush."

494   "To Run, To Win?" Economist, July 18, 1992,
25-26. Photo. Clinton's convention bounce and
Perot's withdrawal as a candidate obscured the main
political story--the decline of the Bush presidency.

495   Alter, Jonathan. "How He Would Govern: Style."
Newsweek, July 20, 1992, 40-42. Illus. Speculation
on how Clinton would govern based on the following
areas, which are critical to successful presidents:
vision, temperament, congressional relations,
communications, and tone. There was also speculation
if Clinton could achieve as much as he hoped for in
his first 100 days. The public generally disdains
politicians, but a good president needs to be a good
politician. A more negative assessment of Clinton is
that he "'pays lip service to proposals. Then the
lobbyists chip away. Then he declares victory.'"
Accompanying article entitled "At Work and Play in a
Clinton White House" speculates on who might serve in
a new administration and lists some Clinton pastimes.

496 Bilski, Andrew. "Baby Boom Ticket: Clinton and
Gore Signal the Emergence of a New Generation of
American Leaders." (Cover story). Maclean's, July 20,
1992, 24-25. Photo. Written before the Democratic
Convention and after Al Gore's selection as Clinton's
vice presidential running mate. Discussed the pluses
and minuses of this choice (balance out the character
issue a plus, two candidates from the same region a
negative). Besides presenting a Canadian perspective
on the American campaign, the article noted Canadian
interests such as Gore's strong environmental record
and his support for NAFTA.

497 "'Change is Very Painful': Interview."
Newsweek, July 20, 1992, 28-29. Photos. Among the
topics discussed were: what people should know about
Clinton, the label of "Slick Willie," G.O.P. attacks
on his character, his expectations of the campaign,
Bush's and Perot's strengths, choice of a Supreme
Court justice, Republican portrayals of his wife, the
impact of the campaign on his daughter Chelsea,
whether Clinton ever contemplated quitting the
campaign (which he never did), and if he could
deliver real change as opposed to just minor reform.

498 Clift, Eleanor. "Hillary Then and Now: Profile."
Newsweek, July 20, 1992, 38-39. Photo. Attempt by
Clinton campaign to portray Hillary Clinton as a
homemaker was mocked by G.O.P. political consultant
Roger Ailes. The race had taken a toll. She did not
like to talk about personal matters, transforming
such questions into a discussion of policies. Voters
should get accustomed to the idea that she would play
a significant role in a Clinton administration.

499 Fineman, Howard. "Sixties: Coming of Age."
Newsweek, July 20, 1992, 32-35. Photo. 1960s'
influence on Clinton as a politician.

500 Fotheringham, Allan. "Why Can't Americans Accept
Strong Women?" (Column). Maclean's, July 20, 1992,
52. Photo. It would be interesting to see how the
American electorate responds to two intelligent,
successful, and knowledgeable political spouses like
Hillary Clinton and Tipper Gore as well as to a
ticket composed of southerners.

501 Greenfield, Meg. "The Democratic
Fortysomethings." Newsweek, July 20, 1992, 70.
Comments favorably on the selection of Al Gore on the
Democratic ticket. Clinton and Gore were dedicated
policy/issues oriented politicians.

502 Klein, Joe. "Clinton the Survivor." Newsweek,
July 20, 1992, 22-25. Photos. While Clinton
demonstrated his political resilience in surviving
the primary season, he still was in a relatively weak
position politically due to the controversies he had
endured. Contains background on Clinton, including
the New Hampshire primary, which he survived since
New Hampshire was similar to Arkansas in terms of
population, according to James Carville. Clinton was
still relatively unknown and distrusted. Thus, he
would not win until he started to reveal more about
his personal history.

503 Kramer, Michael. "Clinton's Second Chance."
(Cover story). Time, July 20, 1992, 22-24. Photo.
Clinton got a second chance due to a boost in the
polls and his selection of Al Gore as vice president.
Article focuses on that selection and Clinton's
revised economic plan. Democratic ticket was
preparing for a difficult fall campaign. Written
prior to the Democratic National Convention.

504 Mackenzie, Hilary. "A Blueprint for Change."
(Cover story). Maclean's, July 20, 1992, 32-33.
Photo. Clinton's plan for "economic renewal"
represented a reversal of Reaganomics. This plan and
Clinton's selection of Al Gore allowed the Arkansas
governor to portray himself as an instrument of
change. And, for some voters, Clinton's resilience
in withstanding attacks on his character was in
itself a test of his character.

505 McMurdy, Deirdre. "The Political Wife: Hillary
Clinton Redefines Her Role." (Cover story).
Maclean's, July 20, 1992, 34. Photo. Hillary Clinton
adjusted to being a presidential candidate's wife and
defining a role for herself as a political adviser
and partner. Mrs. Clinton helped rescue Clinton from
allegations about marital infidelity. Since a
considerable part of a voter's choice is determined
by personality, a candidate's wife is also a measure
of character.

506 Muller, Henry and John F. Stacks. "An Interview
With Clinton." Time, July 20, 1992, 25-27. Photos.
Informative interview with Clinton on the eve of the
Democratic convention. Topics included: Clinton's
criticism of Republican personal attacks, Dan Quayle
and family values, the selection of Al Gore as
running mate, Democratic unity and support for his
candidacy, his economic plan and the deficit,
entitlements, tax proposals, the use of force

overseas, and speculation on a three candidate race.

507 "Running Mates." (Cover story). Newsweek, July
20, 1992, 18-21. Photos. Photo essay reflecting
boost Clinton received by selecting Al Gore as his
vice presidential running mate. Together, they
conveyed a centrist, moderate image of the Democratic
Party, which perhaps had finally put the New Deal
behind it. The upcoming fall campaign promised to
exceed prior expectations.

508 Taylor, John. "The Blues Brothers: The
Clinton-Gore Ticket." ("The National Interest"
column). New York, 25, 28(July 20, 1992), 9-10.
Photo. Favorable article on Clinton's selection of
Al Gore as his vice presidential running mate.

509 Turque, Bill. "The Three Faces of Al Gore:
Profile." Newsweek, July 20, 1992, 30-31. Three
sides of Al Gore were: a stiff and smug exterior, the
forceful debater, and a man with a sense of humor.
Clinton selected Gore due to these advantages which
he brought to the ticket: military service, foreign
policy experience, a thoroughly examined personal
life in the 1988 campaign, appeal in southern and
border states necessary for the fall election, and a
positive counterpoint to Dan Quayle. Also provides
background information on Gore and his family.

510 Wills, Garry. "Beginning of the Road" (cover
story). Time, July 20, 1992, 32-34, 55-57, 59. Major
article on Clinton's Arkansas background. Political
scientist Diane Blair described Arkansas as a very
difficult state to govern, yet Clinton had done
rather well. Clinton's background could be best
related in terms of his four "hometowns": Hope, Hot
Springs, Fayetteville, and Little Rock. As governor,
Clinton had hoped to continue the reforms of
progressive Republican governor Winthrop Rockefeller
(1966-1970), who benefited from a federal government
which believed in the Great Society, but the federal
government was retrenching fiscally. Clinton also
had hoped that fellow southerner Jimmy Carter, as
president, would benefit Arkansas. Instead, Carter's
decision to house Cuban refugees in Fort Chaffee hurt
Clinton politically. Clinton's Arkansas experience
could serve him well as president since he labored
under financial constraints, established priorities,
and concentrated on basic tasks. And Clinton was
accustomed to the public's antigovernment mood.

511 Steinem, Gloria. "Why I'm Not Running for

President: Revolution From the Bottom Up." <u>Nation</u>,
July 20-27, 1992. Clinton's greatest quality was his
ability to listen, besides being the superior
candidate on racial and sexual equality and the
environment, among many other issues. He would not
be an obstacle to the women's movement.

512 "Forget Dukakis: The Campaign." <u>Economist</u>, July
25, 1992, 26. Reports on post-convention bounce for
the Clinton-Gore ticket and their successful midwest
bus trip. The Democrats in 1992 would learn the
lessons of the unsuccessful 1988 Dukakis campaign.

513 Alter, Jonathan. "It's Change Versus Trust."
<u>Newsweek</u>, July 27, 1992, 35. In the fall campaign,
Clinton's message would be change and Bush's, trust.

514 Bentley, P.F. "Behind the Scenes of a Campaign."
<u>Time</u>, July 27, 1992, 34-38, 43. The "From the
Publisher" section on p. 4 of this issue introduced
the black and white photographs (accompanied by
captions) taken by Bentley, providing a unique
behind-the-scenes look at the Clinton campaign.
Bentley's photos appeared in subsequent issues of
<u>Time</u> and a selection of them was compiled into a book
entitled <u>Clinton: Portrait of Victory</u>.

515 Blumenthal, Sidney. "The Reanointed: Bill
Clinton, Survivor." <u>New Republic</u>, July 27, 1992,
10-12, 14. Illus. From the New Hampshire primary to
Democratic convention, Clinton had two personas--one,
fighting off personal attacks on his character and
the other, developing policy. Just as the convention
was to convene, these two personas meshed to form a
"whole candidate."

516 Borger, Gloria. "Clinton Breaks Out." (Cover
story). <u>U.S. News & World Report</u>, July 27, 1992,
20-29. Photos. Upbeat assessment of the successful
Democratic convention, enhanced by Perot's
withdrawal. Clinton established in his acceptance
speech the link between his past and what he planned
to do as president. The outline of the fall campaign
was emerging. Clinton wanted the debate to center on
change while Bush wished to focus on risk. The
campaign would be difficult because both candidates
had to prove the negatives of their opponents.

517 Carlson, Margaret. "Bill's Big Bash." <u>Time</u>, July
27, 1992, 34, 38, 43. A major objective of the
convention was to give a more complete picture of the
Democratic nominee's character following the attacks

Clinton endured during the primaries and those likely
to come before the fall election.

518 Cooper, Matthew. "Words and Pictures Larger than
Life." ("Outlook" column). U.S. News & World Report,
July 27, 1992, 4-5. Photos. Clinton emerged from the
Democratic convention as a "new candidate" by
introducing the American public to his personal
history, which was important to know as an indication
of what kind of leader he would be now.

519 "The Democrats Can Win--But Not Without These
People." Business Week, July 27, 1992, 30-31.
Clinton could win if he attracts the voters who
abandoned the Democratic Party after 1976. Besides
Reagan Democrats, Clinton also needed to get a high
voter turnout from blacks and pro-choice advocates.
A sampling of voters was taken from Georgia, San
Francisco, Michigan, and Chicago.

520 Fineman, Howard. "Minus Perot: The New Math."
Newsweek, July 27, 1992, 24-27. Campaign strategy
after Perot's withdrawal from the presidential race.

521 "Front Runners." (Cover story). Newsweek, July
27, 1992, 24. Photo essay on the successful
Democratic National Convention. While the convention
furnished the Democrats with a dramatic boost in the
polls, the fall campaign against Bush promised to be
very difficult.

522 Gergen, David. "Wanted: Two New Covenants."
(Editorial). U.S. News & World Report, July 27, 1992,
72. In his acceptance speech, Clinton called for a
"New Covenant" to make a better relationship between
government and the citizenry. Gergen also called for
a "more personal new covenant between politicians and
the people" by which the political parties would stop
making (and the media stop reporting) personal
attacks on political candidates and, in turn,
politicians would be more truthful with the public,
even on unpopular issues and proposed measures to
solve them (like the deficit). Americans wanted to
believe in Clinton, but he had to earn their trust.

523 Klein, Joe. "The Relentless Suitor." Newsweek,
July 27, 1992, 34. Clinton's acceptance speech at
the Democratic convention helped introduce the
candidate to the country. It reflected three aspects
of Clinton--policy expert, politician, and person.
As a policy wonk, Clinton fared least well because
the more traditional Democratic constituencies were

represented at the convention and thus were not as
favorable to some of his "New Democrat" ideas such as
national service.   Clinton the politician did better.
His speech was "politically adept" and he enjoyed a
"spectacular week" at the convention.   More important
than policy or politics, however, was the
reintroduction of Clinton as a person to the American
public while, in contrast, Perot withdrew from the
campaign and Bush was on the political sidelines.

524 Kondracke, Morton. "Apprentices' Sorcerer:
Clinton's Best Idea." New Republic, July 27, 1992,
14, 16.   Credited Bill and Hillary Clinton with
proposing to do something positive for an often
overlooked group: the approximately 60% of high
schools graduates who either did not attend college
or did not finish.   With the advice of his wife and
economic advisers Ira Magaziner and Robert B. Reich,
Clinton made enhancing worker skills a key component
of his program both as Arkansas' governor and as a
candidate.   Clinton agrees with their view that
training initiatives constitute the best means to
increase U.S. productivity and competitiveness.

525 Kramer, Michael. "Front and Center." Time, July
27, 1992, 28-31.   The Clinton campaign received a
great boost from the convention due to its centrist
platform, an effective Clinton biographical film, and
his acceptance speech.   In the fall, the G.O.P.
planned to attack Clinton on character, his Arkansas
record, and ideology.   Regarding character, besides
holding the option of bringing up again the Flowers
and draft incidents, this area also encompassed
depicting Clinton as too willing to please.   The
Republicans also would portray Clinton as a failed
governor who was a tax and spend liberal.

526 Magnusson, Paul. "What Clinton Expects From
'Senator Science.'" Business Week, July 27, 1992, 29.
Photo.   Vice presidential candidate Al Gore's plans
for a high-tech industrial strategy was an important
component of the campaign.   Among the issues of
interest to Gore were the following: computer
superhighway, environmental cleanup, high-tech
industrial policy, and defense conversion.

527 Noonan, Peggy. "Behind Enemy Lines." Newsweek,
July 27, 1992, 32, 34.   Noonan, a former Reagan and
Bush speech writer, comments on the Democratic
convention, which reminded her more of a Republican
convention due to its orderliness and relative lack
of political rancor.   Her commentary discussed, among

other topics and people, Jesse Jackson, Mario Cuomo, Ann Richards, the film introducing Clinton, and, of course, Clinton himself.

528   Taylor, John. "'It's Time for a Change': Clinton's Defining Moments Redefine the Democrats." New York 25, 29(July 27, 1992): 24-29. Photos. Democratic convention reconstituted the party by demonstrating a pragmatic desire of Democrats to look toward the election.   While Clinton had been appealing to Reagan Democrats, Republicans who might vote for Clinton could tip the balance.

529   Walczak, Lee, Richard S. Dunham, Douglas Harbrecht, and Howard Gleckman. "What Could Stop Clinton: It's the Dems' Best Chance in Years, But..." Business Week, July 27, 1992, 26-28.   Despite the optimism and surge generated by the Democratic convention, there were factors (such as impending Republican attacks and if the economy improved before the election) which could still have an adverse effect on Clinton.   Democratic electoral strategy also was discussed by region of the country.

530   Will, George F. "Labels Do Matter." Newsweek, July 27, 1992, 64.   Assesses Clinton in terms of political ideology, believing him to be an advocate of "middle liberalism."

531   "The Dawn of the Living Dems" (cover feature). Village Voice, July 28, 1992, 22-43.   Iconoclastic irreverent look at the Democratic convention, comprised of several articles related to Clinton and the convention.   Other articles are on Clinton's appeals to the youth vote and criticism of Clinton on issues like gay rights and the death penalty.

532   Schroth, Raymond A. "Clinton Reaches Out to the Nation for a Hug." National Catholic Reporter 28, 35(July 31, 1992): 3-4.   About the Democratic convention, whose prime goal was to make Clinton "look good" to a public which generally still did not fully trust him to be their leader.   Schroth criticized Clinton's pro-choice stance and that of the convention.   Despite some reservations, Schroth thought Clinton could "bring more justice and community into our national life."

533   Breen, Bill. "In the Dumpster (Campaign '92)." Garbage: The Practical Journal for the Environment 4, 4(July/August 1992): 66.   Editorial favorable to Jerry Brown and negative to Bush.   Most environmental

reviews of Arkansas placed Clinton ahead of Bush, but
not by much. While Clinton had been exploring ways
to make ecology and employment compatible, Arkansas
ranked last in environmental protection and
enforcement according to an Institute for Southern
Studies' 1991 survey of the environment.

534 "The Campaign and the Press at Halftime: The
People, the Press & Politics, Campaign '92."
(Supplement). Columbia Journalism Review 31,
2(July/August 1992): 1-7. Study of the campaign at
mid-point by the Times Mirror Center for The People &
The Press, Washington, D.C. A section is devoted to
"The Clinton Character Issue" and the impact of the
press on the campaign. Regarding coverage emphasis,
press respondents assessed three stories--Clinton's
front runner status, a campaign appearance by George
Bush, and business dealings by the Clintons in
Arkansas. Much statistical data is presented as well
as an explanation of survey methodology.

535 Ehrenreich, Barbara. "Who's on Main Street?"
Mother Jones 17, 4(July/August 1992): 40-46, 75-77.
View of the campaign from a leftist perspective,
including a consideration of Jerry Brown.

536 "Should Progressives Support Clinton? Current
Debate?" Tikkun 7, 4(July/August 1992): 29-34.
Reflects debate among leftists and progressives on
whether or not to vote for Clinton. Letty Cottin
Pogrebin makes the case for Clinton in an article
entitled "The Purist Trap" (pp. 29-32) while Bob
Fitch made the case against ("Bob Fitch: The
Not-So-Lesser Evil," pp. 32-34). Pogrebin responded
to Fitch on p. 34.

537 Abbott, Shirley. "Hillary Speaks to Her
Mythologizers." Glamour 90, 8(August 1992): 208-209,
268-270. Photos. Abbott explores the myths
surrounding Hillary Rodham Clinton. From her middle
class background in community activities and public
service, Hillary Clinton was much more similar to
Barbara Bush than Gloria Steinem.

538 "Clinton Wows Delegates to NEA Representative
Assembly." Arkansas Educator 17, 10(August 1992): 16,
13. Clinton discussed educational issues and
received in July the NEA's overwhelming endorsement
for president. Among topics addressed were
educational vouchers (which Clinton opposed), the
Secretary of Education position, and comprehensive
health care reform. Clinton also noted his support

for the National Education Goals for the year 2000, especially since he helped formulate them in 1989.

539 Marill, Michele Cohen. "First Partner." <u>Atlanta</u> 32, 4(August 1992): 32-35, 85-86, 88. Photo. Well before the issue regarding the role of first ladies arose in the 1992 campaign, Jimmy and Rosalynn Carter established the tone for the "partner-presidency."

540 Neimark, Jill. "Forget Hillary: The Other Women in Bill Clinton's Life." <u>Mademoiselle</u> 98, 8(August 1992): 86, 88, 90. Photo. Inside look at the Clinton campaign leading up to the New York primary.

541 "Mr. Clinton, Meet Mr. Kinnock." (Editorial). <u>Economist</u>, August 1, 1992, 12-13. Although similarities (economic conditions) existed between Great Britain and the U.S., the Labour Party still lost the election because voters did not believe that it could fulfill its promise on spending without raising taxes. Clinton should heed this lesson.

542 Barnes, Fred. "They're Back! Neocons for Clinton." <u>New Republic</u>, August 3, 1992, 12, 14. About Reagan Democrats (or neoconservatives) like Richard Schifter who were either going to support Clinton or were leaning in that direction.

543 Blumenthal, Sidney. "The Wonks: Clinton-Gore's History." <u>New Republic</u>, August 3, 1992, 10-11. Gore's selection signified that the Democratic ticket had no geographical restrictions and was ready to contest all regions.

544 Drew, Elizabeth. "Letter From Washington." <u>New Yorker</u>, August 3, 1992, 66-72. Assessment of the campaign as of July 23. Drew comments favorably on the Clinton-Gore bus trip following the Democratic convention. This success overshadowed the "astonishing" decline in Bush's political position.

545 Fineman, Howard. "Keeping the Big Mo Rolling: How Clinton and Gore Will Try to Stay Ahead." <u>Newsweek</u>, August 3, 1992, 27-28. The Clinton campaign planned to maintain the momentum generated by the convention with these strategies. Clinton would attempt to preempt the Republicans on issues like taxes and crime. More bus trips were planned into America's heartland, where Clinton needed to win back Democratic voters. The campaign wanted to remain "'on message,'" emphasizing economic themes like jobs and economic policy. An aggressive

campaign strategy was foreseen such as in Texas.

546 Goodgame, Dan. "Quayle vs. Gore." <u>Time</u>, August
3, 1992, 38-39. Unlike Dan Quayle, Al Gore had
gained in political ability and public approval. The
bus tour through the midwest was very successful,
with Gore playing an important role. Gore was a very
effective running mate. For Democrats, there was a
consensus that the "synergy" between Clinton-Gore
would enhance the potential for the ticket's
electoral success in November.

547 "The Importance of Being Earnest." (Editorial).
<u>New Republic</u>, August 3, 1992, 7. The Democrats were
earnest about winning the White House, largely due to
the efforts of Clinton and Gore.

548 McNamara, Robert S. "On Avoiding the Draft."
<u>Newsweek</u>, August 3, 1992, 28. McNamara, secretary of
defense under presidents Kennedy and Johnson,
defended Clinton's 1969 letter on the draft.

549 Zuckerman, Mortimer B. "Clinton's Golden
Opportunity." (Editorial). <u>U.S. News & World Report</u>,
August 3, 1992, 64. With the Bush administration
unable to deal with the economy and Perot's
withdrawal, the Democrats had an opportunity to
improve the economy and be the agents of change.

550 "Tongue Twisting." (Editorial). <u>Nation</u>, August
3/10, 1992, 121. Suggested that two themes from the
Democratic convention (centrism and change)
represented a contradiction that would be difficult
to reconcile. Doubted whether Clinton could cast off
the party's "social welfare/civil rights legacy" and
still retain its core constituencies and base.

551 "Green and Glamorous: Environmental Politics."
<u>Economist</u>, August 8, 1992, 21, 24. The election
would determine to what extent ecology was an
important issue for American voters. Gore would
appeal to environmentalists in the key state of
California and he helps to balance Clinton's
relatively poor environmental record in Arkansas.
The <u>Economist</u>, however, believed that most Americans
would support the more moderate environmental views
of Bush EPA director, William Rielly.

552 "The Merry Wives of Washington." <u>Economist</u>,
August 8, 1992, 26. The subject of this article is
Barbara Bush and Hillary Clinton.

553   Barone, Michael. "Free Trade: The Autumn
Showdown." <u>U.S. News & World Report</u>, August 10, 1992,
27. Photo.   Clinton had to decisively support NAFTA
to enhance its chances of passage.   Otherwise,
Clinton would be playing politics and it eventually
would die.

554   Blumenthal, Sidney. "Party Time: The Rise of the
Democrats." <u>New Republic</u>, August 10, 1992, 16-17.
The Democratic convention was successful because the
Democratic Party had resuscitated itself as the
"party of practical government" for most voters.
Clinton represented a "return to government as an
agent for helping the middle class."   The potential
for the final revival of the party depended on a
Clinton victory and reinvigorating the presidency.

555   "Bush vs. Clinton: Technology Imperatives."
<u>Computerworld</u> 26, 32(August 10, 1992): 25.   Presents
the views of Bush and Clinton on technology.   Clinton
called for a national strategy to invest in
technology and civilian research and development.   It
was also vital to invest in education and training.
He predicted his administration would "create a
revolution in lifetime learning" via a National
Service Trust Fund, a National Apprenticeship
Program, and require business training investment.

556   Gest, Ted. "The New Crime (Talk) Wave." <u>U.S.
News & World Report</u>, August 10, 1992, 23.   The
Clinton and Bush campaigns tried to take the
initiative on the crime issue.   Unlike the 1988
campaign, the G.O.P. did not enjoy a distinct
advantage in 1992.   Clinton supported an additional
100,000 police officers, gun control, "boot camps,"
and treatment for drug addicts.

557   Kramer, Michael. "Amateurs, But Playing Like
Pros." <u>Time</u>, August 10, 1992, 27. Photo.   Following
the Democratic convention and two weeks prior to the
Republican convention, the Clinton campaign was
running smoothly while the Bush camp was on the
defensive.   This was due to the Clinton campaign's
quick responses to Bush attacks on Clinton.

558   Krauthammer, Charles. "The Pornography of Self-
Revelation." <u>Time</u>, August 10, 1992, 72.   The
"politics of autobiography" was dominating American
politics too much as reflected in Clinton and Gore's
acceptance speeches at the Democratic convention.
This was used to make a candidate more appealing and
link "biography with policy,"   which should not be

the proper way for a candidate to win an election.

559 "Lawyers Go For Clinton." National Law Journal
14, 49(August 10, 1992): 1. Photo. Refers to a
National Law Journal (NLJ)/West Publishing Company
poll of lawyers' political views, indicating a 58 to
30% margin in Clinton's favor.

560 McGeary, Johanna. "One Degree of Separation."
Time, August 10, 1992, 28-29. On foreign policy
issues such as Yugoslavia, Iraq, Russia, the Middle
East, China, and Haiti, there were not many
differences in the positions of Clinton and Bush.

561 Myers, Ken. "His Ex-Students Say Bill Clinton
Was Good, If a Little Distracted." ("Law Schools"
column). National Law Journal 14, 49(August 10,
1992): 4. Recollections of Clinton's tenure as law
professor at the University of Arkansas at
Fayetteville from 1973-1976. Also includes favorable
assessments of Hillary Clinton as a law professor.

562 Blackburn, Thomas E. "How to Get Catholic Vote
Behind Bishop's Backs." National Catholic Reporter
28, 36(August 14, 1992): 15. If Clinton could gain
Catholic vote in the fall, he would win. But Clinton
received a lukewarm reception from Catholics largely
due to his pro-choice position.

563 "Clinton Might Have Already Lost It." ("Inside
NCR" column). National Catholic Reporter 28,
36(August 14, 1992): 2. The Clinton-Gore ticket may
have lost Pennsylvania because Democratic Governor
Robert Casey (a Catholic) was not permitted to speak
at the Democratic convention because he favored
abortion restrictions.

564 Dionne, E.J., Jr. "Hey, the '80s are Over: The
Clinton Bounce." Commonweal, August 14, 1992, 5-7.
Clinton's upswing really began before the convention,
but was overshadowed by the Perot factor and Bush's
difficulties. Once Perot withdrew, resentment
against Bush became more evident, thereby accounting
for the Clinton surge.

565 "Green Ticket or Thicket?" (Editorial).
Commonweal, August 14, 1992: 4-5. Notes potential
conflict between the environmental views of Gore and
Clinton's call for a high growth and wage economy.
Clinton's position on environmental issues was not as
clear as Gore's (contained in Earth in the Balance).

566   "Bring on the Dancing Girls: Conventions."
Economist, August 15, 1992, 21. While party
platforms and nominees are decided beforehand,
political conventions still can provide a significant
bounce in the polls. This occurred for the Clinton
campaign and Bush needed a similar bounce from the
Republican convention.

567   "Shock, Horror." Economist, August 15, 1992, 22.
Photo. The campaign already had become personal.
Considering the lack of a domestic Bush record to run
on, the only alternative election strategy was to
conduct a negative campaign against Clinton.

568   "Unpicking the Republican Lock: The Campaign."
Economist, August 15, 1992, 20-21. Despite Clinton's
big lead in the polls, he still had a way to go to
secure electoral votes. Thus, he needed a southern,
a western strategy, and a suburban strategy.

569   Dentzer, Susan. "Why Workers Have Little to
Cheer." U.S. News & World Report, August 17, 1992,
26-27. Photo. Both Clinton and Bush did not have
adequate plans to create significant job growth due
to fiscal limits imposed by the budget deficit and
soaring health costs.

570   Gergen, David. "Don't Count Bush Out."
(Editorial). U.S. News & World Report, August 17,
1992, 64. Although Clinton maintained a large lead
in the polls, his support was still very soft. While
Clinton was an "innovative governor" and could take
some harsh criticism, he still had to prove his
leadership abilities, which would be tested should
Bush give him a strong challenge. It was not enough
for Bush to just go negative by attacking Clinton's
economic plan and record as governor.

571   Klein, Joe. "On the Road Again." Newsweek,
August 17, 1992, 31, 33. Photo. On the second
Clinton-Gore bus trip, originating from St. Louis.

572   Shapiro, Walter. "The Team Behind Bill &
Hillary." Time, August 17, 1992, 30-33. While Bill
and Hillary Clinton had the final say on how the
campaign should be operated, they were ably supported
by three key strategists (James Carville, George
Stephanopoulos, and Betsy Wright) who deserved
recognition for a tighter more effective campaign.

573   Taylor, John. "Pawing the Dirt: Bush Lukewarms
Up." New York 25, 32(August 17, 1992): 16-17. The

Republican negative campaign against Clinton had
begun before the Republican convention, including a
controversial Bush-Quayle news release issued by Mary
Matalin, the campaign's deputy director. Unlike
1988, negative attack ads would not work in 1992.

574 Walsh, Kenneth T. "George Bush on Attack." U.S.
News & World Report, August 17, 1992, 21, 24.
Interview with George Bush, including his views on
Clinton. A Clinton administration would just be a
repeat of the Carter presidency. Clinton had made
too many promises and shifted his position on too
many issues. Since Clinton attacked his record, Bush
believed that it was only fair to scrutinize
Clinton's Arkansas record. Bush described the
Clinton economic plan as a clear "tax-and-spend
program," which did not deal with the deficit. Bush
also criticized the environmental views of Al Gore.

575 Kinsley, Michael. "Air on an L String." ("TRB
From Washington" column). New Republic, August 17 &
24, 1992, 6. A key component of Republican strategy
was to depict Clinton as a liberal.

576 Kopkind, Andrew. "Doctor Reich's Economic Rx:
Bobby's in the Basement." Nation, August 17-24, 1992,
166-168. Criticism of Robert Reich's economic
policies, which were inadequate.

577 Alter, Jonathan. "Sex, Abortion and Hypocrisy:
Media." Newsweek, August 24, 1992, 28. 1992's
"unmistakable consensus" was for the privacy of
candidates. Also discusses alleged media bias.

578 Cooper, Matthew and Kenneth T. Walsh. "Land
Mines on the Track." U.S. News & World Report, August
24, 1992, 16. Photo. Possible obstacles for Clinton
could be his draft history, a land deal with a failed
savings and loan, campaign staff, and the resurfacing
of the pandering charge.

579 Dentzer, Susan. "Economic Gladiators at War."
U.S. News & World Report, August 24, 1992, 29-31.
Illus., photo. Clinton and Bush campaigns on the
budget deficit, economic growth, financing health
care, taxes, job growth, and entitlements.

580 Leo, John. "Al Gore's Global Vision." ("On
Society" column). U.S. News & World Report, August
24, 1992, 20. Republican criticism of Earth in the
Balance would probably follow the argument made by
Gregg Easterbrook in the July 6, 1992 issue of the

New Republic, which criticized Gore's environmental
views. Leo, however, generally defends them.

581   Roberts, Steven V. "The Moody Swings of Anxious
Voters." U.S. News & World Report, August 24, 1992,
32-34. U.S. News poll results were largely favorable
to Clinton. However, while Bush had problems holding
the Reagan coalition, it could coalesce again if
doubts about Clinton persisted. Election outcome
depended on whether voters would be willing to take a
risk on a relative unknown (Clinton) or stay with
someone they knew (Bush).

582   Raban, Jonathan. "Bill Clinton, Simplified." Los
Angeles Times Magazine, August 30, 1992, 12-14, 16,
18, 20, 22, 24, 26-27, 44, 46. Long, detailed, and
insightful article about Clinton. Factors
contributing to his resurgence were the biographical
film (produced by Hollywood producer Linda
Bloodworth-Thomason) on Clinton shown at the
convention, the selection of Al Gore as vice
president, and the Clinton-Gore bus tours. Also
discussed the Jerry Brown and Perot campaigns.

583   Barrett, Laurence I. "Pulpit Politics." Time,
August 31, 1992, 34, 43. Bush-Quayle ticket had more
competition in 1992 than in 1988 from the Democrats
for the evangelical Protestant vote because both
Clinton and Gore are Southern Baptists. The
Democratic ticket had a chance to win almost 50% of
the white evangelical vote, which could prove
decisive in the south and beyond.

584   Cloud, Stanley W. "Here Come the Big Guns."
Time, August 31, 1992, 28-33. Photos. Following the
G.O.P. convention, Bush campaign aides acknowledged
that the only way for Bush to defeat Clinton would be
to criticize him on spending, taxes, defense cuts,
and health care.

585   Furman, Jesse. "Broken Records: Clinton's
Hypocrites." New Republic, August 31, 1992, 18.
Criticism of Clinton's Arkansas record (environment,
taxes, and economy) by two Republican governors,
Massachusetts' William Weld and South Carolina's
Carroll Campbell. This was part of a coordinated
strategy to have surrogates question Clinton's record
so that Bush could appear to be taking the high road.

586   Glynn, Patrick. "Closing the Loop: A Foreign
Policy Realignment?" New Republic, August 31, 1992,
22-23. Speculation on how Clinton would handle

foreign policy on such issues as Bosnia. Clinton
might take a harder line on Bosnia than Bush, but
would act pragmatically and not rush to intervene.

587 Reich, Robert. "Clintonomics 101: And Why It
Beats Bush-Reagan." New Republic, August 31, 1992,
23-25, 28. Reich makes the case for Clinton's
economic plan, whose major component was "investment
in education, training, and infrastructure."

588 Baer, Donald. "The Race." U.S. News & World
Report, August 31-September 7, 1992, 34, 37-40.
Photo. G.O.P. Convention revived Bush, who argued
that while Clinton called for change, he was more
trustworthy to oversee that change.

589 Leo, John. "Hillary's Children's Crusade." ("On
Society" column). U.S. News & World Report, August
31-September 7, 1992, 28. G.O.P. criticism of Mrs.
Clinton on children's rights was "shameful." She
wrote three moderate articles on this topic from 1973
to 1978.

590 Roberts, Steven V., Dorian Friedman, and Susan
Pastrick. "Issues." U.S. News & World Report, August
31-September 7, 1992, 42-44. The positions of Bush
and Clinton on abortion, capital punishment, crime
and drugs, the deficit, education, environment and
energy, family leave and child care, gays, the Gulf
War, gun control, health care, the military, taxes
and the economy, trade, and urban aid and welfare.

591 Walsh, Kenneth T., Michael Barone, and Matthew
Cooper. "The Media Battle." U.S. News & World Report,
August 31-September 7, 1992, 49, 51. The Bush and
Clinton campaigns geared their television messages to
issues that commanded attention in local media
markets. The dominance of national television
networks and print media would decline.

592 Barry, Herbert, III and Paul Elovitz.
"Psychobiographical Explorations of Clinton and
Perot." Journal of Psychohistory 20, 2(Fall 1992):
197-207. Important presidential leadership skills
include empathy, wisdom, and confidence. Clinton was
strong in the first two skills but had both strengths
and weaknesses as a confident leader.

593 Campbell, James E. and Thomas E. Mann.
"Forecasting the 1992 Presidential Election: A User's
Guide to the Models." Brookings Review 10, 4(Fall
1992): 22-27. Clinton surmounted questions of

marital infidelity and the draft and won the
nomination. His election prospects improved
considerably with the selection of Gore, a successful
convention, and a well-publicized post-convention bus
tour. Predicted a Clinton victory in November.

594 Jentleson, Bruce W. "A Clinton Administration:
Foreign Policy For a Post-Cold War World." Brookings
Review 10, 4(Fall 1992): 32, 34. Future American
foreign policy should be maintained by four basic
precepts. One, the U.S. must continue being a world
leader. Two, the U.S.'s international position
requires a stronger domestic policy. Three, issues
such as nonproliferation and the global environment
should be given a higher priority. Four, the country
must promote democracy throughout the world.

595 Wood, James E., Jr. "Religion and the U.S.
Presidential Election of 1992." (Editorial). Journal
of Church and State 34, 4(Autumn 1992): 721-728. In
this consideration of the increased influence of
religion in the 1992 campaign and the Republican
convention, Wood also noted Clinton's position on
church and state matters as indicated in his speech
at Notre Dame during the fall campaign.

596 Agron, Joe. "Taking It to the Top." American
School & University 65, 1(September 1992): 27, 29,
31. Photos. Clinton (and Bush administration
education secretary Lamar Alexander) on plans for
education, federal funding and its role in education,
school choice, and conditions in public schools. The
value of this interview was Clinton's responses to
specialized questions on education.

597 "The Candidates Speak Out." American Legion
Magazine 133, 3(September 1992): 36-39, 70. Photo.
Clinton and Bush on health care, education benefits
for Gulf War veterans, military cuts, flag burning,
resolution of the POW/MIA issue, foreign lobbying's
influence on the U.S. economy, and homeless veterans.

598 Carey, Benedict. "The Candidates on Health: A
Voter's Guide." Health 6, 5(September 1992): 53-55.
Clinton and Bush on national health insurance,
abortion, and child care.

599 "Election '92 Will Determine the Future of
Higher Education." NEA Advocate 10, 1(September
1992): 1. Notes the NEA's endorsement of Clinton for
president. Deals with Clinton's educational record
as governor. Preparing students for college was step

one in Clinton's strategy and step two was making higher education accessible to students. While educational reform did not constitute an Arkansas "'miracle,'" important progress was made.

600 Ivins, Molly. "Of Conventional Wisdom and Bliss." ("Small Favors" column). Progressive 56, 9(September 1992): 46. Illus. Includes comment on the turn-around of Clinton's political fortunes following the Democratic convention and his absence from a George McGovern convention reunion.

601 Ledbetter, James. "BOBers, Bushleaguers, and the Billbus: The Best and Worst Among the Presidential Press Corps." Campaigns & Elections 13, 3(September 1992): 24-27. Noted shortcomings concerning media coverage of the 1992 presidential campaign. Criticized Joe Klein (New York magazine and then Newsweek) and Hendrik Hertzberg of the New Republic as being too favorable to Clinton. Among the "best" reporters were William Schneider, CNN, and George Will, ABC. The "worst" were: R.W. Apple, New York Times; Sidney Blumenthal, New Republic (now the New Yorker); David Broder (CNN and Washington Post); Cokie Roberts, ABC and NPR; Mark Shields, CNN and PBS' "MacNeil/Lehrer NewsHour"; Michael Duffy, Time; and Jack Germond, CNN and Baltimore Sun.

602 Mitchell, Chris. "Gang of Three: Meet the Real Democratic Party Bosses, Teachers' Unions, Government Employees, and the AARP." Washington Monthly 24, 9(September 1992): 23-26. Despite Clinton's ties to the moderate Democratic Leadership Council, which attempted to move the Democratic Party beyond its traditional constituencies, Clinton and the party were still beholden to unions like AFSCME (American Federation of State, County, and Municipal Employees), AARP (American Association of Retired Persons) and national education unions.

603 Peters, Charles. "Tilting at Windmills" (column/editorial). Washington Monthly 24, 9(September 1992): 6. Endorsement of Clinton-Gore because in "values and ability" they were superior to the Republican ticket.

604 Schifter, Richard and Thomas Sowell. "Have the Democrats Really Changed?: A Debate." Commentary 94, 3(September 1992): 23-32. Reagan Democrat (neoconservative) debate over which presidential candidate to support. Richard Schifter argued for Clinton and Thomas Sowell for Bush.

605   Raskin, Jamin. "Inside Clinton Headquarters:
Campaigns & Elections Interviews James Carville."
Campaigns & Elections 13, 3(September 1992): 28-30.
James Carville's election strategy.

606   Urquhart, Rachel and George Kalogerakis. "Covert
Activism." Vogue 182, 9(September 1992): 396, 398,
402, 404. These writers posed as Bush and Clinton
volunteers in New York City in early summer 1992 to
relate their experiences for this article.

607   "Talk-Radio Meets Rock-TV." Economist, September
5, 1992, 32. Illus. While Rush Limbaugh supported
Bush, MTV's political reporter Tabitha Soren helped
Clinton by interviewing him in mid-June when he had
been mired in third place in the polls.

608   Reed, Roy. "Clinton Country." New York Times
Magazine, September 6, 1992, 32-35, 40, 44-45.
Photos. While Clinton portrayed himself as a
centrist, he began his political career as a
"populist liberal," as reflected in his involvement
in the 1972 George McGovern campaign and his first
bid for public office in 1974. While moderating his
progressive rhetoric, he never really left his
populist leanings. This progressive populism has
historical roots in Arkansas and Clinton (and other
Democrats like William J. Fulbright, Dale Bumpers and
David Pryor as well as moderate Republican Governor
Winthrop Rockefeller) were part of this legacy. So
when Clinton advocated health care reform, tax the
wealthy, and more funding for education and jobs, he
was drawing on Arkansas' populist tradition.

609   Klein, Joe. "Fighting the Squish Factor."
("Public Lives" column). Newsweek, September 7, 1992,
39. While Bush was losing the election, Clinton had
not yet cinched it. Clinton's true character
question was his tendency to finesse issues, which
reflected his desire to keep the Democratic Party
united behind his candidacy.

610   Shapiro, Walter. "So Happy Together." Time,
September 7, 1992, 30-31. Photo. On the "synergy"
between the Clintons and Gores on the campaign trail.

611   Thomas, Rich. "One Issue, Two Fantasies."
Newsweek, September 7, 1992, 32, 34. The Bush and
Clinton economic plans would not improve the economy
and largely ignored the deficit. Accompanied by a
comparison of their positions on the budget, taxes

and growth, jobs and education, and health care.

612 "Bill Clinton's Bad Habits." Economist,
September 12, 1992, 34. Illus. Insightful article on
Clinton, who tended to be evasive (Clinton's
explanation of his draft record) and to please
everyone. Clinton would be tested by NAFTA, which
would be opposed by some Democrats and their
constituencies (labor and environmentalists).

613 "Who's Best: The Economy." Economist, September
12, 1992, 28, 33. Compares the Bush and Clinton
economic plans. Clinton and Bush held fairly similar
positions on tax breaks for business investment and
research and development, training, enterprise zones,
the budget deficit, monetary policy and trade.

614 Alter, Jonathan. "Whose Gut Is It, Anyway?"
Newsweek, September 14, 1992, 33. Clinton had the
edge over Bush on most issues, especially health
care, jobs, and financing college, which were even
more important to voters than other issues like the
deficit, trade, banking, crime, and patriotism.

615 Barone, Michael. "Litmus Tests for the
Democrats." ("On Politics" column). U.S. News & World
Report, September 14, 1992, 45. Tort reform and
judicial restraint were two tests for Clinton.

616 Carlson, Margaret. "All Eyes on Hillary." (Cover
story). Time, September 14, 1992, 28-33. Photos.
Republican strategy to consolidate Bush's
conservative base by portraying Hillary Clinton as an
extreme feminist could alienate working women.

617 Clift, Eleanor. "How the Candidates Play to
Gays." Newsweek, September 14, 1992, 40. While
Clinton welcomed gay support for his campaign, most
Americans would not give support to candidates on
either pole of this sensitive issue.

618 Cooper, Matthew. "All Things to All Voters: In
Search of Clintonism." U.S. News & World Report,
September 14, 1992, 32-33. Photos. Doubts continued
about Clinton and he seemed to shift his positions on
issues. Clinton was having difficulty defining
himself and what he believed in (such as NAFTA and
abortion). Cooper defined some key elements of
"Clintonism" in terms of what David Osborne called
"'activist but not necessarily big government'" and
the notion that education was a key to economic
growth. However, Clinton had not explained his

beliefs nor his evolution from a McGovern liberal to a leader of the moderate Democratic Leadership Council. Clinton also sought the political middle ground on too many issues.

619 Fineman, Howard. "The Caricature Wars." Newsweek, September 14, 1992, 29. Photo. The fall campaign amounted to a contest to define Clinton and would determine the outcome of the election. The G.O.P. wanted to deflect attention from Bush's record by demonizing the opposition. Fineman also outlined potential pitfalls the Clinton campaign wished to avoid such as the character issue.

620 Greider, William, P.J. O'Rourke, Hunter S. Thompson, and Jann S. Wenner. "Bill Clinton: The Rolling Stone Interview." Rolling Stone, September 17, 1992, 40-44, 47, 51, 53, 55-56, 108-109. Topics addressed included voter discontent, the political year, health care, crime, drug enforcement, AIDS, the banking system, the global economy, economic growth, jobs, lobbyists, Clinton's view of Bush, foreign policy (Iraq, the former Yugoslavia), the Supreme Court, the Congress, and the Democratic Party.

621 Wenner, Jann S. "Bill Clinton for President." (Editorial). Rolling Stone, September 17, 1992, 15. Endorsement of the Clinton-Gore ticket, which stood for: civil rights for women and minorities, environmental protection, responsible appointments to the Supreme Court, health care, national service for college students, dealing directly with the nation's economic problems, and child care.

622 "The Leading Question." Economist, September 19, 1992, 25-26. Draft and trust issues continued to plague the Clinton campaign as did the Iran-contra affair for the Bush campaign.

623 Clift, Eleanor. "Hillary Clinton's Not-So-Hidden Agenda." Newsweek, September 21, 1992, 90. Questioned charges made against Hillary Clinton at G.O.P. convention based on a 1973 Harvard Educational Review article entitled "Children Under the Law."

624 Fineman, Howard. "Stumbling Blocks on the Draft: Clinton May Face New Questions on an Old Subject." Newsweek, September 21, 1992, 48. Photo. The draft was the only issue since the New York primary that had thrown Clinton off stride. The Republicans used this issue to question Clinton's trustworthiness.

625   Gold, Steven D. "Tax Increases Under Governor
Bill Clinton: If the Bean Counters Are Wrong, What is
Right?" Tax Notes 56, (September 21, 1992):
1653-1656. Includes an analysis of Clinton's
Arkansas record on taxes.

626   Kinsley, Michael. "128 Skidoo." ("TRB From
Washington" column). New Republic, September 21,
1992, 6, 49. Criticizes Bush's claim that Clinton
raised taxes in Arkansas 128 times, which was
inaccurate and thereby also tested Bush's character.

627   Klein, Joe. "Clinton, Soul on Ice: In a 'Big
Election, Why Are His Themes So Small?" Newsweek,
September 21, 1992, 46-48. Photos. The Clinton
campaign had became overly cautious. It concentrated
on promptly responding to Republican attacks and
portrayed Clinton as a new kind of Democrat. Clinton
retreated from his inventiveness as governor
(celebrated in David Osborne's Laboratories of
Democracy) and his theme of change.

628   Kramer, Michael. "The Lies of George and Bill."
("The Political Interest" column). Time, September
21, 1992, 26. Besides avoiding the draft, of more
concern was Clinton's not directly explaining the
situation, which might reflect a character flaw.

629   Didion, Joan. "Eye on the Prize." New York
Review of Books 39, 15(September 24, 1992): 57-66.
Illus., photos.

630   Wills, Garry. "A Doll's House?" New York Review
of Books 39, 17(October 22, 1992): 6, 8-10. Illus.

631   Edsall, Thomas Byrne. "Clinton's Revolution."
New York Review of Books 39, 18(November 5, 1992):
7-8, 10-11. Illus.

The New York Review of Books' coverage of the fall
campaign by Didion and Edsall. Gary Wills writes
about Hillary Clinton.

632   Garvey, John. "Appalling, Depressing, Revolting:
The Presidential Election." Commonweal, September 25,
1992, 9-10. Garvey would not vote for any of the
presidential candidates and implied that others
should not do so. Clinton's support for capital
punishment was sufficient reason not to vote for him.

633   Kass, Stephen L. and Michael B. Gerrard. "The
Records of Bush and Clinton: Environmental Law." New

York Law Journal 208, 61(September 25, 1992): 3-4.
Bush was moving away from environmental protection
while Clinton was moving toward it.

634 "Missing the Bus: Black Votes." Economist,
September 26, 1992, 25-26. Charles Rangel noted that
the Clinton-Gore bus trips did not visit urban areas.
If the campaign were to ignore the black vote, this
could be of critical importance since this voting
block was concentrated in some key electoral states.

635 Barone, Michael. "Who is Paddling with the
Current?" ("On Politics" column). U.S. News & World
Report, September 28, 1992, 48. Although Clinton led
in the polls, victories which had been predicted for
the Social Democrats in the former East Germany, the
Sandinistas in Nicaragua, and the Labour Party in
Great Britain did not materialize. The same could
happen to Clinton who spoke less and less of his
"'new covenant'" proposals that distinguished him
from "big-government Democrats" who had been defeated
in three consecutive elections.

636 Birnbaum, Norman. "One Cheer for Clinton:
Thoughts on the Election." Nation, September 28,
1992, 318-320. Speculates on how the left could
influence a Clinton presidency and some issues (such
as human rights, foreign policy, and relations with
Congress) which might arise under Clinton.

637 Cooper, Matthew. "An Ill Draft Blows Over
Clinton's Camp." U.S. News & World Report, September
28, 1992, 44, 46. Illus., photo. The draft issue
kept recurring and was important as an indication of
Clinton's honesty and had implications if he were to
be elected, perhaps affecting his calls for
responsibility, passage of his national service plan,
and ability to serve as commander-in-chief.

638 Drew, Elizabeth. "Letter From Washington." New
York, September 28, 1992, 104-109. Campaign update
as of September 17. Clinton and Bush were on the
defensive at the beginning of the fall campaign,
reflecting their tenuous political positions. They
had not yet captured the voter's imagination and were
still attempting to transcend their weaknesses. The
electorate harbored serious misgivings about them.
The Clinton campaign's two major tasks were to get
people to feel more comfortable with the candidate
and portray him as "'a different kind of Democrat'"
and not as a liberal who taxed and spent for
traditional Democratic Party constituencies.

639 Greenwald, John. "Neither Bush Nor Clinton is Confronting the Hard Numbers, But At Least Each is Proposing...Baby Steps." Time, September 28, 1992, 39-40. Clinton was more willing than Bush to deal with fundamental economic problems and propose long-range solutions. Positions of Bush and Clinton on economic growth, jobs, taxes, spending, the deficit, health care, and trade were presented.

640 Kaus, Mickey. "A Clinton Nightmare: It's March 1995 in America..." New Republic, September 28, 1992, 20-23. Hypothetical piece on what went wrong with the Clinton presidency from the perspective of March 1995. Kaus predicted a budget stalemate with Congress and Republican control of the Senate and Democratic losses in the House due to the 1994 congressional elections. Result: gridlock and a repeat of the Carter years.

641 Lind, Michael. "The Fission Thing: The Future Foreign Policy Fight." New Republic, September 28, 1992, 18-20. Clinton believed the Democratic Party should promote democracy and make a commitment to multilateral institutions and economic revival domestically. Lind, however, noted potential pitfalls in a future Clinton foreign policy.

642 McLoughlin, Merrill. "Giving One's Life for One's Country." ("Outlook" column). U.S. News & World Report, September 28, 1992, 12-13. The issue of national service was at the heart of the controversy over Clinton's draft history. There were many ways to serve the country, besides military service. Clinton served his state first as attorney general and then as governor. During the campaign, Clinton called "'service a way of life'" whereby college students could repay educational grants by performing public service. This constitutes a different kind of sacrifice from those who died for their country. In this new time, however, when domestic problems need to be dealt with (rather than war overseas), national service made sense, a view shared by Marian Wright Edelman, head of the Children's Defense Fund.

643 Rauch, Jonathan. "Supply-Side Democrat: Clinton's Blow-Dried Reaganomics." New Republic, September 28, 1992, 23, 26-27. Clinton's economic plan was similar to Reagan's.

644 Rosen, Jeff. "Court Test: Clinton's Opportunity." New Republic, September 28, 1992, 15-16, 18. Speculation on Clinton Supreme Court

appointments. Rosen hoped Clinton would advocate
judicial restraint and not Warren court activism.
Includes Clinton's record in Arkansas regarding the
judiciary and the mention of Ruth Bader Ginsburg as a
good candidate for the Supreme Court. (When the
opportunity arose early in his presidency, Clinton
did select Ginsburg, who was easily confirmed).

645 Shapiro, Walter. "Countdown Mentality: Why
Clinton's Cautious Team is Focusing on How Many Days
Remain Until the Election." Time, September 28, 1992,
43. Photo. The caution exhibited by the Clinton
campaign was based on the notion of not tinkering
with a winning formula--the economy. Clinton toned
down the activities of the "war room," where
Republican charges were quickly countered because he
was concerned that constant rebuttals to these
charges overshadowed his larger message. Clinton was
in the process of preparing for the first debate,
especially on his two most potentially problematical
areas--his record as governor and foreign policy.
The goal of this preparation was to give him an
underlining theme for his debate responses.

646 Taylor, John. "Robocandidate: Clinton Drives
On." ("The National Interest" column). New York 25,
38(September 28, 1992): 12-13. Photo. The Clinton
campaign was determined to stay "on message" by
focusing on the economy, viewing other issues as
secondary and distracting. But trying to ignore and
not addressing such questions had the effect of
perpetuating questions like Clinton's draft history.
Written within the context of appearances by both
candidates at the National Guard Association
convention in Salt Lake City.

647 "Does Clinton Have an Answer?" (Book review).
Tikkun 7, 5(September/October 1992): 71-75. Two
reviews of the book Reinventing Government: How the
Entrepreneurial Spirit is Transforming the Public
Sector by David Osborne and Ted Gaebler
(Addison-Wesley, 1992, 405 pp.). This book
influenced Bill Clinton's thought on government.
Question remained whether Clinton's policies could
solve the country's problems.

648 Foster, Douglas. "Yes, It Matters" (Editor's
Note). Mother Jones 17, 5(September/October 1992): 2.
Clinton offered advice to the Dukakis campaign in
1988 (on how to appeal to Reagan Democrats), but was
largely ignored. Clinton now had the opportunity to
put his own advice into practice in 1992.

649   Lerner, Michael. "The Politics of Meaning Meets the Democrats." Tikkun 7, 5(September/October 1992): 9-12. Clinton-Gore's appropriation of the rhetoric of the "politics of meaning" was criticized.

650   Lydon, Christopher. "A Walk Through the Garden." Columbia Journalism Review 31, 3(September/October 1992): 9-14. Observations on the Democratic convention and the press' treatment of Clinton. Lydon criticized New Republic's Sidney Blumenthal (now of the New Yorker) and especially Joe Klein (formally of the magazine New York and now of Newsweek) for being advocates for Clinton and included Larry King's opinion of the candidate.

651   "The Men Who Would Be President." Buzzworm: The Environmental Journal 4, 5(September/October 1992): 30-34, 36. Bush and Clinton on air pollution, endangered species, energy policy, global warming/ozone depletion, water pollution/wetlands, population, agriculture/food production, transportation, wilderness, and foreign environmental policy. Accompanied by smaller articles on Clinton's environmental record in Arkansas (p. 33), Gore's views on the environment (p. 31), and those of then Colorado Senator Tim Wirth (pp. 35, 89).

652   Rancourt, Linda M., comp. "How Green is Your Candidate? National Parks Compares Bush and Clinton on Environmental Issues." National Parks 66, 9-10(September/October 1992): 22-23. Clinton pledged to improve on Bush's environmental policy. While Clinton as governor made accommodations with the timber and animal agriculture industries on issues affecting water quality, his personal inclinations appeared to favor a firm environmental policy. Clinton bolstered his position on the environment with his selection of Gore.

653   "Saving America: Special EcoReport--Election '92." Buzzworm: The Environmental Journal 4, 5(September/October 1992): 28-29. Editorial introducing a special section on the election contained in this issue, including the environmental views of Jerry Brown.

654   Adams, James Ring. "Clinton's Bert Lance?" American Spectator 25, 10(October 1992): 18-24. Indepth story on Arkansas banker Jackson Stephens, who was involved in BCCI, has had influence on Presidents Carter, Reagan, and Bush, and continued to wield influence on both presidential candidates. The

Stephens family had dominated the political and economic history of Arkansas for almost five decades, including Clinton's tenure as governor.

655 Betsky, Aaron. "Bush or Clinton: What's In It For the Architect?" Architectural Record 180, 10(October 1992): 44-45. View of the election from the field of architecture. Examines the positions of Bush and Clinton on land use, urban planning, infrastructure, and other related issues.

656 "Bill Clinton: Convention Acceptance." Congressional Digest 71, 10(October 1992): 230, 232. Excerpts from Bill Clinton's acceptance speech at the Democratic National Convention on July 16, 1992.

657 "Bush and Clinton: Comparing the Candidates." Physics Today 45, 10(October 1992): 101-102, 105-107. Bush and Clinton on "science, technology, arms control, energy and the environment, and government participation" in research and development (R&D).

658 "Bush v. Clinton: The Candidates on Legal Issues." ABA Journal 78, (October 1992): 57-64. Bush and Clinton on: appointment of federal judges, special attempts to chose more women and minorities for judicial positions, prompt filling of judicial vacancies, federal funding for civil legal services for the poor, restrictions on types of legal services receiving Legal Services Corporation (LSC) funding, appointments to the LSC Board, the justice system, possible legal remedies to the drug problem, gun control, the prison system and the costs involved, the role the federal government should play in the tort liability system, tax simplification, congressional proposals like the Family Medical Leave Act, indigent defense funding, lawyers and the civil justice system, and, a constitutional amendment to abolish the Electoral College and adopt a direct popular election system.

659 "Bush vs. Clinton: The Candidates Debate." Reader's Digest, October 1992, 58-65. Photo. Clinton and Bush on character, congressional term limits, health care reform, and the role of First Lady.

660 Clark, Jane Bennett. "The Candidates' Prescriptions for Reform." ("Health & Fitness" column). Kiplinger's Personal Finance Magazine 46, 10(October 1992): 100, 102-103. Clinton and Bush on health care reform in terms of expanded coverage, controlling costs, improved service, reducing paper

work, and the viability of their respective plans.

661 "Clinton's Record in Arkansas." American Teacher
77, 2(October 1992): 3. Arkansas had made
significant progress in education (comparing 1978 to
1990) as confirmed by a national educational analyst,
Kern Alexander. Clinton was able to achieve results
in a state with limited financial resources. Time
magazine in 1989 ranked Arkansas as one of two states
whose educational system had improved most
significantly in the 1980s. Listed other educational
achievements during the Clinton years in Arkansas.
Accompanied by another article entitled "The Truth
About Those Taxes," which rebutted Bush campaign
allegations. Based on a Michael Kinsley column.

662 Draper, Robert. "StateWide, Donkey Business:
Small-Town Texas Gets a Taste of National Politics Up
Close." Texas Monthly 20, 10(October 1992): 95-96,
98. Report on the Texas Clinton-Gore bus tour in
August 1992.

663 Dumas, Ernest. "The Democrat: Bootstrapper or
Just Busy?" Planning 58, 10(October 1992): 9-11,
13-15. Cover story with accompanying articles,
including a parallel one on George Bush. Dumas
presents a favorable account of Clinton's Arkansas
record. Arkansas was faring better in 1992 than when
Clinton was first elected governor in 1978. While he
had not been able to make substantial improvements in
the poor Mississippi River delta area, significant
change had taken place in the rest of the state.
This was specially the case regarding education and
training as well as encouraging private and public
capital formation. Dumas summarized Clinton's
programs as follows: "investment tax credits,
apprenticeship training for high school students who
aren't college-bound and aid for those who are,
enterprise zones, tougher work rules for those on
welfare, heavy investment and transportation."
Clinton also passed "two major education tax programs
and three transportation tax programs." Perhaps
Clinton's greatest contribution to Arkansas was his
foresight to develop its human capital via education
and training. For this investment in human resources
to make a discernable difference in the state
economy, a considerably longer period of time would
be required.

664 Eastland, Terry. "On the Bus With Bill and
Hillary." ("Presswatch" column). American Spectator
25, 10(October 1992): 48-50. Eastland maintained

that a pro-Clinton bias in the media (and conversely
the media's bias against the G.O.P. as typified by
its coverage of the Republican convention) could
backfire, producing a backlash against the media
which might help Republican chances in the election.
G.O.P. strategy also targeted Hillary Clinton for
criticism.

665   Galo, Daniel P. "Bush and Clinton Speak Out on
Europe." Europe (October 1992): 22-29. Bush and
Clinton on the European economic market, the European
Community, GATT, NAFTA, NATO's new functions, war in
the Balkans, Russia and other former Soviet
republics, Eastern Europe, Maastricht, American
investment in Europe, and their respective general
foreign policy views.

666   Jaben, Jan. "President Bush is Marketers'
Choice." Business Marketing 77, 10(October 1992): 6,
174.

667   Jaben, Jan. "Marketing Execs Move Toward
Clinton." Business Marketing 77, 11(November 1992):
11, 128.

668   Jaben, Jan. "Clinton Wins at the Tape With
Marketing Execs." Business Marketing 77, 12(December
1992): 22, 27, 52.

Presents results of national presidential polls and
exit polls conducted by Business Marketing among
marketing executives. While Bush led in the earlier
polls, Clinton prevailed over Bush by a close margin
(44.4 to 41.7%) in the exit poll conducted on
election day.

669   Kaus, Mickey. "The Challenge to Merit: Having
Both Merit and Equality." Current 346(October 1992):
4-9. Reprint of citation in entry 465.

670   Lasch, Christopher. "Hillary Clinton, Children
Saver: What She Values Will Not Help the Family."
Harper's Magazine 285, 1709(October 1992): 74-82.
Extensive article which criticizes Hillary Clinton's
advocacy of children's rights, which Lasch argued
undermined parental authority. Garry Wills' article
on Hillary Clinton published in the New York Review
of Books is also noted. Among the works analyzed are
articles contained in these edited books: Children's
Rights and Beyond the Looking Glass.

671   Lichtman, Allan J. "President Bill?

(Prediction)." <u>Washingtonian</u> 28, 1(October 1992): 45.
Lichtman co-authored a book with Ken DeCell entitled
<u>The 13 Keys to the Presidency</u> (Madison Books, 1990).
DeCell predicted a Bush victory, but Lichtman
forecasted a Clinton win based on a key system, which
essentially measures presidential performance.

672   "Our Farmer Poll Gives Clinton the Edge Over
Bush." <u>Successful Farming</u> 90, 10(October 1992): 28.
Results of a "call-in" presidential poll among
farmers from 26 states--Clinton 50%, Bush 41%, and
Perot 9%. Most of the article contained comments
from farmers who supported Clinton, Bush, and Perot.

673   "Revitalizing Higher Education: Bill Clinton Can
Help Do It." (Editorial). <u>NEA Advocate</u> 10, 2(October
1992): 1. Noted the deterioration of American higher
education since 1980. Believes that two Clinton
proposals could reinvigorate higher education--a
National Service Trust Fund and a corporate training
mandate. In a related item in this issue is a NEA
endorsement of the Clinton-Gore ticket on the
"Political Action" page (p. 8). This item also
includes a summary of the Bush record on education,
family and medical leave, the environment, Head
Start, and employment, comparing Bush's pledges on
these issues with his record.

674   Rothschild, Matthew. "Beyond the Lesser Evil:
The Case Against Clinton." <u>Progressive</u> 56, 10(October
1992): 18-22. Illus. Rothschild presents the reasons
why he would not vote for Clinton from a leftist
perspective. Besides his support for capital
punishment and the Gulf War, Clinton was too
conservative and diverted Democrats from their
traditional causes. Much of the article is devoted
to a treatment of leftwing third party movements as
alternatives to Clinton.

675   Smith, S.L. "Time For a New Team?" <u>Occupational
Hazards</u> 54, 10(October 1992): 92-95, 97. Photos.
Reviews Clinton's mixed labor and environmental
record as governor. Labor groups believed he did not
press hard enough on worker safety and environmental
matters so to attract business, although he did
receive a presidential endorsement from the Arkansas
AFL-CIO. Defenders of Clinton's record maintain that
he struck a balance between jobs, the economy, and
the environment. Al Gore had a favorable record on
issues of worker safety and the environment.
Accompanied by these smaller complementary articles:
"Clinton/Gore on Environment," "Clinton/Gore on

Labor," and "Al Gore: Politics and the Environment."

676 "Sports Afield Questions the Candidates:
Presidential Race '92." Sports Afield 208, 4(October
1992): 12, 14. Clinton and Bush on hunting, gun
ownership, and the environment.

677 Thompson, Garland L. "Debating the Future in
Prime Time." Crisis 99, 7(October 1992): 8.
Thoughtful analysis from an Afro-American
perspective. Thompson saw some parallels with the
1932 election between Roosevelt and Hoover, who,
like Bush, maintained that the economy would improve
while both Roosevelt and Clinton advocated change. A
Clinton administration probably would not benefit
blacks as much as the New Deal did, considering that
Clinton distanced himself from the black national
leadership during the campaign. While he led in the
polls, it was too early to predict a Clinton victory.

678 Train, Ben. "Air Elvis: Guzzling 'Cinnamon
Decaf,' Playing Seat-O, and Orange Bowling on Bill
Clinton's Plane." ("Vanities" column). Vanity Fair
55, 10(October 1992): 184. Light-hearted look at
Clinton's chartered Boeing 727 campaign plane ("Air
Elvis") with its entourage of reporters, secret
service, staff, and, of course, the candidate.

679 "A Visit With Bill Clinton: The Conflict Between
the 'A Student' and the 'Pol.'" ("Reports & Comment"
section). Atlantic 270, 4(October 1992): 16, 18, 20,
22-23, 26, 28. Interview with Clinton in Little
Rock. In the Democratic primary season, Clinton's
excessive rhetoric contributed to his "'character
problem.'" The typical voter viewed his long
detailed positions as confusing and deceptive.
Reporters perceived that Clinton's multiple-point
answers were made to appeal to various interest
groups rather than reflecting consistent principles.
Among the issues discussed were race, abortion, the
budget deficit, international trade strategy, social
security, health care, and Medicare.

680 "Who Does What? How Each Level of Government
Could Do What It Does Best." ("What I've Learned").
Washingtonian 28, 1(October 1992): 33-34, 38-40.
Interview with Alice Rivlin.

681 Ferguson, Sarah. "More Social Responsibility is
Communitarian Key." National Catholic Reporter 28,
42(October 2, 1992): 8. Interesting analysis which
explains the influence of communitarism on Clinton.

Communitarian William Galston helped write Clinton's
"New Covenant" speech, which focused on
responsibility. In addition, Clinton's platform
seeking to restore the values of family, community
and work reflects traditional communitarian themes as
also was the case when he was governor (workfare).

682 "The Clinton Shuffle: Free Trade." Economist,
October 3, 1992, 28. Clinton had not yet made a
final decision on NAFTA, reflecting his protectionist
tendencies. While unions would oppose free trade and
investment in Latin America, Clinton should not
because of long-term job growth with NAFTA.

683 "To the Tolerant, the Money: Homosexuals and
Politics." Economist, October 3, 1992, 29-30.
Homosexuals could play a decisive role in the
election due to their financial and political
support. Thus, Clinton supported part of their
agenda (such as ending the military ban on
homosexuals and pledging more money for AIDS
research) in return for their support.

684 Barrett, Laurence I. "Three's a Crowd." Time,
October 5, 1992, 28-30. The campaign was going into
its final weeks. The Bush and Clinton camps were
deciding on how to sway undecided voters and which
important battleground states to concentrate on.
Complicating these considerations was the possible
reentry of Ross Perot into the presidential race.

685 Friedman, Betty. "Our Party: Women and the
Democrats." New Republic, October 5, 1992, 16, 18,
20. Relates the progress women made in the
Democratic Party as women's issues came to the fore.

686 Glastris, Paul. "A Democrat's Tough-Love
Lessons." ("On Politics" column). U.S. News & World
Report, October 5, 1992, 46. As a Clinton victory
seemed likely, could he be an effective leader when a
major Democratic constituency (public employee
unions) were opposed to many changes necessary to
make government more effective? Glastris discussed a
dispute in Philadelphia between Democratic Mayor Ed
Rendell and the American Federation of State, County,
and Municipal Employees, which could serve as a
lesson for Clinton. Two of his preferred new
programs (workfare and national service) required
public jobs for nonunion workers (recipients of
welfare and teenagers). Unions would oppose this
unless it involved only busywork. Thus, Clinton
would have to stand up to unions if welfare reform

and national service were to be successful.

687   Taylor, John. "Waiting for Jessica Rabbit: Is
Clinton's Lead Real?" New York 25, 39(October 5,
1992): 16, 22.   Taylor offers reasons for Clinton's
lead in the polls (before Perot's reentry into the
race), mainly due to the fact that approximately 80%
of the public believed the nation was headed in the
wrong direction--meaning that Reagan-Bush policies
had jeopardized the country's economic health.

688   Tyler, Gus. "The Final Battle: Countdown '92."
New Leader 75, 13(October 5-19, 1992): 5-7.   Predicts
election outcome and explains the polls regarding
Clinton's lead over Bush.   Tyler also discusses the
1948 and 1988 elections.   Regarding the latter, it
could be assumed that Clinton would carry the states
Michael Dukakis did in 1988 and build on that base.
Even once solid Republican states were within
Clinton's reach.   Also discussed Perot.

689   "Promises, Promises." (Editorial). Commonweal,
October 9, 1992, 3-4.   Urged Bush and Clinton to
specify the direction they wished to take the country
in this important election, which would dictate the
country's economic future.   As for Clinton, while
voters wanted change, they were still wary of his
credibility and character.   Bush's neglect of
domestic issues and political cynicism, however, also
called his character into question.

690   Wilber, Charles K. "Bread, Butter &
Infrastructure: Economic Issues in the Campaign."
Commonweal, October 9, 1992: 11-16.   Analyzed
policies needed for long-term economic improvement
and then assessed the economic policies advocated by
Bush and Clinton within that context.   Among the
issues discussed were trade policy, the deficit,
economic growth, taxes, and employment.

691   "The FOBs Meet the SOBs." Economist, October 10,
1992, 32.   Clinton's character was being
transformed--from a candidate to a
"president-in-waiting."   Speculated on a future
Clinton presidency, including appointments and his
relations with Congress.

692   "If It's Broke, Fix It--But How?" (Editorial).
America, October 10, 1992, 235-236.   The economic
plans of Bush and Clinton would be hard to implement.
So whatever the election outcome, there was no easy
long-term solution to improve the economy.

693 Fineman, Howard. "Mixing It Up--Again."
<u>Newsweek</u>, October 12, 1992, 26-29. Discussion of the
potential impact of the debates on the presidential
race. The Bush campaign was most eager to see Perot
reenter the race and participate in the debates, but
it conceded that while Perot could alter the race, he
could not reverse it. While voters were not yet
totally convinced to support Clinton, he maintained
his edge in the electoral vote count.

694 Gergen, David. "Why the Debates Matter."
(Editorial). <u>U.S. News & World Report</u>, October 12,
1992, 88. The presidential debates would enable the
eventual winner to develop a mandate to govern and
establish the basis for a strong presidency by
focusing on a few specific goals. Clinton risked the
same mistake Jimmy Carter made--dealing with too many
issues from too many perspectives.

695 Gwynne, S.C. and Stephen Koepp. "Head to Head."
<u>Time</u>, October 12, 1992, 44-46. Debate between key
economic advisors for the Clinton and Bush campaigns,
Roger Altman and Richard Darman, respectively,
concerning the economic plans of their candidates.

696 Hage, David. "Paving Over the Pain." <u>U.S. News &
World Report</u>, October 12, 1992, 59-62. A well
planned infrastructure program, as Clinton carried
out in Arkansas, would be helpful to the economy.

697 Kaus, Mickey. "Welfare Waffle: What's That Plan
Again, Bill?" <u>New Republic</u>, October 12, 1992, 10-12.
The issue of welfare reform could contribute to a
Clinton victory. Reviews Clinton's Arkansas record
on welfare. Kaus hoped for a genuine reform of
welfare and believed that having made this
commitment, Clinton would truly transform the system
in his first term, if only out of political
considerations--to win over the middle class.

698 Kramer, Michael. "Why Bush Welcomes Perot."
("The Public Interest" column). <u>Time</u>, October 12,
1992, 48. The Bush campaign was hoping to create a
"reasonable doubt" among voters over Clinton's
domestic proposals and then frame the campaign as a
referendum on his character. Since this strategy had
not yet worked, the Republicans' only hope was that
Perot's reentry into the race would change the
dynamics of the election.

699 Linden, Eugene. "The Green Factor." <u>Time</u>,
October 12, 1992, 57-58, 60. Bush campaign attempted

to depict Clinton as a prisoner of environmental
interests, who was willing to sacrifice jobs for the
environment. Dan Quayle was the point man in this
strategy and his major target was Al Gore. In
contrast, Clinton-Gore emphasized that good
environmental policy would encourage economic growth.
Gore's Earth in the Balance is also discussed.

700 Taylor, Elizabeth. "Al's O.K., You're O.K."
Time, October 12, 1992, 60. Photo. Traces Gore's
transformation from an unsuccessful 1988 presidential
candidate to a successful vice presidential running
mate in 1992.

701 Taylor, John. "Betting the Ranch." ("The
National Interest" column). New York 25, 40(October
12, 1992): 14-15. Discusses the respective
strategies of the Clinton, Bush, and Perot campaigns
regarding the presidential debates. Perot's presence
could help Clinton because Perot would focus on
Republican fiscal mismanagement.

702 Twersky, David. "Jews for Bill: A Constituency
Coup." New Republic, October 12, 1992, 12-13. Jewish
support would be significant in several key states
for Clinton, who was aware that he could gain the
Jewish vote by indicating that he would be more
favorable to Israel than Bush had been.

703 "What Perot Really Wants." U.S. News & World
Report, October 12, 1992, 19. Perot may have
endorsed Clinton prior to his reentry into the
presidential race if the Clinton campaign had gone as
far as Paul Tsongas did on deficit reduction.

704 Wills, Garry. "Clinton's Hell-Raiser." New
Yorker, October 12, 1992, 92-96, 98-101. Detailed
story on James Carville, who developed into the "real
coordinator" of Clinton's campaign. Among those also
discussed were Mary Matalin, an important Bush
campaign aide, and Paul Begala, Carville's political
consulting partner. Traced Carville's background and
political career.

705 "Science Policy: The Candidates' Response."
Science 258, 5081(October 16, 1992): 385, 493.
Presents Clinton's positions on national science
policies, which would have an impact on disease
control, international economic competitiveness, and
the environment. Among the topics Clinton addressed
were: science funding, "'big science' versus 'little
science,'" the Environmental Protection Agency, the

biodiversity treaty of the Rio Earth Summit, White House science policy, and science education in grades K through 12.

706 "Beyond Debate." Economist, October 17, 1992, 25-26. Illus. Assessment of the campaign less than three weeks before the election.

707 "Bill's Best Buys." Economist, October 17, 1992, 88. Speculation on how financial markets might react to a Clinton victory. Unlike past Democratic presidents, Clinton would have little leeway to boost economy via more spending due to the federal deficit.

708 "Conforming to What? The Suburban Vote." Economist, October 17, 1992, 36. Clinton had a chance to do well in suburbs, as typified by Du Page county near Chicago and Macomb county near Detroit.

709 "On a Knife-Edge: Texas." Economist, October 17, 1992, 29-30. Assessment of a close presidential race in Texas, with a consideration of Perot's potential impact. Texas Democrats maintained that Clinton's chances would be enhanced if he devoted more attention to the state.

710 "Peas in a Pod." Economist, October 17, 1992, 38. On the Gore-Quayle vice presidential debate and the differences and similarities between the two.

711 Alter, Jonathan. "The Smear Heard 'Round the World." ("Between the Lines" column). Newsweek, October 19, 1992, 27. Photo. Refers to Bush's questioning of Clinton's 1969 Moscow trip and his antiwar activities in England. Bush's charges, made on the Larry King show, reflected desperation. Fortunately, the public could distinguish between genuine issues like NAFTA and health care reform and simply campaign issues like Bush's personal attacks on Clinton. Alter also considered the media's role and responsibility in its coverage of such attacks.

712 Barnes, Fred. "What It Takes: Al Gore's Campaign Makeover." New Republic, October 19, 1992, 22-24.

713 Peretz, Martin. "The Other Al: Gore in Private." New Republic, October 19, 1992, 19-20, 21.

714 Shabecoff, Philip. "Green Giant." New Republic, October 19, 1992, 20.

The New Republic focused on Al Gore in this issue.

Peretz writes favorably of Gore. Shabecoff defends
Gore's environmental record and contends that he is
not an "'environmental extremist'" as the Republicans
portrayed him. Barnes presents a more negative view
of Gore, maintaining that Gore toned down some of the
positions he took in his book Earth in the Balance
for political reasons (that is, so to get elected).

715 Barone, Michael. "The Making of a New Majority."
("On Politics" column). U.S. News & World Report,
October 19, 1992, 40. While Clinton's task in
maintaining a Democratic majority had been helped by
the decline of the right and left within the
Democratic Party, he still faced a great challenge--
promote economic growth, pass health care legislation
(without a significant increase in taxes), show that
the Democrats can be moderate on social issues, and
make government more efficient without alienating
various Democratic constituent groups like public
employee unions, trial lawyers, and feminists.

716 Beck, Melinda. "Painful Remedies." Newsweek,
October 19, 1992, 31.

717 Easterbrook, Gregg. "Who Would be Cleaner?"
Newsweek, October 19, 1992, 36.

718 Kantrowitz, Barbara and Pat Wingert. "Different
Choices on School Choice." Newsweek, October 19,
1992, 32.

719 Kaus, Mickey. "False Hopes for the Cities?"
Newsweek, October 19, 1992, 35.

720 Warner, Margaret Garrard and John Barry. "The
Global Vision Thing." Newsweek, October 19, 1992, 34.

Clinton, Perot, and Bush on health care, education,
foreign policy, urban policy, and the environment.

721 Byron, Christopher. "Spooked: Clintonphobia on
Wall Street." ("The Bottom Line" column). New York
25, 41(October 19, 1992): 22, 24. The economy may
fare worse under a Clinton administration and would
be reflected on Wall Street.

722 Cooper, Matthew. "10 Key Decisions for the Next
President." U.S. News & World Report, October 19,
1992, 30-32, 34-35. Presents 10 crucial decisions
for whoever was elected president: economic stimulus
package, health care reform, winter crises (whether
in the former Yugoslavia or Russia), the Middle East,

reduction in defense budget, NAFTA, a potential
December bank crisis (which did not materialize),
court appointments and cases, possibility of new
outbreaks of racial tension, and selection of
individuals to important administration positions.

723 Drew, Elizabeth. "High Noon: Letter From
Washington." New Yorker, October 19, 1992, 48, 50,
54-56, 59. Assessment of campaign as of October 8.
At this late stage, the two major events were Perot's
reentry into the race and the presidential debates.
Drew doubted the value of debates, which had little
connection with being a good president.

724 Fineman, Howard. "Face to Face to Face."
Newsweek, October 19, 1992, 20-24. Photo. Analysis
of the first presidential debate, including the
performances of Clinton, Perot, and Bush.

725 Gould, Stanley W. "Quayle vs. Gore." Time,
October 19, 1992, 34-35. Gore had been criticized
for stubbornness and arrogance and his 1988
presidential bid was viewed by some as ambitious.
Since then, Gore's status had risen, especially since
he had provided a real boost to Clinton as his
running mate. Gore compensated for some of Clinton's
weaknesses such as his Washington experience, lack of
serious marital difficulties, service in Vietnam, and
support for the Gulf War. And Gore was aware that
vice presidential experience could serve as a future
stepping stone to the presidency.

726 Greenwald, John. "Anatomy of a Smear." Time,
October 19, 1992, 28-29. Photo. On Republican
efforts to bring up Clinton's past draft history both
in the U.S. and England, his 1969 trip to Moscow, and
the tampering of his passport records. These efforts
were designed to raise new doubts among voters about
Clinton just prior to the first presidential debate.

727 Gwyne, S.C. and Elizabeth Taylor. "'We're Not
Measuring the Drapes': Al Gore Holds Forth on the
Campaign, Television's Damaging Impact and Dan
Quayle." Time, October 19, 1992, 36. Interview with
Gore on Quayle's depiction of his environmental
positions, plans for the first 100 days of a Clinton
administration, U.S. policy toward Iraq prior to its
Kuwaiti invasion, and his compatibility with Clinton.

728 Hood, John. "Clinton's Record." National Review
44, 20(October 19, 1992): 35-37. Negative assessment
of Clinton's Arkansas record based on the economy,

the budget, education, welfare, the environment,
health care, crime, and transportation.

729 Kinsley, Michael. "178 and Counting." ("TRB From
Washington" column). New Republic, October 19, 1992,
6, 49. Criticism of the Bush campaign for distorting
Clinton's tax and economic record in Arkansas.

730 Klein, Joe. "Bush's Desperate Game." ("Public
Lives" column). Newsweek, October 19, 1992, 26.
Bush's strategy of personal attack, including his
"Red-baiting" of Clinton on the Larry King show, was
a "sorry spectacle."

731 Kramer, Michael. "It's Clinton's to Lose."
(Cover story). Time, October 19, 1992, 26-30. Photo.
Assessment of the fall campaign following the first
presidential debate, which allowed voters to get a
better sense of the candidates but did not alter the
dynamics of the election. Clinton did best on his
strength, which was policy. Kramer also provided an
overview of the Bush administration and the early
part of the campaign for Clinton.

732 Roberts, Steven V. "Clinton, Oxford and the
Draft: Clinton Still Shows His Ambivalence About
Those Painful Years." U.S. News & World Report,
October 19, 1992, 36, 38-39. The Vietnam War's
shadow continued to follow Clinton, whose conduct in
response to that war became a focus of the Bush
campaign. Bush argued that Clinton was unqualified
to be president based on avoiding military service,
participating in antiwar protests, and going to
Moscow during the conflict. (See also brief
accompanying article "Moscow Connection: School Days"
on p. 38). Clinton had underestimated the negative
impact this issue would have on his candidacy.

733 Schwartz, Herman. "Unpacking the Supreme Court:
What Clinton Could Do." Nation, October 19, 1992,
434-437. Clinton's potential impact on the federal
judiciary regarding appointments, a past antiabortion
litmus test for Supreme Court nominees, and social
welfare and civil rights laws.

734 Zoglin, Richard. "Ad Wars." Time, October 19,
1992, 40, 45. Assessment of the presidential media
campaigns. Clinton's was run by Greer, Margolis,
Mitchell, Grunwald & Associates with assistance from
Democratic media consultants. This collective effort
had been focused and effective, placing ads on a
state-by-state basis.

735 Zuckerman, Mortimer B. "Loony-Tune Economics."
(Editorial). <u>U.S. News & World Report</u>, October 19,
1992, 82. Clinton's economic program would deal with
the recession and reverse some tax inequities,
although it did not adequately address the deficit.

736 Drinan, Robert F. "Clinton Background Puts
Jesuit Issues Up Front." <u>National Catholic Reporter</u>
29, 1(October 23, 1992): 5. If Clinton were to be
elected, he would be the only graduate of a
Catholic-Jesuit college to be president.

737 "Clinton for Government-Aided Reform."
<u>Economist</u>, October 24, 1992, 21-22. MIT economist
Rudiger Dornbusch made the case for Clinton. The
U.S. needed government-initiated change and Bush
could not meet the economic challenges the country
faced, but Clinton would. The Clinton economic
program included public sector investment, education,
welfare reform, and health care.

738 "Keeping His Mouth Shut: Clinton and the Fed."
<u>Economist</u>, October 24, 1992, 24-25. Possible impact
of a Clinton victory on U.S. financial markets.

739 Alter, Jonathan. "How He Would Govern." (Cover
story). <u>Newsweek</u>, October 26, 1992, 22-26. As the
election approached, speculation grew as to what kind
of president Clinton would be. This article was
accompanied by a smaller one entitled "Who Would Get
the Jobs?" speculating on who might get key posts in
a Clinton administration.

740 Baer, Donald. "Can Anyone Stop Clinton? A
Debate-A-Thon Helped Democrats, Rehabilitated Perot
and Left Republicans with Nightmares." <u>U.S. News &
World Report</u>, October 26, 1992, 38-40, 42-44, 46-47.
Photos. Status of the campaign following the vice
presidential debate and the first two presidential
debates--the most important week of the campaign
because the debates were the G.O.P's last opportunity
to make any headway since their earlier attacks on
Clinton as a tax-and-spender, his character, and
record in Arkansas had not worked. In the debates,
Clinton held his own. Regarding how Clinton would
govern if elected, he and Democrats would have to
produce by breaking the Washington gridlock.

741 Brodkey, Harold. "Box Populi: Couch Reporter."
<u>New Yorker</u>, October 26, 1992, 55-57. The second
presidential debate was the "decisive encounter,"
in which Clinton excelled. Brodkey was critical of

Bush and Perot, but, in contrast, very praiseworthy
of Clinton, likening him to Truman.

742 "Candidates Bush and Clinton Talk About Jobs,
Racism, Affirmative Action." Jet 83, 1(October 26,
1992): 4-9. The black vote could be crucial to the
election. Notes positions of Bush and Clinton on
employment, racism, and affirmative action.

743 "Crunch." (Editorial). New Republic, October 26,
1992, 9. Urges Clinton to deal with the deficit.

744 Fineman, Howard. "The Inner Circles: Clinton's
Team." Newsweek, October 26, 1992, 28-31. Illus.,
photos. Consideration of Clinton's friends and
professional contacts, divided into the following
sections: Arkansas, college days, Oxford, Yale, the
antiwar crusade, the governors, Renaissance (Weekends
in South Carolina), the DLC, and the campaign.

745 Gergen, David. "The Awful Dilemma Awaiting
Clinton." U.S. News & World Report, October 26, 1992,
50. Photo. The cruxt of the dilemma which could
follow a Clinton victory was that if he started off
with a large deficit reduction, he would be compelled
to ask for sacrifices which would be unpopular and go
beyond what he had discussed in the campaign. On the
other hand, if Clinton delayed too long, he may lose
the opportunity to accomplish anything. And if he
did nothing, the economy would continue to be flat so
that in 1996 Clinton would be as vulnerable on the
economy as Bush had been in 1992.

746 Klein, Joe. "The Bill Clinton Show." ("Public
Lives" column). Newsweek, October 26, 1992, 35.
Photo. While Bush was out of his element in the
second debate, Clinton might be the "ultimate
American talk-show host." Clinton could provide a
different kind of leadership--that of "hosting the
presidency." Klein then noted a similarity between
Roosevelt and Clinton, as reflected in what Rabbi
Stephen Wise wrote to Felix Frankfurter about FDR.

747 Klare, Michael T. "Know Them By Their Enemies:
Clinton and Bush on Defense." Nation, October 26,
1992, 461-464. While the positions of Bush and
Clinton were similar on foreign policy, they diverged
regarding countries which would most likely face
hostility from the U.S. Bush's enemies list would
include Iraq, North Korea, Libya, and Iran while
Clinton's would be Syria, South Africa, and China.

748 Kramer, Michael. "Playing Out the End Game."
("The Political Interest" column). <u>Time</u>, October 26,
1992, 43. Clinton should build a consensus on a few
concrete definable principles, but this was not his
forte, the national service plan being an example.
His administration could resemble Carter's--many
disparate policies with no underlining vision.

749 Turque, Bill. "How to Stay in the Loop: Gore."
<u>Newsweek</u>, October 26, 1992, 27. Photo. On Gore's
possible influence in a Clinton administration.
Clinton promised Gore policy areas like the
environment, technology, and national security. In
the long run, Gore could take solace since being vice
president could lead to a bid for the presidency.

750 Wingo, Walter S. "Bush, Clinton Square Off on
Technology: November's Winner May Determine What Many
Engineers Design in the 1990s." <u>Design News</u> 48,
20(October 26, 1992): 25-26. Photo. Bush and Clinton
on technology, defense and space, industrial output,
energy and environment, and the budget and taxes.

751 Goldstein, Richard. "Sweet William." (Cover
story). <u>Village Voice</u>, October 27, 1992, 29-33.
Clinton's ability to overcome negative personal
images could serve as a preview to how he would
govern the nation. Clinton managed to attract the
traditional (John F.) Kennedy vote with the themes of
renewal and change. The title of the article was
coined by Clinton journalist critic, John Robert
Starr, and Goldstein included a brief summary of
Clinton's political career in Arkansas. Written in
the usual irreverent <u>Village Voice</u> style.

752 Tomasky, Michael. "Clinton Torches Hotlanta."
<u>Village Voice</u>, October 27, 1992, 35-37. Good article
about the Clinton-Gore campaign in Georgia, which
led in the polls for the same reasons it was ahead
nationally: an intelligent campaign and Bush's poor
one, the anemic economy, and the choice issue. Also
includes an assessment of Clinton by Republican
ideological opponent Newt Gingrich.

753 Drinan, Robert F. "It's Good to Protest Abroad
for a Good Reason." <u>National Catholic Reporter</u> 29,
2(October 30, 1992): 23. Defended Clinton's right to
have protested overseas and criticized Bush for
having made it an issue.

754 "Clintonomics Under a Cloud." <u>Economist</u>, October
31, 1992, 71. Criticism of projected Clinton

economic policies as articulated by the National
Association of Business Economists.

755 "A Spanking From Madonna: The Youth Vote."
Economist, October 31, 1992, 25-26. Youth vote was
gravitating toward Clinton-Gore ticket.

756 "Time to Choose." (Editorial). Economist,
October 31, 1992, 13-14. Despite some reservations
on future Clinton foreign and domestic policies
(based on some aspects of his record as governor),
the Economist endorsed Clinton for president.

757 Regardie, William A. "George Bush, It's Time to
Retire to Kennebunkport." Regardie's Magazine 12,
7(October/November 1992): 7. Regardie's endorses
Clinton for president due to the Bush
administration's inattention to the economy.

758 Anthony, Joseph. "Bush & Clinton: Their Plans
for Your Health." American Health 11, 9(November
1992): 84-85. Bush and Clinton on family leave,
child care, senior care, AIDS, and abortion.

759 Auletta, Ken. "Loathe the Media: An
Election-Year Anatomy of an Institution in Decline."
Esquire 18, 5(November 1992): 107-112, 177, 179,
181-182. Among the factors which contributed to the
public's dislike of the media (and linked directly to
the Clinton candidacy) were "mindless reportage" in
the form of "pack campaign journalism" and an
"obsession with the character issue." Also includes
James Carville's thoughts on the press. Insightful
critique of media coverage late into the campaign.

760 Bloom, Mark. "Taking the Presidential Pulse: Are
Bush and Clinton in Good Health?" American Health 11,
9(November 1992): 81-83, 86. Photo. Within the
context of an overview of past presidents' health
histories, those of Bush and Clinton were discussed.

761 Brown, Christiane N. "What Women Should Know
About the Candidates Before They Vote!" Good
Housekeeping 215, 5(November 1992): 267-268. About
issues pertaining to the family (family and medical
leave, child support, and domestic violence/child
abuse), working women (discrimination/harassment),
child care (day care and preschool programs),
education (school reform, college costs, and college
alternatives), abortion (Roe v. Wade, Freedom of
Choice Act, and gag rule), and health care (health
insurance, fetal-tissue research, and RU 486).

762 Conant, Jennet. "Who Puts Women and Children
First?" Redbook 180, 1(November 1992): 92-93,
145-147. Bush and Clinton answered 10 questions
relating to women and children. Conant noted that
the candidates differed most on abortion and sex
education while both agreed on health care reform,
although they disagreed on the means to control
costs. Other issues discussed: American national
character, focus on the personal life of candidates,
working women, decline of the American family, Roe v.
Wade, education and schools, drugs, and the Clarence
Thomas-Anita Hill hearings.

763 "Dread October." (editorial). American Spectator
25, 11(November 1992): 18. Disparaging editorial
predicting that by November Clinton would be a
"goner" and lose the election.

764 Edwards, Lee. "Bush vs. Clinton: Who Will It
Be?" World & I 7, (November 1992): 24-33. In the
volatile election year of 1992, the electorate seemed
prepared to opt for change and chose a "'different
kind of Democrat,'" Bill Clinton. As with other
elections, this one amounted to a "referendum on
continuity versus change." The focus was on the five
fundamental aspects of all political campaigns
(money, organization, candidates, issues, and media)
and both Clinton and Bush were "graded." Their
scores were the equivalent of a rather close 53 to 47
popular victory and a firm 325 to 213 electoral
college win for Clinton. It is important to note
that this article was written before the debates were
formalized and Perot's reentry into the campaign.

765 "First Arkansan Elected President: Bill Clinton
Goes to the White House." Arkansas Educator 18,
3(November 1992): 1.

766 "Message to AEA From the President-Elect of the
United States of America." Arkansas Educator 18,
3(November 1992): 2.

767 McHenry, Cara D. "Education in a Post-Clinton
Era." Arkansas Educator 18, 4(December 1992): 2.

Coverage of Clinton's election and beyond from the
AEA's official publication.

768 Jaffe, Harry. "Mr. In-Between." Washingtonian
28, 2(November 1992): 64-67, 105-108. Detailed
profile of Ron Brown, who was instrumental in uniting
the Democratic Party behind Clinton.

769 Norquist, Grover. "The Coming Clinton Dynasty."
American Spectator 25, 11(November 1992): 24-27.
Some Republican conservatives believed that their
longer-term interests would best be served if Clinton
defeated Bush in the election because he would raise
taxes, impose regulations, increase inflation,
hamstring the economy, and emphasize social issues,
thereby uniting a Republican opposition who would
defeat him in 1996. Norquist, president of Americans
for Tax Reform, however, cautioned against this rosy
conservative scenario, believing that the Clinton
administration would not be a "rerun" of the Carter
administration. Just as Democrats have retained
their power in Congress, Clinton would seek to retain
power as well by not repeating the mistakes of the
Carter years.

770 Peña, Nelson. "Here's the Ticket: For Cycling
Issues, Bush/Quayle or Clinton/Gore?" ("Bike
Advocate" column). Bicycling 33, 9(November 1992):
44. Bicycling sought the views of both campaigns on
bicycling and the environment in general, integrated
with commentary by Peña, who concluded that Clinton's
"overall environmental record...is mixed."

771 "Report From Chicago: Presidential Candidates
Woo Legionnaires at the 74th National Convention...."
American Legion 133, 5(November 1992): 32, 35. Photo.
Clinton and Bush spoke separately on August 25 at the
American Legion's National Convention. Clinton,
while acknowledging that he had not served in the
military, hoped that Legionnaires would not allow the
past to hinder their looking to the country's future,
which Clinton thought he best could serve. As a 1963
Boys Nation graduate, the Democrat gave credit to the
Legion for starting his career in politics. Clinton
also promised to make Veterans Affairs more
responsive to the veterans it was designed to serve.

772 Schnepper, Jeff A. and Bob Leduc. "Escaping the
Budget Quagmire." ("The Economic Observer" column).
USA Today (Magazine) 121, 2570(November 1992): 19.
Discusses the deficit reduction plans of Bush and
Clinton. The authors believe in supply side
economics and disagreed with Clinton's economic plan.

773 Sturgis, Ingrid and Matthew S. Scott.
"African-Americans Ponder Where To Place Votes."
Black Enterprise 23, 4(November 1992): 20. Photo.
The 1992 election represented the first one since
1960 when the black vote was not actively courted by
either the Republican or Democratic parties. Neither

party addressed the concerns of the Afro-American
community. Clinton and Bush's positions on the
economy, education, and health care are presented.
The article closes with the opinions of several
prominent Afro-Americans on the election, including
those of Alexis Herman, who was deputy chair of the
Democratic National Committee (and is now Clinton's
Director of Liaison for Public Outreach).

774 Vidal, Gore. "Goin' South: Clinton and Gore
Offer a Busted Country One Last Deal." GQ
(Gentleman's Quarterly) 62, 11(November 1992):
226-231. Vidal wrote a cynical appraisal of the
prospects for the impending Clinton victory. The
political system is no more effective than the
economic system. Problems have become systemic and
are no longer cyclical. Vidal made some predictions
which turned out to be wrong, predicting that over
half of the electorate would not vote and that tax
rates would not be increased for the rich by
Congress. Vidal believed that Clinton and Gore,
being southern conservatives, were tied to the
military-industrial complex, but Clinton would have a
great opportunity for defense conversion due to
defense cutbacks. Clinton was compared to F.D.R. in
that the latter helped shore up the economic and
political system, which Clinton also needed to do.
Like Roosevelt, Clinton was "equally unprincipled."

775 "Where the Candidates Stand on Health Reform."
Consumer Reports 57, 11(November 1992): 696-697.
Photo. Presents the positions of Bush and Clinton on
health care in terms of three components considered
by Consumer Reports to be essential--universal
access, cost controls, and quality care. Neither the
Bush nor Clinton reform plans sufficiently met these
criteria because they both favored insurance
companies and health-care providers, but not the
public. Instead, this publication called for a
"single-payer health-care system."

776 Yates, Brock. "Sticking with George." Car and
Driver 38, 5(November 1992): 18. Endorsement of Bush
for president. Yates depicted Gore's environmental
positions as "anti-car" due to stricter CAFE
standards, electric cars, and calls for eliminating
the internal-combustion engine in the next 25 years.

777 Barrett, Laurence I. "The Fat Lady Hasn't Quite
Sung." Time, November 2, 1992, 24-27. Bush
questioned Clinton's presidential qualifications,
character, and trustworthiness. Clinton needed to

show that he was a reliable candidate for change in contrast to Perot. Despite a tightening of the race, Clinton could still win an electoral landslide, even with only a popular vote plurality.

778 Borger, Gloria. "How Would Clinton Manage Congress? It's Not Clear the Party's Ready for Prime Time." U.S. News & World Report, November 2, 1992, 33. Dan Rostenkowski declared that "'Clinton already knows more about the Hill than Jimmy Carter ever did.'" The early legislative agenda for a Clinton administration would include an economic stimulus plan, health care reform, and a long-term deficit reduction plan. Just prior to the election, however, Democrats had not yet reached a consensus on the specific ways to deal with such issues, although they agreed on more general goals--lower expectations, decide on a few priorities, gain early victories, thereby setting precedents for later victories.

779 "The Character Thing." (Editorial). New Republic, November 2, 1992, 7. The Bush campaign's questioning of Clinton's 1969 trip to Moscow was likened to McCarthyism and red-baiting. The Republicans resorted to the so-called character issue because it was the only one they had left to use against Clinton and since they could not run on the Bush record. On the other hand, the character question was legitimate in the sense that this editorial urged Clinton to be more direct and forthcoming in his responses to questions about his past and where he stood on issues and principles.

780 Church, George J. "The Long Road." (Cover story). Time, November 2, 1992, 28-38, 43. Describes how a mixture of good fortune, determination, and a strong message made Clinton into the frontrunner for the presidency in 1992. This late campaign assessment presents a good overview of the Clinton campaign. (Another highlight was the accompanying photos by P.F. Bentley). Although the race tightened toward the end, Clinton had come a long way. (See also "From the Publisher" section, p. 4).

781 Cockburn, Alexander. "Clinton, Labor and Free Trade: The Executioner's Song." Nation, November 2, 1992, 489, 506-509. Cockburn criticizes Clinton's record on labor as governor of Arkansas, which is a "right to work" state. Clinton's labor record in Arkansas could have national implications if Clinton won the election. North American Free Trade Agreement (NAFTA) is discussed within this context.

782   "Conservatives for Clinton." New Republic,
November 2, 1992, 22-23. Conservatives Joshua
Muravchik, John Frohnmayer, and Arthur B. Laffer
present their reasons for voting for Bill Clinton.

783   Cooper, Matthew. "Now, It's Down to the Wire:
Clinton's Dream Time." U.S. News & World Report,
November 2, 1992, 28, 30-31. Photo. Reports on the
Clinton campaign in the final stage of the race.
While the Clinton camp did not want to become
overconfident, there was talk of a landslide and
Clinton asked voters for a mandate. The campaign was
concentrating on midwestern battleground states and
promoting its economic message. Ads were geared to
increase both the number of "'persuadable voters'"
and the "GOTV" index, to "'get out the vote'" in
strong electoral areas.

784   Dentzer, Susan. "What Should Bill Clinton Do
First?" ("On the Economy" column). U.S. News & World
Report, November 2, 1992, 52. Clinton had such a
large agenda that it could never be fulfilled even at
the end of a second Al Gore term as president, let
alone at the close of Clinton's first. Even before
the election, Dentzer cautioned against an economic
stimulus package and spending on new infrastructure
as a means to spur the economy because they could
lead to the funding of "pork" projects.

785   Drew, Elizabeth. "Endgame: Letter from
Washington." New Yorker, November 2, 1992, 56-58, 60,
61. Dated October 22, Drew provides a good overview
and analysis of the last stages of the election,
especially the three presidential debates and one
vice-presidential debate. Clinton did well in the
debates. Clinton maintained a relatively good lead,
but his campaign was apprehensive of complacency and
blowing the lead in the polls. There were still some
doubts in the public's mind about Clinton's character
and his tendency to equivocate on answers, which
could cause him some difficulties should he be
elected. This election engaged the voters and
addressed important issues.

786   Egan, Jack. "A Clinton Watch on Wall Street."
("On Money" column). U.S. News & World Report,
November 2, 1992, 92. A Clinton administration would
not adversely affect Wall Street and could give the
economy a temporary boost, spurring confidence. Wall
Street had already had "come to terms with a Clinton
presidency" and appeared "relatively unworried."

787 Fineman, Howard. "Running Scared: Perot's
Eleventh-Hour Surge Could Hurt Both Clinton and
Bush." Newsweek, November 2, 1992, 46-48. Photo.
Last issue of Newsweek published before the election.
An "October Surprise" materialized after all--the
reemergence of Ross Perot. Fineman reported on
Perot's surge in the polls toward the end of the
campaign, which tightened the race. Included an
assessment of the likely impact of Perot's resurgence
on Clinton (lower both Clinton's percentages in the
polls and the popular vote). And if Clinton did win,
he would have Perot and the deficit to deal with.

788 Klein, Joe. "Prisoner of the People." Newsweek,
November 2, 1992, 58. Photo. In the 1992 election
year, the public wanted a serious discussion of
issues and leadership. As the election approached,
however, neither Clinton nor any other politician
could meet the public's increasingly unrealistic
expectations of what their leaders could deliver.
Klein also looked to the future beyond the election.

789 Roberts, Steven V. "That Sinking Feeling:
Drowning in Economic Woes, Voters Seem Willing to Try
a New Rescue." U.S. News & World Report, November 2,
1992, 22-24, 27. Illus. Based on a U.S. News October
20-21 poll, Clinton led Bush 45 to 31%, with 20% for
Perot. The poor economy harmed Bush and boosted
Clinton's electoral chances with these voting
groups--young voters, working women, Reagan
Democrats, white collar suburbanites, and Clinton
Republicans. Accompanied by a small article entitled
"Campaign Currents: Under the Surface," which noted
the strengths of the Clinton campaign and the
weaknesses of the Bush campaign based on the economy,
swing voters, debates, attributes, and salesmanship.

790 Tobias, Andrew. "How to Invest in a Clinton
Win." ("Money Angles" column). Time, November 2,
1992, 53-54. Personal finance in terms of a
"four-pronged investment technique," especially as it
related to a likely Clinton victory in the election:
"liquid money," "inflation hedge," "deflation hedge,"
and "prosperity hedge." Perhaps a Democrat could get
Congress to change welfare into workfare, cut Social
Security for those who could afford it, and provide
investment incentives.

791 Turque, Bill. "The Clinton File Mystery Grows: A
Key Figure Talks, But Many Questions Remain."
Newsweek, November 2, 1992, 49. Controversy over an
improperly conducted search of Clinton's passport

file by senior State Department officials in hopes of
finding information harmful to him. Newsweek
interviewed Elizabeth Tamposi, Assistant Secretary
for Consular Affairs, about the incident, but
questions remained. The negative political fallout
enabled the Democrats to decry this as a scandal
toward the end of a tightening presidential race.

792 Weisberg, Jacob. "Southern Exposure: Clinton as
Sitcom." New Republic, November 2, 1992, 13-15.
Photo. Influence of T.V. producers Harry and Linda
Bloodworth-Thomason on the Clinton campaign.

3

Transition Period, November 4, 1992-January 19, 1993

NEWSPAPERS (NOVEMBER 4, 1992-JANUARY 19, 1993)

Arkansas Times (weekly newspaper)

793 Brummett, John. "Anatomy of a Miracle: Even Bill Clinton Had Reservations About the Run That Changed America." November 5, 1992, 17.

794 Leveritt, Mara. "Arkansas Will Never Be the Same: Get Ready; What's Ahead Could Be Amazing." November 5, 1992, 21.

795 Martin, Richard. "Glory Days: Arkansans Share In Clinton Triumph." November 5, 1992, 16, 18-20. Photo.

796 Brummett, John. "The 'Big Chill' Presidency." November 12, 1992, 16-17. Photo.

797 Brummett, John. "Eyes of the World: From Sweden to Salt Lake City, Journalists Asked Crazy Things." November 12, 1992, 5.

798 Wells, George. "Lost Jobs and New Opportunities at the Courthouse: Federal Appointments Also On Clinton's Agenda." November 12, 1992, 12.

799 Brummett, John. "Clinton's Little Men: Stephanopoulos, Lindsey and Reich--Small Guys With Major-League Clout." November 19, 1992, 5.

800 Brummett, John. "The World's Biggest Story: Catching Up On Bill Clinton's Future; From the

Grandiose To the Mundane." November 19, 1992, 16-17. Photo.

801 Brummett, John. "The Clinton Watch." December 3, 1992, 18-19.

802 Brummett, John. "Reagan Democrat: President-Elect Clinton Looks to the Gipper As a Role Model." December 3, 1992, 6.

803 Dumas, Ernest. "The Urgency of Health Care: Clinton Should Press Issue Now." December 3, 1992, 31.

804 Brummett, John. "McLarty Revealed: The New White House Chief of Staff Mixes Propriety, Passion and Humor." December 17, 1992, 7.

805 Brummett, John. "Washington Watch, The Transition." December 17, 1992, 13-14. Photo.

806 Brummett, John. "No Betsy [Wright] in D.C.: The President-Elect's Defender Says She'll Go Her Own Way." December 24, 1992, 6.

807 Brummett, John. "Our Real Favorite Son: Mack McLarty Goes To Washington With One Piece of Heavy Baggage--The Gas Company He Leaves Behind." December 24, 1992, 24-25.

808 McCord, Robert S. "Why Resent Hillary's Help?" December 24, 1992, 29.

809 Brummett, John. "The Year To Come." December 31, 1992, 6.

810 Dumas, Ernest. "Clinton Picks Strong Cabinet." December 31, 1992, 23.

811 Brummett, John. "No More 'Spin': The Campaign Is History; Bill Gets the Awful Truth." January 7, 1993, 6.

812 Brummett, John. "This Group Is Really Chic--Homefolks: They're the 'Arkansas Travelers'..." January 7, 1993, 13.

813 Brummett, John. "A Guide To D.C." January 14, 1993, 5.

814 Mabury, David. "Waiting For Bill: Inauguration." January 14, 1993, 12-13.

815   Christian Science Monitor

816   Los Angeles Times

817   New York Times

818   USA Today

819   Washington Post

Extensive newspaper coverage of the Clinton transition period.

SPECIALIZED POLITICAL JOURNALS

820   Congressional Quarterly Weekly Report

821   National Journal

Provides detailed information and analysis of the Clinton transition.

CONSERVATIVE POLITICAL MAGAZINES

822   American Spectator

823   Insight on the News

824   National Review

Provides considerable coverage of the Clinton transition period from a conservative perspective.

FINANCIAL/ECONOMIC ORIENTED MAGAZINES

825   Business Week

Economist

826   "Getting His Way." (Editorial). November 7, 1992, 15.

827   "No Margin for Error." November 7, 1992, 27-29.

828   "The Bill Clinton Nobody Knows." November 7, 1992, 38.

829   "After the Market." (Editorial). November 7,

1992, 13-14.

830 "Keeping an Eye for <u>The Economist</u> on the President-Elect: The Economy." November 14, 1992, 26.

831 "101 Uses for a Dead Nine Weeks." November 21, 1992, 25-26.

832 "Keeping an Eye for <u>The Economist</u> on the President-Elect: The Underclass." November 21, 1992, 26.

833 "Out of the Locker: Homosexuals and the Military." November 21, 1992, 26-27.

834 "Ignore Blue Touch Paper and Retire." November 28, 1992, 23-24.

835 "Keeping an Eye for <u>The Economist</u> on the President-Elect: Health Care." November 28, 1992, 24.

836 "Keeping an Eye for <u>The Economist</u> on the President-Elect: Education." December 5, 1992, 26.

837 "Hillary Clinton, Trail-Blazer." December 5, 1992, 30.

838 "He's No Paul Volcker: But There are Virtues To Be Made Out of the Vices of Lloyd Bentsen, America's Next Treasury Secretary." December 12, 1992, 18-19.

839 "The World In His Lap." December 12, 1992, 29.

840 "Keeping an Eye for <u>The Economist</u> on the President-Elect: Mandate for Change." December 12, 1992, 30.

841 "Lloyd Bentsen, Horse for a Course." December 12, 1992, 36. Illus.

842 "World Cop?" (Editorial). December 19, 1992, 13-14.

843 "The No-Hard-Choices Summit." December 19, 1992, 23-24. Photo.

844 "Ron Brown, Man of Parts." December 19, 1992, 30.

845 "Arkansas Comes to Washington: Some Lessons for the Capital From the Land of Opportunity." December 26, 1992-January 8, 1993, 27-28.

846   "Everybody Happy? Appointments." December 26,
1992-January 8, 1993, 30.

847   "When the State Picks Winners." (Editorial).
January 9, 1993, 13-14.

848   "Formidable Baton to Pass." January 9, 1993, 23.

849   "Southwards, Look." January 9, 1993, 24.

850   "Greener and Browner." January 9, 1993, 25-26.
Photo.

851   "Working On It." January 9, 1993, 26.

852   "Magic Trick or Sacrifice?" January 16, 1993,
27-28.

853   "Clinton's Options." January 16, 1993, 28.

854   "A Glance at the Clock: Free Trade." January 16,
1993, 28-29. Photo.

The Economist's coverage of the transition period.

855   Forbes

856   Fortune

In addition to specific citations contained elsewhere
in this bibliography, the reader also should consult
Forbes and Fortune during the transition period.

NATION'S CITIES WEEKLY

857   Shafroth, Frank. "Clinton Promises 'New
Beginning' For America." 15, 45(November 9, 1992): 1,
6.

858   Barnes, Bill. "Stimulus is Focus of Major Policy
Debate." 15, 46(November 16, 1992): 2.

859   Shafroth, Frank. "Local, State Leaders Agree on
Message of Support to...Clinton As He Takes on Tough
Issues." 15, 46(November 16, 1992): 1, 6.

860   Barnes, Bill. "Clinton Must Confront Balancing
Act: The Deficit Versus the Economy." 15, 47(November
23, 1992): 10, 22.

861   Shafroth, Frank. "Partners in Community

Investment." 15, 47(November 23, 1992): 7.

862 Shafroth, Frank. "President-Elect Begins to Map Agenda that Includes Cities." 15, 47(November 23, 1992): 10, 12. Photo.

863 Baker, Denise. "Transition Team Members Meet With NLC Board at Congress of Cities." 15, 48(December 7, 1992): 1, 3, 11.

864 Shafroth, Frank. "Clinton Cabinet Takes Shape Under 'Investment' Theme." 15, 49(December 14, 1992): 1, 11.

865 Arndt, Randy. "Economy Tops Local Officials Concerns." 16, 2(January 11, 1993): 1, 4.

866 Barnes, Bill. "Local Matters in Economic Policy." ("Opinion"). 16, 2(January 11, 1993): 2.

867 Shafroth, Frank. "Rare Opportunity Awaits Clinton, 103rd Congress: A Time to End Gridlock." 16, 2(January 11, 1993): 10, 12.

868 Shafroth, Frank. "Clinton Economic Nominees Offer Plans Similar to NLC's Deficit Reduction Strategy." 16, 3(January 18, 1993): 4.

Coverage of transition by Nation's Cities Weekly.

NATIONAL CATHOLIC REPORTER

869 "Americans Stand Together at Crossroads of the World." 29, 4(November 13, 1992): 28.

870 Castelli, Jim. "Catholics Were Key Element in Coalition to Elect Clinton." 29, 6(December 4, 1992): 9.

871 "Catholics Must Include Abortion in Moral Agenda." 29, 6(December 4, 1992): 28.

872 Chittister, Joan. "Along the Line, Progress Became the Holy Grail." 29, 6(December 4, 1992): 22.

873 Drinan, Robert F. "Clinton Could Be Man of Destiny and Eliminate World Hunger." (Column). 29, 9(December 25, 1992): 14.

874 "It's Time to Start Creating Jobs for the Urban Poor." (Editorial). 29, 10(January 8, 1993): 24.

875 "Let Poor Children Form the Ark of Clinton's New
Covenant." (Editorial). 29, 11(January 15, 1993): 32.

National Catholic Reporter's coverage of Clinton.

ANNOTATED ENTRIES (INCL. ARTICLES, BOOKS, NEWSPAPERS)

876 Glass, Andrew J. "Changing the Power Process."
New Leader 75, 14(November 2-16, 1992): 3-4.
Prospects for campaign finance reform and curbing
lobbyists' influence in a Clinton administration.

877 Barnes, Fred. "The New Covenant: Clinton's
Religious Strategy." New Republic, November 9, 1992,
32-33. Religion was the "stealth issue" of the
presidential race, second only to the economy.
Clinton's comfort with discussing his religious
beliefs in public could help Clinton win.

878 "Clinton for President." (Editorial). New
Republic, November 9, 1992, 7. Illus. New Republic's
endorsement of Clinton for president. Makes the case
against Bush both in domestic and foreign policy.

879 Cockburn, Alexander. "Clinton as Dog."
"Clintonspeak." "Investing in Clinton." Nation,
November 9, 1992, 530-531. Cockburn continued to
criticize Clinton, asserting that Jimmy Carter had
more political principle and a Clinton administration
would be similar to Carter's, followed by a return of
the Republicans. Also noted Clinton's support of the
Cuban Democracy Act and called the Democrat a "Likud
man" due to his support for Israel.

880 "The Election and Beyond." (Editorial). Nation,
November 9, 1992, 525, 527-529. Written just before
the election. Includes some of the positive aspects
of the expected Democratic/Clinton victory--reversal
of conservative appointees to the federal judiciary,
gay rights, greater protection for women's
reproductive rights, health care reform, and greater
support for the arts and civil liberties. However,
progressives still needed to pressure Clinton to go
beyond these minimal benefits. Clinton was not
"committed to produce...substantive change."

881 Kinsley, Michael. "Endgame." ("TRB From
Washington" column). New Republic, November 9, 1992,
6. Makes the case for Clinton--and against Bush.

882 Burd, Stephen, Colleen Cordes, Scott Jaschik,

and Jim Zook. "For Many Leaders in Higher Education, 'President Clinton' Has a Good Ring to It." Chronicle of Higher Education 39, 12(November 11, 1992): A23. Clinton's election would be good for higher education because it was a key element of his economic plans, including national service and scientific research. But a Clinton administration could enforce more rigorously federal regulations on civil rights, the environment, taxation, and immigration as well as add economic costs to higher education through medical and family leave. Formed part of a special section, including articles on Georgetown's reaction to its famous alumni's victory, suggestions for appointments to the new administration, and the Democratic ticket's appeal to the youth vote.

883   "Changes on Horizon: Lawyers Predict Boost in Business Under Clinton." New York Law Journal 208, 93(November 12, 1992): 5, 7.   Survey conducted by this publication of business law experts on their expectations of a new Clinton administration.

884   Hamilton, David P. "Clinton's Technology Agenda." Science 258, 5092(November 13, 1992): 1076-1078. Photo.   A Clinton administration could mean a significant shift in federal government policy toward science and technology with a new focus on the development of technology, a major role for the vice president in this development, and the funding of scientific research.   Includes complementary listings of those prominent scientists and engineers who supported the Clinton/Gore ticket (p. 1077) and speculation on who would gain or lose science positions in the new administration (p. 1078).

885   Alter, Jonathan. "President Best Friend." ("Between the Lines" column). Newsweek, November 16, 1992, 49. Photo.   Clinton needed to set limits on influence peddling and lobbying such as a five year ban on former government officials and a lifetime ban on former officials working for foreign interests.

886   Auster, Bruce B. "Fighting Tomorrow's Wars: Clinton Must Make the Military Smaller, Cheaper and More Versatile." U.S. News & World Report, November 16, 1992, 77-78.   Speculation on the Clinton administration's military/defense policy.

887   Baer, Donald. "The Graying of the Clintons." U.S. News & World Report, November 16, 1992. 61, 63. Photos.   Experiences gained from difficulties the Clintons endured during the campaign may help them in

the new administration, including Hillary Clinton's role as First Lady.

888   Barnes, Fred. "Cool Hand Bill: Clinton's Confidence Trick." New Republic, November 16, 1992, 12-13.   Barnes admitted that he had greatly underestimated Clinton's campaigning skill and that Clinton was he a good politician.

889   Byron, Christopher. "Depending on the Kindness of Strangers: Clinton and the Deficit." ("The Bottom Line" column). New York 25, 45(November 16, 1992): 30-31.   Byron noted Wall Street's skepticism of the Clinton economic policy, including an elaboration of Clinton's economic options such as deficit reduction and short term stimulus.

890   Carlson, Margaret. "A Different Kind of First Lady." Time, November 16, 1992, 40-41. Photo. Carlson ponders what Hillary Clinton's role as First Lady would be.   She had learned the "lessons of accommodation" as First Lady in Arkansas and perhaps could draw on lessons learned then.

891   Clift, Eleanor. "Hillary's Ultimate Juggling Act: As First Lady, She's Free to be Herself." Newsweek, November 16, 1992, 42. Photo.   On Hillary Clinton's new role as First Lady, making a difficult transition from "activist to public symbol."

892   Cook, William J. "Sparking the Future." U.S. News & World Report, November 16, 1992, 90, 92-93. Clinton agenda on technology and industry.

893   Dentzer, Susan. "Bill Clinton, Productivity President." ("On the Economy" column). U.S. News & World Report, November 16, 1992, 48.   To improve American productivity, Clinton and Congress had to cut the deficit and control consumption spending, particularly for growing health programs like Medicare and Medicaid.   This translates into significant changes in health care, reductions in a number of government-spending programs, and, most likely, tax increases.   Clinton needed to persuade the public to make sacrifices now for a later payoff (economic productivity and growth).

894   Gergen, David. "The People Have Great Expectations." ("On Politics" column). U.S. News & World Report, November 16, 1992, 88. Photo.   Not only was a new president elected in November, but also a "new father figure" and a "therapist for the national

psyche" because Clinton recognized that he raised
people's hopes and expectations. Clinton was as a
"truly remarkable political figure," whose
presidential prospects were already being assessed
immediately following the election. Gergen advised
Clinton to act as decisively at the outset of the
transition as he had during the end of the campaign.

895 Isaacson, Walter. "A Time For Courage." Time,
November 16, 1992, 26-29. Photo. Conjecture on what
Clinton would try to accomplish. If Clinton were to
carry out change, he could not be concerned with
pleasing people and would have to displease some.
Now that the voters had the courage to vote for
change, it was Clinton's turn to demonstrate
political courage. Clinton's new covenant involved a
combination of "conservative values such as
responsibility and self-help with liberal ones like
tolerance and generosity." Clinton needed to succeed
because another unsuccessful one-term administration
would signal that government could not govern and the
economy was inexorably declining. It also would
constitute a further setback to the two-party system,
leading the way "to a stronger Perot or Perot-like
candidacy in 1996."

896 Kinsley, Michael. "Stay Mad." ("TRB From
Washington" column). New Republic, November 16, 1992,
6. Kinsley argued that every criticism (like trust,
character, and "waffles") Bush leveled at Clinton was
even more applicable to Bush.

897 Klein, Joe. "Magic and Mystery." Newsweek,
November 16, 1992, 34-38. Photos. Speculation on
Clinton as president. Reaching consensus would be a
key to the Clinton presidency. In this sense,
Clinton's model would be Lyndon Johnson. Clinton
understood the interrelationship between policy and
politics. Clinton might run into problems when he
cannot not find consensus and has to make a stand on
a particular issue. As governor, Clinton had been
making national policy because in the 1980s federal
responsibilities had been transferred to the states,
which had limited resources. Also, as governor,
Clinton gained experience by achieving consensus
among his fellow governors and lobbying Congress to
express state concerns.

898 Kramer, Michael. "What He Will Do." Time,
November 16, 1992, 30-34, 36, 38. Despite budget
restraints, Clinton believed that he needed to
stimulate the economy prior to fulfilling his pledges

(health care reform and job retraining). Kramer
identified potential pitfalls Clinton might be facing
such as the banking system, Russia, and short-term
health care problems. Kramer also made an
observation on the future implications of the
transition period. "The first 100 days cannot be
successful without an intense interregnum."

899 Quinn, Jane Bryant. "What To Do Next." Newsweek,
November 16, 1992, 56-57. A Clinton administration
cannot produce an "economic miracle." Advise on
personal finance with a "money outlook" on taxes, tax
withholding, jobs, and mortgages, and stocks.

900 Robbins, Carla Anne. "A New Kind of Leadership."
("On Foreign Policy" column). U.S. News & World
Report, November 16, 1992, 80. While in the campaign
Clinton held that his main foreign policy goal was to
improve the U.S. economy, major threats to American
security included "refugees, AIDS, the environment,
hunger, population, weapon proliferation, ethnic
warfare and other crises." Clinton's first foreign
policy challenges would be peacemaking and
peacekeeping such as in Bosnia and Cambodia.

901 Shapiro, Walter. "The Final 48 Hours." Time,
November 16, 1992, 44-45. Photos. A diary form
account of the last two days of the Clinton campaign
as it went to 14 cities and covered 5,000 miles.

902 Taylor, John. "What Now?" New York 25,
45(November 16, 1992): 40-45. Illus. Includes
speculation on the new administration's prospects.

903 Turque, Bill. "The Transition: Setting the
Tone." Newsweek, November 16, 1992, 36-37. Insights
into the nature and importance of presidential
transitions. Following an election victory, the
transition "can be a tedious and sour second act."
The Clinton transition ultimately would be judged by
whether it prepared him to move quickly and surely
after he is sworn in.

904 Walcott, John. "Entering Sniper Alley: A
Troubled World Won't Wait for the New Administration
to Get Organized." U.S. News & World Report, November
16, 1992, 73-74. Discusses the foreign policy issues
and areas President Clinton would have to deal with
such as world trade talks, Russia, the Middle East,
NAFTA, the Balkans, the START agreement, and GATT.

905 Walsh, Kenneth T. "Thinking About Tomorrow: The

Clinton Era Begins." U.S. News & World Report,
November 16, 1992, 30-32, 36-37, 40-41, 43, 45.
Photos. Looks ahead to a new administration in which
politics and governing would be inseparable--the
"permanent campaign" to promote Clinton's policy
agenda following Reagan's strategy of concentrating
on specific issues. Clinton was intrigued with the
idea, as elaborated by Franklin Roosevelt, that the
president should serve the role of teacher by
providing moral leadership and clarifying the key
issues affecting the nation.

906 Zuckerman, Mortimer B. "Let's Wish Clinton
Well." (Editorial). U.S. News & World Report,
November 16, 1992, 108. Clinton had to face several
challenges, including public mistrust in government.
As president, Clinton needed to "level" with the
public to enact difficult policies.

907 Abelson, Philip H. "Jobs, Technology, and
Change." (Editorial). Science 258, 5086(November 20,
1992): 1287. In June 1992, candidate Clinton pledged
to create eight million jobs as well as restore the
U.S.'s position as an industrial and technological
leader. An important Clinton campaign policy
document (released on September 18, 1992) entitled
Technology: The Engine of Economic Growth was noted
as was Clinton's assignment of Al Gore as coordinator
of the administration's technology policy.

908 Alter, Jonathan. "The Double Bubba Double
Standard." ("Between the Lines" column). Newsweek,
November 23, 1992, 29. Photo. The press will hold
Clinton accountable for controlling influence
peddling and raising high expectations on what
government can achieve.

909 Baer, Donald. "A Network for the Nineties: The
Retreat That Spawned a Presidency." U.S. News & World
Report, November 23, 1992, 42. Photo. On the annual
New Year's Eve "Renaissance Weekend" retreats held at
Hilton Head, South Carolina, which Bill Clinton and
his family have attended since the mid-1980s along
with other public figures like David Gergen.
Clinton's participation at the 1993 retreat was even
more significant because he was president-elect.
Accompanied by an article entitled "The Friends of
Bill--Not!" by Warren Cohen, in which he identified
individuals who definitely were not "friends of
Bill," most of whom were from Arkansas--Larry Nichols
(who broke the Gennifer Flowers' story), Sheffield
Nelson (Clinton's Republican opponent in the 1990

gubernatorial race), Cliff Jackson (former Oxford student), John Robert Starr (<u>Arkansas Democrat-Gazette</u> columnist and long-time Clinton antagonist and critic), and Gennifer Flowers.

910 Barone, Michael. "How To Do the Transition Right." ("On Politics" column). <u>U.S. News & World Report</u>, November 23, 1992, 50. Barone offers advice to Clinton regarding potential pitfalls to avoid and ones that befell past transitions such as those of John F. Kennedy and Jimmy Carter.

911 Barry, John and Daniel Glick. "Crossing the Gay Minefield." <u>Newsweek</u>, November 23, 1992, 26.

912 Hackworth, David H. "The Key Issue is Trust." <u>Newsweek</u>, November 23, 1992, 27.

On Clinton's struggle over his promise to lift the ban on homosexuals in the military. Barry and Glick noted potential problems for Clinton over this issue. Hackworth, who opposed lifting the ban, urged Clinton to review the issue via a presidential commission.

913 Byron, Christopher. "Son of Malaise? Clinton's Summit." <u>New York</u> 25, 46(November 23, 1992): 22, 24. Criticized Clinton's decision to hold an economic summit, citing the failure of similar past meetings (held by Ford in 1974 and Carter in 1979). Instead, Clinton should increase "confidence in his economic leadership" among consumers and Wall Street.

914 Cockburn, Alexander. "Beat the Devil: Depression, Prediction, Compassion." <u>Nation</u>, November 23, 1992, 618. Criticizes Clinton for business as usual politics and welfare reform. Also discusses health care.

915 Corn, David. "Beltway Bandits." <u>Nation</u>, November 23, 1992, 620, 630-632. Corn's prescription for good government and "de-Reaganizing" in Bill Clinton's first seven days in office--acting immediately on the federal regulatory system, abortion, environmental measures, campaign finance reform, and reducing defense spending.

916 Cooper, Matthew. "Beyond the Bushes." <u>U.S. News & World Report</u>, November 23, 1992, 6-7. Photo. The transition period indicated what Clinton's governing style (including his decision making process) would be. Because Clinton made his own decisions and people were able to come to him directly to express

their views, Clinton would not have a powerful chief
of staff, which also was the case when Clinton was
governor and during the campaign.

917 Dentzer, Susan. "Clinton's Big Test." U.S. News
& World Report, November 23, 1992, 26-28, 30. Photo.
The eventual outcome of the budget, the economy and
Clinton's first term will depend on controlling
medical costs.

918 Fineman, Howard. "Help Wanted." Newsweek,
November 23, 1992, 24-26. Photos. Discusses the push
by Democrats to serve in the Clinton administration
and reports favorably on Clinton's first
post-election news conference. Like Ronald Reagan,
Clinton was expected to view his first months in
office as an continuation of the campaign.

919 Greenwald, John. "How Much Can He Do? The
Transition." Time, November 23, 1992, 24-26. Photo.
Discusses Clinton's options on economic policy for
his upcoming administration regarding deficit
reduction and a short-term economic stimulus. These
options would be limited by the downturn in the
global economy. Included consideration of Clinton's
first post-election news conference and plans for a
conference on the economy in Little Rock in December.

920 Hage, David and Sara Collins. "Reaching Out For
Help." U.S. News & World Report, November 23, 1992,
67-68, 70-71. Many white-collar workers supported
Clinton, including some Republicans. With corporate
downsizing, there was not much Clinton could do in
the short-term. Clinton did create an Economic
Security Council, analogous to the National Security
Council, to coordinate longer-range economic policy.
While Clinton believed in the power of government (as
Lyndon Johnson had), there are now more constraints
on government power than in the past.

921 Henwood, Doug. "Clinton and the Austerity Cops:
Stimulus or Stagnation." Nation, November 23, 1992,
626, 628, 630. Advised Clinton to support a greater
economic stimulus than he had proposed and described
Clinton's "Putting People First" economic program as
an "activist version of supply-side economics," which
could make him an "ideal austerity President."
Henwood also criticized Clinton's welfare reform.

922 Kaplan, David A. "No More Hacks or Cronies."
Newsweek, November 23, 1992, 64. Clinton should
select a nonpartisan attorney general, unlike

previous politicized Justice Departments such as the
one under former Attorney General Ed Meese.

923   Kramer, Michael. "Building a World-Class Team."
("The Political Interest" column). _Time_, November 23,
1992, 27.   Clinton was elected president "to fix the
economy."   To achieve this goal, it was essential he
select a quality economic team that worked well
together.   A foremost consideration was the precise
role the Economic Security Council would play.
Kramer noted several potential candidates for
Treasury Secretary (Paul Volcker, Lloyd Bentsen,
Robert Rubin, and Roger Altman).

924   Goodgame, Dan. "Clinton's Economic Idea Man."
("Clinton's People"). _Time_, November 23, 1992, 29-30.

925   Painton, Priscilla. "A Faithful Friend and
Confidant." ("Clinton's People"). _Time_, November 23,
1992, 28-29.

Profiles of key Clinton advisers--Robert Reich and
Bruce Lindsey, respectively.

926   Kinsley, Michael. "Election Day Fraud on
Television." _Time_, November 23, 1992, 84.   Kinsley
argued against press self-censorship regarding making
public election day exit polls before election sites
closed in the western U.S.   By the afternoon of
November 3, it became clear that Clinton was going to
win the election.

927   Roberts, Steven V. "A Little Self-Restraint: How
Liberals Could Cause Some of Bill Clinton's Earliest
Problems." _U.S. News & World Report_, November 23,
1992, 41.   If Clinton were to govern as a new kind of
Democrat, he had to say no to liberals and find
middle ground.   Roberts identified the following
areas in which liberals would probably want Clinton
to go further than he otherwise would want to--family
leave, abortion, education, civil rights, District of
Columbia statehood, and campaign finance reform.
Clinton's position on these issues would indicate his
"presidential character."

928   "Take Five." (Comment). _New Yorker_, November 23,
1992, 4, 6.   Noted overly critical press coverage of
President-elect Clinton following the election,
including criticism that his plans, like health care,
would not work.

929   Clift, Eleanor and Mark Miller. "Hillary: Behind

the Scenes." Newsweek, November 28, 1992, 23-25.
Photo. Hillary Clinton would play an important role
behind the scenes in a Clinton administration since
she is Bill Clinton's "most important adviser,"
thereby serving as an "unofficial chief of staff."
Some Clinton aides wanted Hillary to take on an issue
like health care which would be "at the heart of the
Clinton presidency" (and that did take place).

930 Alter, Jonathan. "Clinton's Challenge."
Newsweek, November 30, 1992, 27-29. Photos. The
transition period was an "anxious interregnum" in
which special interests position themselves to
influence the new president and his administration.

931 Carlson, Margaret and Michael Duffy. "Mr.
Clinton Goes to Washington: The Transition." Time,
November 30, 1992, 28-31. Photos. About Clinton's
36-hour whirlwind trip to Washington where he met
with President Bush, congressional leaders, and
visited a Washington neighborhood. (Mrs. Clinton met
with Barbara Bush). Also contained speculation over
which economic course Clinton would follow (deficit
reduction and/or economic stimulus).

932 Carlson, Margaret. "Alter Boy at the Power
Center." ("Clinton's People"). Time, November 30,
1992, 35-36.

933 McAllister, J.F.O. "A Foreign Policy Puritan."
("Clinton's People"). Time, November 30, 1992, 36.

Profiles of George Stephanopoulis and Tony Lake.

934 "Clinton's First Fire Fight." Time, November 30,
1992, 42. Short but prescient piece on Pentagon
criticism of Clinton's proposal to lift the ban on
homosexuals in the military.

935 Dentzer, Susan. "Clinton's Foreign Tax Crusade."
U.S. News & World Report, November 30, 1992, 59.
Clinton had overestimated the amount of revenue that
could be collected from foreign companies located in
the U.S. which had evaded paying taxes.

936 Dershowitz, Alan M. "Open Door to Candidates'
Skeletons: Voters Had Interest in Clinton Files."
Legal Times 15, 28(November 30, 1992): 24. Beyond
the failed attempt by the State Department under
George Bush to undercover any damaging information
from Clinton's file (such as the false allegation
that Clinton considered renouncing his American

citizenship), this famous attorney believed the larger issue was the public's right of access to important information on candidates they were about to vote for via an improved and more efficient Freedom of Information Act (FOIA).

937 "Facing the Powers That Be." Newsweek, November 30, 1992, 30, 32-34, 36. Clinton's future efforts as president might find resistance from four powerful interests--the medical industry, the military, industry, and liberal interests (like the environmental movement and education).

938 "A Fondness for the Gallows." (Comment). New Yorker, November 30, 1992, 4, 6. Following an overview of the issue of capital punishment, including an international perspective, this commentary appealed to Clinton to review his support of the death penalty once in office.

939 Gergen, David. "The Commander's First Minefield." ("On Politics" column). U.S. News & World Report, November 30, 1992, 32. Photo. Gergen refers to Clinton's position on allowing homosexuals to serve in the military. If not handled properly, this issue could hurt both the new president and the military. Clinton had to stand by his pledge. Otherwise, he risked "losing control of his presidency." On the other hand, as commander in chief, he had to understand the military's concerns on this issue and strike a balance. The commission Clinton proposed could help resolve the issue.

940 Hardigg, Viva. "Tipping the Balance of Economic Power: Will Clinton Back a New Plan for the States?" U.S. News & World Report, November 30, 1992, 54-55. Photo. Among the ideas contained in Alice Rivlin's book Reviving the American Dream (Brookings Institution, 1992) was that of shifting more power to the states in relation to the federal government. Clinton was supportive of this idea since he had been a governor and so empathized with state concerns. An accompanying brief article indicated other business/economic related books Clinton was reading.

941 Kinsley, Michael. "Spinach, Please." ("TRB From Washington" column). New Republic, November 30, 1992, 6. Kinsley argues for Clinton to focus on long-term deficit reduction ("spinach") and to avoid a tempting short-term economic stimulus.

942 Klein, Joe. "Clinton and the Tao of BAU."

("Public Lives" column). Newsweek, November 30, 1992,
38. Photo. BAU (business as usual) would prevail as
Clinton came to realize the obstacles to political
reform (especially reform of Congress). The
"immediate transition debate" remained "economic
stimulus vs. deficit reduction."

943 Nader, Ralph. "How Clinton Can Build Democracy:
Taming Corporations." Nation, November 30, 1992, 649,
652-653. Urged Clinton to promote citizens'
interests, which are usually overshadowed by
corporate interests.

944 Neier, Aryeh. "Watching Rights." Nation,
November 30, 1992, 655. Aryeh maintained that if
Clinton would be directly involved in the nominating
process of the State Department's Bureau for Human
Rights and Humanitarian Affairs, then that could
indicate the role Clinton envisioned for U.S. foreign
policy during his term.

945 Taylor, John. "Sex Isn't the Issue: Gays in the
Military." ("The National Interest" column). New York
25, 47(November 30, 1992): 21-22. Argued for lifting
the ban on gays in the military, but foresaw the
difficulties (such as a distraction from reviving the
economy) this issue could cause Clinton as president.

946 Tyler, Gus. "Dear Mr. President: Countdown '92."
New Leader 75, 15(November 30, 1992): 5. Tyler sees
a striking similarity between 1992 and 1932. Had
Roosevelt concentrated solely on deficits, he would
not have been a successful president. Instead, he
promoted economic growth by borrowing and spending.
Clinton should take this lesson into consideration.

947 "Unusual Suspects." (Editorial). New Republic,
November 30, 1992, 7. Described as "unfortunate"
Clinton's appointment of Vernon Jordan and Warren
Christopher to lead the Clinton transition team
because they represented the Washington
establishment. It urged Clinton to make other more
bolder choices.

948 Walsh, Kenneth T. and Matthew Cooper. "The
Education of Bill Clinton." U.S. News & World Report,
November 30, 1992, 24-26. Photos. Report on
Clinton's visit to Washington, which constituted part
of his "education" as he became better acquainted
with Washington. Clinton was anticipating his "role
of national teacher," using the "bully pulpit" to
promote his policies, thus demonstrating presidential

leadership. While Clinton pledged to end gridlock, there was some concern among Democrats that he was too willing to compromise and accommodate, as some contended when Clinton was governor.

949 Will, George F. "Purring Along the Potomac." Newsweek, November 30, 1992, 96. Will is skeptical whether Clinton could get Congress to reform (such as pass a line-item veto, or even enhanced recision, and cut congressional staffs by 25%).

950 Zuckerman, Mortimer B. "America's Midlife Crisis." U.S. News & World Report, November 30, 1992, 84. Clinton had campaigned against both "failed conservatism" and "failed liberalism," seeking a "more harmonious reconciliation of individual freedom and public duty." Clinton was qualified to take on this task.

951 Broyles, William, Jr. "Draft: Campaign Issues." Columbia Journalism Review (CJR) 31, 4 (November/December 1992): 42-43. Photo. Assesses press coverage of the draft issue and Clinton.

952 Guttenplan, D.D. "Covering a Runaway Campaign." Columbia Journalism Review (CJR) 31, 4 (November/December 1992): 23-33. Contains a useful "Campaign Timeline" consisting of a weekly survey of the campaign and coverage of it from the week of February 10-16, 1992 to September 21-27, 1992.

953 Hatchett, David. "Clinton's At the Helm: Where To From Here?" Crisis (November-December 1992): 8, 10-11. Hatchett first provided an overview of how Clinton was influenced by ideas (such as welfare reform, national service, national health insurance, and capital punishment) emanating from the Democratic Leadership Council. Clinton's approach was not to devise programs specifically for minorities, but to propose legislation that would encompass a wider spectrum of people. Hatchett skillfully presents the views of political analysts considering Clinton's prospects as president. Pressure to reduce the deficit could temper Clinton's investment plans, workfare could conflict with public employee union interests, and the success of Clinton's presidency could depend on his ability to stem the loss of U.S. manufacturing jobs overseas and reduce the deficit. Just as Roosevelt developed the New Deal due to popular protest, Clinton also may have to be pressured in a similar way.

954 "How He Won: The Untold Story of Bill Clinton's Triumph." (Special Election Issue). <u>Newsweek</u> (November/December 1992). "Inside story" of the presidential campaign, including: when Clinton was just one of several Democratic hopefuls, allegations of scandal which nearly derailed the Clinton campaign, the challenge posed by Paul Tsongas, how Clinton rebounded from a slump in May and June, and several stories on the fall campaign.

955 Hoyt, Mike. "Talk Radio: Turning Up the Volume." <u>Columbia Journalism Review</u> (CJR) 31, 4(November/December 1992): 45-50. Illus. Talk radio and the presidential campaign, including the positive impact in the New York primary campaign of Clinton appearances on the Phil Donahue and Don Imus shows.

956 Ivins, Molly. "The Pundit's Secret." <u>Mother Jones</u> 17, 6(November/December 1992): 8, 10-11. Political columnist/humorist Ivins commented on the 1992 campaign. Regarding Clinton, she points to the so-called "conventional wisdom" which lacked consistency. The May 4 <u>New Republic</u> explained "Why Clinton Can't Win" and the April 20 <u>Time</u> declared Clinton politically dead on the issue of trust. Yet, two months later both publications declared that Clinton was a sure winner.

957 Menéndez, Albert J. "The Voter's Guide to Church-State Issues." <u>Humanist: A Magazine of Critical Inquiry and Social Comment</u> 52, 6(November/December 1992): 21-23, 36. Analyzes the positions of the Democratic and Republican parties on church-state/religious issues. Clinton supported the Democratic Party platform on abortion rights, freedom of choice, and protection of public education (on the latter issue, by opposing private school vouchers). Also provides religious background on Clinton and Gore as Southern Baptists and noted the use of religious imagery in Clinton's "New Covenant" acceptance speech at the Democratic Convention.

958 "President-Elect Clinton's Foreign Policy Statements, December 12, 1991-November 4, 1992." <u>Foreign Policy Bulletin: The Documentary Record of United States Foreign Policy</u> 3, 3(November/December 1992): 2-23. Special feature consisting of a compendium of Clinton's remarks on foreign policy, mostly during the campaign. Contents: A New Covenant for American Security, Georgetown University, December 12, 1991; Foreign Policy Association Speech, April 1; Statement on the Situation in Iraq, July 23;

Statement on Haitian Refugees, July 29; Los Angeles
World Affairs Council Speech, August 13; Statements
on the Crisis in Somalia, August 8 and 28; Statement
on Establishment of No-Fly Zone in Iraq, August 26;
Statement on the Shooting of Demonstrators in Ciskei,
September 8; Statement on Most-Favored-Nation Status
for China, September 14; American Foreign Policy and
the Democratic Ideal, Institute of World Affairs,
University of Wisconsin-Milwaukee, October 1; and
Statement After Election (Excerpt), November 4.
Clinton's guiding foreign policy principle was the
promotion of democracy.

959   Rosen, Jay. "Discourse: Campaign Issues."
Columbia Journalism Review (CJR) 31,
4(November/December 1992): 34-35.   Photo.   Notes
media's tendency "to wound and humiliate" reflecting
a "feeding frenzy" in regard to political candidates.
Rosen used Clinton's April 1, 1992 appearance on the
Donahue show to illustrate this point.

960   "Clinton's EPA." Occupational Hazards 54,
12(December 1992): 15.   Speculation on who would be
selected to head the Environmental Protection Agency.

961   "'Don't Stop Thinkin' 'Bout Tomorrow': New
Beginnings for American Higher Education."
(Editorial). NEA Advocate 10, 3(December 1992): 1.
Presents the views of NEA lobbyist Joel Packer on the
prospects of higher education with a Clinton
administration, whose highest priorities would be
national service, health care, and the economy.

962   Ehrenhalt, Alan. "What If a Real Governor Became
President? For Better or Worse, We're About to Find
Out." Governing 6, 3(December 1992): 6-7.   Clinton's
experience as a southern governor in the 1980's
during the Reagan-Bush period influenced his
perspective and governing style, but it remained to
be seen whether it would make him a good president.

963   "The Face of Victory." Life 15, 14(December
1992): 10-15. Photos.   Photo highlights from Little
Rock of the Clintons and the Gores on election night.

964   Fallows, Deborah. "First Choice." Washington
Monthly 24, 12(December 1992): 15-17.   Chelsea
Clinton should attend public school in Washington,
D.C. because it would help focus national attention
on public education.

965   Graves, Earl G. "A Mandate For Clinton."

("Publisher's Page"). <u>Black Enterprise</u> 23, 5(December 1992): 9.   Called for investment in urban America.

966   Isaacs, John. "New President; New Policy?" <u>Bulletin of the Atomic Scientists</u> 48, 10(December 1992): 10, 52.   Clinton's national security policy would not differ appreciably from Bush's.

967   Jaben, Jan. "Marketing Execs Eagerly Await Impact of New Administration." (Cover story). <u>Business Marketing</u> 77, 12(December 1992): 25. Advertising and marketing executives generally expressed cautious optimism about the potential impact of the new administration on their industries.

968   Jaben, Jan. "Marketers to Clinton: Initiate the Age of 'Teledemocracy.'" (Cover story). <u>Business Marketing</u> 77, 12(December 1992): 26.   Presents the opinions of marketing executives on how Clinton could "best market and sell his proposals" to the public, which included electronic town meetings, "'teledemocracy,'" "'interactive communications,'" and infomercials.   Others cautioned Clinton against the overuse of marketing and call-in talk shows and advocated the continued use of press conferences.

969   Looker, Dan. "What U.S. Farmers Can Expect From Bill Clinton: He'll Keep Most Farm Policies But May Act Faster On Problems." <u>Successful Farming</u> 90, 12(December 1992): 4.   Prospects under Clinton for farm policy, which likely would be similar to Bush's in terms of the 1990 farm bill, trade, federal support for ethanol, and a national wetlands policy.

970   Minter, Stephen G. "The New Team's Challenge." (Editorial). <u>Occupational Hazards</u> 54, 12(December 1992): 6.   Speculation on Clinton regarding worker safety and the environment.

971   Postrel, Virginia I. "Training Wreck." (Editorial). <u>Reason: Free Minds and Free Markets</u> 24, 7(December 1992): 4-5.   From a libertarian perspective, criticism of Clinton's proposal for a corporate training mandate.

972   Segal, David. "Bill and Friends' Excellent Adventure." <u>Washington Monthly</u> 24, 12(December 1992): 11-14.   While Bush tried to make Oxford an issue in the campaign by playing on its elitist image, it did not have much of a negative impact on Clinton.

973   Tritch, Teresa. "How President Clinton Will

Change Your Taxes." (Cover story). <u>Money</u> 21,
12(December 1992): 72-75. Illus. Notes tax changes
which Clinton would likely make in the following
areas: alternative minimum tax, deductions,
retirement plans, social security and Medicare, the
self-employed, and tax-favored investing.

974 "What Marketers Want From Clinton: Wish Lists
Refined as Economic Spirits Rise." (Cover story).
<u>Business Marketing</u> 77, 12(December 1992): 24. Based
on interviews with a national cross section of
marketing and high-tech executives, who generally
advocated "investment tax credits, R&D tax
incentives, and public-private partnerships." A good
example of the latter was Al Gore's sponsorship of
the High Performance Computing and Communications
Initiative. The survey also indicated that soaring
health care costs were of great concern to small
business and that Clinton should not be overly
concerned with details since leadership should be
emphasized over management.

975 "What Should the President Read?" <u>Reason</u> 24,
7(December 1992): 20-31. <u>Reason</u> asked 24 people to
recommend three books for President-elect Clinton to
read during the transition period.

976 Galston, William A. "Clinton and the Promise of
Communitarianism." ("Point of View"). <u>Chronicle of
Higher Education</u> 39, 15(December 2, 1992): A52.
Photo. Explains the influence on both Clinton and
Gore of communitarianism, which is defined as a
"movement that seeks to balance rights and
responsibilities and to nourish the moral ties of
family, neighborhood, workplace, and citizenship as a
basis for innovative public policy." Galston served
as a policy adviser to the Clinton transition team
and domestic policy adviser to President Clinton.

977 Friedman, Benjamin. "Clinton's Opportunity." <u>New
York Review of Books</u> 39, 20(December 3, 1992): 44-48.
Illus. The economic challenge facing Clinton was
great as was the need to meet that challenge. Urged
Clinton to take bold action and political risks.

978 Cooper, Matthew. "Clinton's Boy Wonder." <u>U.S.
News & World Report</u>, December 7, 1992, 34, 38.
Portrait of key Clinton campaign and transition
communications official, George Stephanopoulos.

979 Corn, David. "Beltway Bandits: Bursting
Bubbles." <u>Nation</u>, December 7, 1992, 692. On Clinton

appointees. Corn and other liberals were concerned
that neoconservative Joshua Muravchik (who supported
Clinton) might be considered for Assistant Secretary
of State for Human Rights and Humanitarian Affairs.

980 Dentzer, Susan. "What's Cooking, Mr. Clinton?"
("On the Economy" column). U.S. News & World Report,
December 7, 1992, 63. Photo. On Clinton transition
team's (headed by Robert Reich) economic options on a
stimulus, deficit reduction, and possible
international economic cooperation.

981 "Ending the Ban." (Editorial). New Republic,
December 7, 1992, 7. Clinton should lift the ban on
gays in the military by allowing for a transition
period so that the military could prepare and plan to
implement this change in policy.

982 Gergen, David. "'Thinking for a Living.'" U.S.
News & World Report, December 7, 1992, 83. About a
report entitled America's Choice: High Skills or Low
Wages and a book, Thinking for a Living by Ray
Marshall and Marc Tucker, which argued for long-term
education/training for American workers, which would
also benefit economic growth and job creation.

983 Hage, David. "Diving Deep For Treasure: Clinton
is Struggling to Find Investment Dollars." U.S. News
& World Report, December 7, 1992, 56-58. Illus.
Recommended programs and areas which could be cut or
reduced: corporate subsidies, the federal work force,
farm subsidies, and "'impact aid'" to richer school
districts. It was time for Clinton to take action.

984 Kaus, Mickey. "The Policy Hustler: The
Politicized Economy of Robert Reich." (Cover story).
New Republic, December 7, 1992, 16-18, 20, 22-23.
Critique of the economic ideas of Robert Reich.

985 Klein, Joe. "Copping a Domestic Agenda."
("Public Lives" column). Newsweek, December 7, 1992,
29. Clinton's national service plan would include a
Police Corps, consistent with his goal of restoring a
"national sense of community" and responsibility.

986 Levinson, Marc. "Uphill Battle." Newsweek,
December 7, 1992, 38-40. Clinton's most difficult
economic challenge would not be improving the
economy, but addressing the growing gap in income
distribution. The best way to alleviate this problem
would be training and education.

987 Lewis, Charles. "The Rainmakers in Bill's
Parade: Outing the Insiders." <u>Nation</u>, December 7,
1992, 693-694. Individuals who would either benefit
from a Clinton administration or who might receive
posts within it included Paula Stern, Ron Brown,
Roger Altman, and Samuel Berger. Also proposed that
Clinton introduce major political ethics legislation.

988 "Nervous Service." (Editorial). <u>Nation</u>, December
7, 1992, 687-688. Foreshadowed Clinton's "first
crisis"--lifting the military's homosexual ban.

989 Roberts, Steven V. "Clinton and the Lobbyists'
Curse: Washington Braces For a New Balance of Power."
<u>U.S. News & World Report</u>, December 7, 1992, 30-31.
Illus., photo. During the campaign, Clinton pledged
to set new limits on lobbying activities.
Ironically, though, concern among vested interests
over what the new administration might do could
trigger even more lobbyists. In addition, the
Clinton transition team placed great emphasis on
ethics reform, which would have an impact on
potential Clinton appointees. Campaign finance
reform also falls under this category. Clinton's
first key tests on lobbying would occur as he
proposes reform of taxes, trade, and health care,

990 Samuelson, Robert J. "Is the Summit Necessary?"
<u>Newsweek</u>, December 7, 1992, 41. Photo. Clinton's
December 14-15 economic summit was not needed because
his economic advisers could provide him with a clear
idea of the economy.

991 Shuger, Scott. "American Inquisition: The
Military Vs Itself." <u>New Republic</u>, December 7, 1992,
23, 26, 28-29. Supports Clinton policy to end gay
ban in the military and argues against the military's
attempt to identify and discharge gays in its ranks.

992 Watson, Russell. "Troops to Somalia?" <u>Newsweek</u>,
December 7, 1992, 24-27. Photo. Clinton supported
Bush's commitment of U.S. troops to Somalia, a
decision which ultimately could backfire on Clinton.

993 "Whoa, It's Not Over Yet." (Editorial). <u>Nation</u>,
December 7, 1992, 685. Calls for a "single-payer,
Canadian-style health plan" in contrast to Clinton's
more moderate approach of "'managed competition.'"

994 Winkler, Karen J. "A Scholar Seeks the
Multicultural Middle Ground: Finding the Moral
Center." <u>Chronicle of Higher Education</u> 39,

16(December 9, 1992): A6, A8-A9. Profile of Charles
Taylor, one of the major proponents of
communitarianism, an intellectual movement which has
had an impact on Bill Clinton and Al Gore in their
political thought on community service, common
purpose, and a "New Covenant."

995 Abramowitz, Morton. "For Clinton, a Messy Hand:
Foreign Policy Will Demand Swift Attention."
<u>Newsweek</u>, December 14, 1992, 41. Clinton needed to
deal with the following areas in foreign
policy--Russia, Haiti, Somalia, Iraq, and Bosnia.

996 "Bill's Blue Pencil." (Editorial). <u>New Republic</u>,
December 14, 1992, 7. Case for the line item veto.

997 Boroughs, Don L. "Fixing the Job Machine." <u>U.S.
News & World Report</u>, December 14, 1992, 59-61. About
Clinton's investment tax credit proposal.

998 Corn, David. "Dealing With Bill." (Editorial).
<u>Nation</u>, December 14, 1992, 724. Discusses position
of progressive Democrats like Minnesota Senator Paul
Wellstone vis-à-vis a Clinton administration.
Pressure from the left would be applied to Clinton on
issues like economic stimulus, campaign finance
reform, health care, choice, and gay rights.

999 Duffy, Michael. "A Public Policy Entrepreneur."
("Clinton's People"). <u>Time</u>, December 14, 1992, 51.

1000 Goodgame, Dan. "A Prophet of Innovation."
("Clinton's People"). <u>Time</u>, December 14, 1992, 50-51.

Profiles of Al From, president/executive director of
the Democratic Leadership Council and transition
domestic issues coordinator, and David Osborne,
author of <u>Laboratories of Democracy</u> and coauthor with
Ted Gaebler of <u>Reinventing Government</u>, books which
influenced Clinton on government and policy making.

1001 Gergen, David. "The Burdens of a Superpower."
<u>U.S. News & World Report</u>, December 14, 1992, 110.
Foreign policy challenges facing Clinton.

1002 Hage, David. "Stepping Up for a Standoff in the
Sky: President-Elect Clinton Says that in Aviation
and Other Industries America Won't Give Unless It
Gets." <u>U.S. News & World Report</u>, December 14, 1992,
61-62, 64. Possible Clinton administration policy on
job creation and the airline industry.

1003   Klein, Joe. "When Everyone's an Amateur."
("Public Lives" column). Newsweek, December 14, 1992,
42.   Clinton faced foreign policy problems in Haiti,
Bosnia, and Somalia.   Clinton should set parameters
on U.S. intervention overseas.

1004   Kramer, Michael. "The Best Pols Money Can Buy."
("The Political Interest" column). Time, December 14,
1992, 49.   Comedian Eddie Murphy's role in the movie
"The Distinguished Gentleman" provided Kramer with an
opportunity to discuss campaign finance reform, which
Clinton supports.   The views of Clinton and some of
his aides are presented.

1005   Powell, Bill. "The Trade Hawks: Circling In on
Clinton." Newsweek, December 14, 1992, 61.   Discusses
two books--Who's Bashing Whom: Trade Conflict in High
Technology Industries by Laura D'Andrea Tyson, who
later was selected for the Council of Economic
Advisers in the Clinton administration, and The
Highest Stakes: The Economic Foundations of the Next
Security System by Michael Borrus, John Zysman and
five other Berkeley professors whose ideas could
influence Clinton on trade and competitiveness.

1006   Rosenblatt, Roger. "Hillary's Kids: An
Interview With Mrs. Clinton." New Republic, December
14, 1992, 12-14.   Hillary Clinton's views on
children's rights and family issues.   Refers to Mrs.
Clinton's writings/speeches on these matters.

1007   Shapiro, Walter. "Clinton and the Stones of
Venice." ("Essay"). Time, December 14, 1992, 78.
Post-election reflections on Bill Clinton.

1008   "Term Extension." (Comment). New Yorker,
December 14, 1992, 4, 6.   Calls for Clinton to resist
short-term economic stimulus at the expense of a
long-range economic policy, even though the former
might be more expedient for reelection in 1996.

1009   Weisberg, Jacob. "Nowhere Man: The Hit List."
New Republic, December 14, 1992, 10.   First of a
series of assessments on people New Republic believed
Clinton should not select for his administration.
Weisberg made the case against appointing Indiana
Senator Lee Hamilton as Secretary of State.

1010   Clift, Eleanor. "Clinton's Cabinet: Beyond
White Men." Newsweek, December 21, 1992, 37.   Clift
discusses the appointment of women to the Clinton
administration in the name of diversity--for economic

posts, Alice Rivlin, deputy budget director, and
Laura D'Andrea Tyson, head of the Council of Economic
Advisers; Donna Shalala, Health and Human Services;
and Carol Browner, Environmental Protection Agency.
Also noted that Clinton was considering a woman or a
minority for attorney general.

1011   Corn, David. "Beltway Bandits: One Big Happy
Family, Beat by the Devils." Nation, December 21,
1992, 764.   Criticized selection of Penn Kemble to
lead transition team for the U.S. Information Agency
due to his advocacy for the contras in Nicaragua
during the Reagan administration, but approved of the
selection of James Cheek on the transition team for
the State Department.

1012   Dentzer, Susan. "Bill Clinton's Capital Gang."
("On the Economy" column). U.S. News & World Report,
December 21, 1992, 54.   Clinton economic team agreed
on issues of deficits and investments.

1013   Goodgame, Dan. "Bill's Dream Team of
Supersalesmen: The Transition." Time, December 21,
1992, 37, 40. Illus.   Clinton appointments to his
economic team (called the National Economic Council)
reassured the financial markets.   Clinton planned to
implement a short-term fiscal stimulus along with a
deficit reduction package.

1014   Hage, David, Robert F. Black, and Sara Collins.
"Finding a Fast Track for the Economy: Clinton Must
Read the Signals Carefully If He Wants to Deliver
Growth on Schedule." U.S. News & World Report,
December 21, 1992, 49-52. Illus.   Presents three
possible economic scenarios for the Clinton
administration along with policy options and
consequences--stagnant growth, slow growth, and
surprising growth.   Accompanied by a smaller article
on Federal Reserve Chairman Alan Greenspan (p. 52).

1015   Judis, John B. "Trader: The Hit List." New
Republic, December 21, 1992, 9-10. Illus.   Judis
argues against appointing Paula Sterns as U.S. Trade
Representative because of her lobbying activities.

1016   Klein, Joe. "Chilly Scenes of Winter." ("Public
Lives" column). Newsweek, December 21, 1992, 42.
Photo.   Some liberal observers, like author Joan
Didion, argued that the centrist positions espoused
by the Democratic Leadership Council and its think
tank, the Progressive Policy Institute, (which
Clinton subscribed to in his campaign) were just a

"'marketing strategy'" rather than a governing
philosophy and that he would move left once in
office. Clinton's moderate economic appointments did
not point in that direction. Klein defined four
areas of contention between liberals and
moderates--economics, national security, social
policy (health, education and welfare), and
"legal-lifestyle" issues (like gay rights). Liberals
prevailed on all these fronts except national
security since liberals wanted more cuts in defense
spending. Even more important than issues like
welfare reform and deficit reduction was Clinton's
leadership abilities. In this regard, Clinton had
gotten off to a good start.

1017 Morganthau, Tom. "One for the Hawks: Clinton
Appoints His Economic Team--And Zeroes in on Reducing
the Deficit." Newsweek, December 21, 1992, 34-37.
Photos. Key appointments included Treasury
Secretary, Lloyd Bentsen; Budget Director, Leon
Panetta; Economic Security Adviser, Robert Rubin;
Deputy Budget Director, Alice Rivlin; Deputy Treasury
Secretary, Roger Altman; Council of Economic
Advisers, Laura D'Andrea Tyson; and Labor Secretary,
Robert Reich. Clinton concluded that deficit
reduction was just as important as increasing
investment.

1018 Nelan, Bruce W. "Today, Somalia..." (Cover
story). Time, December 21, 1992, 28-31. U.S.
intervention in Somalia could set a precedent for the
Clinton administration to intervene elsewhere like
Bosnia. Clinton had indicated that as president he
would not hesitate to utilize America power overseas.

1019 Roberts, Steven V. "Team Clinton Kicks Off."
U.S. News & World Report, December 21, 1992, 45-46.
The Clinton economic team had the potential for both
cooperation and confrontation. Profiles are
presented for Lloyd Bentsen, Leon Panetta, Robert
Rubin, Alice Rivlin, and Roger Altman.

1020 Shapiro, Walter. "Worst-Kept Secrets: The
Transition." Time, December 21, 1992, 45. Press
leaks on potential appointees to the administration.

1021 Traver, Nancy. "Stamps of Disapproval:
Investigations." Time, December 21, 1992, 46. To get
his economic program through Congress, Clinton would
need the support of Dan Rostenkowski, the influential
chairman of the House Ways and Means Committee. A
potential complication was that Rostenkowski may be

the subject of a criminal investigation over alleged campaign-fund abuses.

1022 Walsh, Kenneth T. "Life in Transition: Clinton Starts Creating an Eclectic Team and Pondering Foreign Crises." U.S. News & World Report, December 21, 1992, 40-42, 44. Photos. Discusses domestic and foreign policy concerns of the Clinton transition team. Clinton's economic appointments indicated that he would pursue long-range deficit reduction with some action on short-term economic problems.

1023 Duffy, Michael. "They Call Him Mack the Nice." ("Clinton's People"). Time, December 28, 1992, 25. Profile of Thomas "Mack" McLarty, Clinton's appointee for White House chief of staff.

1024 "Interview: 'I Try to Be Who I Am.'" Newsweek, December 28, 1992, 24-25. Photos. Hillary Clinton discussed her upcoming role as First Lady and her status as a role model for women.

1025 Kaus, Mickey. "FOB Story: The Hit List." New Republic, December 28, 1992, 10-11. Illus. Case against appointing attorney/lobbyist Mickey Kantor to any post in the Clinton administration. (Clinton later appointed Kantor as U.S. Trade Representative).

1026 Klein, Joe. "A Blue Christmas for Elvis." ("Public Lives" column). Newsweek, December 28, 1992, 33. Among advice Clinton received at his economic summit was that if he were to do something difficult like budget deficit reduction, he had to do it within the first six months of his new administration. Health care was another issue which had no easy solution. Clinton needed to take a lesson from the Reagan administration--"take your medicine early" (Reagan survived the 1982 recession). The best advice Clinton received at that conference was to combine long-range deficit reduction with a long-range stimulus plan.

1027 "Middling Through." (Editorial). Nation, December 28, 1992, 795-796. The Progressive Policy Institute's (PPI) book, Mandate for Change, recommended programs for the Clinton administration. With its links to the Democratic Leadership Council (DLC), this book provided a "window into the world of Clintonian possibilities." The PPI/DLC tried to steer a middle course between traditional liberalism and rightwing conservatism. Time would tell "just how much Clinton goes by the P.P.I. book."

1028 Offner, Paul. "Workfail: Waiting for Welfare Reform." <u>New Republic</u>, December 28, 1992, 13-15. Analyzes Bill Clinton's position on welfare reform.

1029 Quinn, Sally. "Beware of Washington." <u>Newsweek</u>, December 28, 1992, 26, 28. Photo. Advice for Hillary Clinton on how to survive Washington.

1030 Thomas, Rich. "Issue One: Health Care." <u>Newsweek</u>, December 28, 1992, 32. Clinton indicated at the Little Rock economic conference that control of health care costs had to be the keystone of his whole domestic agenda to reduce the deficit and promote economic growth.

1031 Cooper, Matthew. "Bruce Reed, Bill Clinton's Vicar of Ideas: Helping To Reinvent Liberalism." <u>U.S. News & World Report</u>, December 28, 1992-January 4, 1993, 85. Includes profile of Reed, one of Clinton's main advisers.

1032 "Potomac Peril: Postcard From the Edge." <u>U.S. News & World Report</u>, December 28, 1992-January 4, 1993, 79, 81-83. Illus. Pictorial depictions of Clinton accompanied by famous quotations on these themes: "First Family," "Clinton & Congress," "Clinton & the Press," and "Clinton & the World."

1033 "Predictions." <u>U.S. News & World Report</u>, December 28, 1992-January 4, 1993, 38-39, 42, 44, 46, 52, 54, 67, 69-70, 72, 75. Photos. Predictions for 1993 pertaining to incoming Clinton administration on the economy, a long-term economic package, Hillary Clinton and children, government involvement in education, health and worker safety, government regulation, Al Gore and environmental protection, health care reform and the medical system, criticism of Clinton (from Rush Limbaugh, Perot and conservative churches), and foreign policy (Russia, South Africa, China, and international trade.)

1034 Roberts, Steven V. "State of the Union." <u>U.S. News & World Report</u>, December 28, 1992-January 4, 1993, 34-37. Photo. Clinton's most difficult challenge in his first year would be "managing the conflicting demands of change and continuity."

1035 Walsh, Kenneth T. and Matthew Cooper. "Clinton: Doing It All: He May Overestimate His Ability to Dominate His Administration." <u>U.S. News & World Report</u>, December 28, 1992-January 4, 1993, 18-20. Photo. Clinton believed he could stimulate the economy, cut the deficit, end Washington's gridlock, and restore national self-confidence with the political techniques he had used in Arkansas. Would Clinton's tendency to reach consensus and his attention to detail ultimately be to his detriment?

1036   Zuckerman, Mortimer B. "Bill Clinton, Professor-Elect." (Editorial). U.S. News & World Report, December 28, 1992-January 4, 1993, 116. Clinton needed to reduce the budget deficit to make the U.S. economically competitive again in the world by exercising leadership.

1037   Denitch, Bogdan. "A Foreign Policy for Radical Democrats." Social Policy 23, 2(Fall-Winter 1992): 23-27.   Clinton foreign policy would resemble Bush's.

1038   "Are You Tired of Politics?" (Editorial). Accent on Living 37, 3(Winter 1992): 54-55. Photo. Presents Clinton's positions on issues concerning the physically challenged (health care and insurance coverage).   Clinton also discussed disabled children as well as beneficial legislation (such as the Family and Medical Leave Act, the National Service Trust Fund, and the Motor Voter Act) to this community.

1039   Frampton, George T., Jr. "Does A New Age Now Begin?" Wilderness 56, 199(Winter 1992): 2-5. Frampton listed the ten most significant environmental issues and opportunities facing the Clinton administration accompanied by recommendations to deal with them within the first 100 days.

1040   Wertheimer, Fred. "From Campaign Pledges to Political Action." Common Cause Magazine 18, 4(Winter 1992): 30.   Call for Clinton and Congress to make campaign finance reform a top national priority.

1041   Garten, Jeffrey E. "The 100-Day Economic Agenda." Foreign Affairs 72, 5(Winter 1992/93): 16-31.   An extensive analysis of what Clinton should do in his first 100 days regarding the U.S. economy within a global context.   It was important that Clinton identify as his top foreign policy priority the improvement of the U.S. economy.   Garten identified Clinton's immediate economic goals--reduce the budget deficit, reassure financial markets, coordinate efforts with Japan and Germany concerning an international growth package which includes economic stimulus, promotion of trade (including NAFTA), and monetary stabilization.

1042 Ashley, Liza (as told to Carolyn Huber). <u>Thirty Years at the Mansion: Recipes and Recollections</u>. 2nd ed. Little Rock: August House, 1993. Photos.

1043 Ashley, Liza (as told to Carolyn Huber). <u>Thirty Years at the Mansion: Recipes and Recollections</u>. Little Rock: August House, 1985. Photos.

Liza Ashley, long-time food production manager at the governor's mansion in Little Rock, writes about her recollections on serving many Arkansas governors, including Bill Clinton. This is an updated edition of the original published in 1985. An outstanding feature of the book is its color and black and white photos, including several of the Clintons.

1044 Barton, Mary Ann and Paul C. Barton, comps. and eds. <u>Campaign: A Cartoon History of Bill Clinton's Race for the White House</u>. Fayetteville: University of Arkansas Press, 1993. Illus. Compilation of political cartoons from many of the country's newspapers and magazines with accompanying captions on Clinton's presidential campaign from fall 1991 to Clinton's victory.

1045 Bentley, P.F. <u>Clinton, Portrait of Victory</u>. New York: Warner Books, 1993. Photos. Compilation of black and white photos of the Clinton campaign. Includes a prologue by Roger Rosenblatt and an epilogue by Michael Kramer. Contains over 125 photos with accompanying narrative captions.

1046 Dumas, Ernest, comp. and ed. <u>The Clintons of Arkansas: An Introduction by Those Who Know Them Best</u>. Fayetteville: University of Arkansas Press, 1993. Photos. Published in early 1993. Contains reminiscences about Bill and Hillary Clinton written specifically for this edited volume plus one reprint from Clinton critic Paul Greenberg. Many of the chapters cover Clinton's political career in Arkansas. Contributors included Diane Blair, political science professor at the University of Arkansas and author of <u>Arkansas Politics and Government</u>; Ernest Dumas, the editor of this volume and columnist for the <u>Arkansas Times</u>; George Fisher, former chief editorial cartoonist for the <u>Arkansas Gazette</u> from 1976 to 1991; Mike Gauldin, a former editorial cartoonist and Clinton's press secretary between 1987 and 1992; and Rudy Moore, attorney and municipal judge, who was campaign manager for Clinton's first gubernatorial campaign and later chief of staff in Clinton's first administration.

1047 Germond, Jack W. and Jules Witcover. <u>Mad as</u>
<u>Hell: Revolt at the Ballot Box, 1992</u>. New York:
Warner Books, 1993. Journalistic account of the 1992
presidential election. Includes extensive coverage
of the Clinton campaign on such topics as the bus
trips, campaign strategy, the "character and trust
issue," the debates, the draft/Vietnam issue,
relations with Jesse Jackson, the New Hampshire and
New York primaries, the Tsongas challenge, and
Hillary Clinton. Contains good index but no notes.

1048 Pomper, Gerald M. [et al.]. <u>The Election of</u>
<u>1992: Reports and Interpretations</u>. Chatham, New
Jersey: Chatham House Publishers, 1993. Contains
seven essays on the 1992 election. The most
extensive coverage on Clinton was for the primaries.

1049 Rosenthiel, Tom. <u>Strange Bedfellows: How</u>
<u>Television and the Presidential Candidates Changed</u>
<u>American Politics, 1992</u>. New York: Hyperion, 1993.
Photos. Rosenthiel chronicled ABC's coverage of the
1992 campaign. Aspects of the Clinton campaign
covered include the draft, environmental policy, fall
campaign, and the Flowers incident. Includes a brief
bibliography and an adequate index, but lacks notes.

1050 Barkan, Joanne. "Clinton and the Left."
("Comments and Opinions") <u>Dissent</u> 40, 1(Winter 1993):
5-8. Reservations about Clinton from a leftist
perspective due to his views on capitalism,
government, campaign finance reform, and the economy.

1051 Davis, Derek. "Rebuilding the Wall: Thoughts on
Religion and the Supreme Court Under the Clinton
Administration." <u>Journal of Church and State</u> 35,
1(Winter 1993): 7-17. Includes Clinton's views on
church-state issues. He opposed state-supported
programs of religious teaching in public education
and favored school choice for public schools.
Clinton supported the separation of church and state.

1052 "Don't Cross These Lines: How Conservatives
Will Mobilize Against Clinton." <u>Policy Review</u>
63(Winter 1993): 34-49. Symposium on a planned
conservative Republican response to the Clinton
administration, including the views of Representative
Dick Armey of Texas, Judge Robert H. Bork,
Representative Henry J. Hyde of Illinois, and former
Representative Vin Weber of Minnesota.

1053 Feulner, Edwin J., Jr. "Reading His Lips: How
to Tell If Clinton Really Is a New Democrat." <u>Policy</u>

Review 63(Winter 1993): 4-8. Photo. Identifies five challenges which would test Clinton's commitment to change as a "New Democrat"--the budget deficit and government spending, empowerment of poor and middle income families, tax relief and not tax increases, reduce federal regulation, and health care reform.

1054 Howe, Irving. "A Second Opinion." ("Comments and Opinions"). Dissent 40, 1(Winter 1993): 7-8. In a rejoinder to Barkan (see entry 1050), Howe favored Clinton, but reserved the right to be critical of him, from a leftist perspective, when necessary.

1055 Mann, Thomas E. "From Campaigning to Governing." Brookings Review 11, 1(Winter 1993): 4-5. Illus. On the significance of the transition period.

1056 Bentley, P.F. "Private Time: This is What Running For President Looks Like From the Inside Out." Washingtonian 28, 4(January 1993): 80-85. Photos. Selection of photographs reprinted from Bentley's book Clinton: Portrait of Victory.

1057 Bresler, Robert J. "Some Worthwhile Advice for the New President." ("The State of the Nation" column). USA Today (Magazine) 121, 2572(January 1993): 37. Take painful economic measures early, set and make priorities clear, provide leadership, capture the political center, and exercise military power wisely to attain political goals.

1058 Cembalest, Robin. "Clinton and the Arts: 'He Never Stops Learning.'" ARTnews 92, 1(January 1993): 122-125. Photos. Clinton's intellectual curiosity explained his interest in the arts. He supported art education and opposed censorship.

1059 "Clinton: The World Watches as Foreign Policy Takes a Back Seat." (Cover story). World Press Review 40, 1(January 1993): 9-15. Illus. International press speculation on Clinton foreign policy.

1060 "An Early Reading of the Clinton/Gore Administration." ABA Banking Journal 85, 1(January 1993): 12, 14, 16. Clinton's performance as president vis-à-vis the banking industry cannot necessarily be gauged based on his Arkansas record, though its banking community generally supports him.

1061 Howell, Llewellyn D. "Bill Clinton and the New American Foreign Policy." ("The World Watcher" column). USA Today (Magazine) 121, 2572(January

1993): 45.   Somalia, Bosnia, China, the Middle East,
and NAFTA will be key foreign concerns for Clinton.

1062   Kidd, Philip E. "Construction Finance: Interest
Rates in Clinton's Administration." <u>Architectural
Record</u> 181, 1(January 1993): 35.   Government spending
was unlikely to raise interest rates in short-term.

1063   McCoy, Frank. "New Prescriptions for an Ailing
Economy." <u>Black Enterprise</u> 23, 6(January 1993):
61-62, 64, 66, 68-69.   Includes assessment of Afro-
American prospects under a Clinton administration in
the areas of job growth, urban policy, education,
enterprise zones, and welfare reform.

1064   Matusow, Barbara. "True Grit." <u>Washingtonian</u>
28, 4(January 1993): 87-91, 163. Photos.   Working
women related to Hillary Clinton.   Provides
considerable background on Mrs. Clinton and her
career.   She will serve as a role model and boost the
women's movement through her example.

1065   "Race For the White House." <u>Life</u> 16, 1(January
1993): 9-11, 54-55. Photos.   Photo highlights of the
campaign, which ranged from its nadir in January to a
photograph of a triumphant Clinton on election night.

1066   Rains, Patrick. "Snuffing Out Incineration."
<u>American City & County</u> 108, 1(January 1993): 38-40,
42.   Speculation about the position of the new
administration on incineration and landfills.

1067   Slater, Robert Bruce. "Changing Times."
(Editorial). <u>Bankers Monthly</u> 110, 1(January 1993): 4.
Banking reform would not be on Clinton policy agenda.

1068   Strauss, Bill and Neil Howe. "Our Turn."
<u>Washingtonian</u> 28, 4(January 1993): 74-75. Illus.   The
1992 election resulted in a new generational shift,
whose political implications are considered.

1069   "To: The President-Elect, Re: Your
Infrastructure Plan." <u>Governing</u> 6, 4(January 1993):
45-48, 50-56.   Advice on infrastructure as a good
economic investment versus "pork-barrel spending."

1070   "Watch Out: Memo From Bush's People to
Clinton's People: How to Survive in Washington."
("What I've Learned"). <u>Washingtonian</u> 28, 4(January
1993): 31-35.   Advice for Clinton from former Bush
cabinet members Nicholas Brady and Lynn Martin.

1071 Carlson, Margaret. "The Dynamic Duo: How the Clinton's Turned Their Marriage into a Political Powerhouse." Time, January 4, 1993, 38-41. Photos. Provides background information on the complementary nature of the relationship between the Clintons.

1072 Kramer, Michael. "Moving In." Time, January 4, 1993, 28-30, 33. Photos. Analysis of a December 7, 1992 meeting between Clinton and his economic advisers held at Blair House, which offered insights into his governing style and leadership skills.

1073 Morrow, Lance. "The Torch Is Passed." Time, January 4, 1993, 20-25. Photos. Good reprise of the 1992 presidential campaign. This lead story constituted part of the special section devoted to Clinton as Time's "Man of the Year" cover story.

1074 Muller, Henry and John F. Stacks. "'First, We Have to Roll Up Our Sleeves.'" (Interview). Time, January 4, 1993, 34-37. Photos. Clinton explained how he would make difficult decisions (like the deficit and short and long-term economic policy). He and Hillary discussed their political partnership.

1075 Salholz, Eloise. "Something for Everybody: Clinton's Cabinet is an Exercise in Diversity." Newsweek, January 4, 1993, 19. Photo. Positive assessment of Clinton cabinet appointments.

1076 Samuelson, Robert J. "The Puzzle of Clintonomics." Newsweek, January 4, 1993, 57. Clinton's focus should be on budget deficits, health care, and poverty.

1077 Cockburn, Alexander. "Beat the Devil: Premature"; "By Any Means Necessary." Nation, January 4/11, 1993, 6-7. Criticism of the selection of Lloyd Bentsen as Secretary of the Treasury and Clinton's support for the Cuban Democracy Act.

1078 Kinsley, Michael. "The Prune Book." ("TRB From Washington" column). New Republic, January 4&11, 1993, 6. Kinsley discussed the federal government's United States Government: Policy and Supporting Positions, known as the "Plum Book," which is published every four years following presidential elections and lists all available jobs to be filled by a new president at his discretion.

1079 "Little New in Little Rock." (Editorial). Nation, January 4/11, 1993, 1. Little Rock economic conference turned out to be "conventional" and broke little or no new ground. Also criticized a "'managed competition'" solution to health care.

1080 "Mandate for Change?" (Editorial). New Republic, January 4&11, 1993, 7. While Clinton did well at the Little Rock economic conference, the appointments of Warren Christopher, Donna Shalala, Laura Tyson, and Ron Brown were disappointing.

1081 Nagourney, Adam. "Homophiliac: Clinton and Gays." New Republic, January 4&11, 1993, 16-17. Clinton assumed a cautious approach to gay issues (such as homosexuals in the military and not making AIDS a more central issue).

1082 Greider, William. "New Deal Redux or Great Society II?" Rolling Stone, January 7, 1993, 27-28. Clinton wanted reform, but it remained to be seen whether his administration would resemble Johnson's Great Society or Roosevelt's New Deal. Clinton's plans were more similar to the rather cautious initial measures Roosevelt had tried (the first New Deal) rather than the more far-reaching New Deal.

1083 Anderson, Christopher. "Clinton Picks His Science Adviser: Science Policy." Science 259, 5092(January 8, 1993): 171. On the appointment of John "Jack" Gibbons as White House science adviser.

1084 Baer, Donald. "Diversity, and Perhaps a Lot More." U.S. News & World Report, January 11, 1993, 4-5. Photo. Assessment of selection process for Clinton cabinet appointments. While very capable individuals were selected, time expediency may have led to promotion of "diversity for diversity's sake."

1085 Brockway, George P. "Clinton's Supply Side: The Dismal Science." New Leader 76, 1(January 11, 1993): 13-14. Little Rock economic conference reflected Reagan policy more than Clinton's call for change.

1086 Davidson, Paul. "It's Still the Economy, Mr. President." New Leader 76, 1(January 11, 1993): 9-12. Illus. Davidson maintained that Clinton should stay with his plans for short-term economic stimulus and long-term deficit reduction. If Clinton were to sway from this course, then the economy would stall.

1087 Egan, Jack. "Now, the Stock Picker's Market." ("On Money" column). U.S. News & World Report, January 11, 1993, 66. Stock market prospects and the economic outlook under a Clinton administration.

1088   Glastris, Paul. "Environmental Fights in the Family." ("On Politics" column). U.S. News & World Report, January 11, 1993, 27. Photo. Potential conflicts exist between moderate Democratic environmentalists and activists, who were united against a Republican administration. But their differences could surface into open conflict with a new Democratic administration.

1089   "Global Gunslinger, Global Cops." ("Comment"). New Yorker, January 11, 1993, 4-5. Clinton has an opportunity to fashion a "new foreign policy for the post-Cold War world."

1090   McAllister, J.F.O. "'An Instinct for The Important': Sandy Berger Brings Carter-Era Ideals Tempered by Pragmatism to the New Foreign Policy Team." Time, January 11, 1993, 20. Profile of Sandy Berger, appointed Deputy National Security Adviser.

1091   Miller, Mark. "Hollywood Meets Woodstock." Newsweek, January 11, 1993, 23. Report on preinaugural preparations.

1092   Walsh, Kenneth T. "The Clinton Doctrines: With Surprising Speed, He Has Set Some Foreign Policy Goals To Guide His Team From the Start." U.S. News & World Report, January 11, 1993, 16-18. Photo. On foreign policy issues facing Clinton--Bosnia, Iraq, Somalia, and Russia.

1093   Baumann, Paul. "Clinton Sounds Good: But Now a Word From Scrooge." ("An Editor's Notebook"). Commonweal, January 15, 1993, 4-5. Critique of an article by William A. Galston (see entry 976) in which he was enthusiastic over Clinton's use of communitarian notions and rhetoric such as the "New Covenant." Includes definition of communitarianism.

1094   "Bill Clinton Presidential Scrapbook: A Pictorial History of the Life and Career of Hot Springs' Favorite Son." (Commemorative Issue). Sentinel-Record, January 17, 1993. Special 32-page issue in honor of Clinton's inauguration, a considerable portion of which was devoted to photos (some color) and informative accompanying captions on Clinton's Arkansas political career.

1095   Kelly, Michael and Maureen Dowd. "The Company He Keeps: Six Relationships That Could Make Or Break

the New President." (Cover story). <u>New York Times</u>
<u>Magazine</u>, January 17, 1993, 20-27, 34, 36, 48, 50-52.
Photos. Identifies the six relationships which would
help shape the Clinton administration, including
those Clinton has with Al Gore and Hillary Clinton.

1096 Peters, Charles. "The Second Coming of
Neo-Liberalism: The Father of the Movement Tells the
New President How To Make It Work, This Time." <u>New</u>
<u>York Time Magazine</u>, January 17, 1993, 30-33. Illus.
The best solution to an issue was not necessarily to
be found in the political middle.

1097 Baumohl, Bernard and Dick Thompson. "Paging Dr.
Clinton: Health Care." <u>Time</u>, January 18, 1993, 24-26.
Presents the complexity of health care problems (like
soaring costs) and dilemmas facing Clinton (such as
expanding health coverage while controlling costs).

1098 Carlson, Margaret. "Just a Couple of Hicks With
40 Million Viewers." ("Clinton's People"). <u>Newsweek</u>,
January 18, 1993, 27. Profiles of T.V. producers
Linda Bloodworth-Thomason and Harry Thomason, who
chaired the Inauguration Committee.

1099 Cooper, Matthew. "Clinton's 'Brady Kids': How a
Staff Full of Thirtysomethings Will Run His
Government." <u>U.S. News & World Report</u>, January 18,
1993, 32-33. New White House staff included media
specialists George Stephanopoulos and Dee Dee Myers,
domestic policy adviser Bruce Reed, attorney Thomas
Donilon, future head of the Democratic National
Committee David Wilhelm, researcher Ricki Seidman,
and foreign policy specialist Nancy Soderberg.
Clinton had given this group wide leeway. But, once
in office, Clinton was expected to exert more control
since he lost his 1980 reelection bid for governor
partly due to the inexperience of a young staff.

1100 Corn, David and Mark Perry. "Who's In..."
(Editorial). <u>Nation</u>, January 18, 1993, 39-40.
Critical of R. James Woolsey Jr. for CIA director.

1101 Dentzer, Susan. "Clinton's Taxing Health
Reform." ("On the Economy" column). <u>U.S. News & World</u>
<u>Report</u>, January 18, 1993, 66. Clinton's options in
financing health care reform.

1102 Gergen, David. "He Keeps Going and Going and
Going." ("On Politics" column). <u>U.S. News & World</u>
<u>Report</u>, January 18, 1993, 38. Photo. Expressed
concern over Clinton's "all-consuming" and "personal

style," which slowed the subcabinet and White House staffing process.

1103 Greenfield, Meg. "First Ladyhood." _Newsweek_, January 18, 1993, 66. Speculates on the role of Hillary Clinton as First Lady.

1104 Gross, Michael. "Queen Mother of the Clinton Court: How Pamela Harriman Became Washington's Power Broker of the Nineties." _New York_ 26, 5(January 18, 1993): 24-34. Photo. Extensive profile of influential Democratic fund raiser and Clinton ally, Pamela Harriman.

1105 Hage, David and Sara Collins. "Driving Down the Deficit." _U.S News & World Report_, January 18, 1993, 58-60. Due to the growing deficit problem, Clinton reassessed his position against higher gas taxes.

1106 Herbert, Wray. "Parent's Choice; President's Dilemma." _U.S. News & World Report_, January 18, 1993, 10-11. Photo. Defends Clinton's decision to send his daughter Chelsea to Sidwell Friends (private school).

1107 Kantrowitz, Barbara. "The Right Choice for Chelsea." _Newsweek_, January 18, 1993, 53. Photo. The Clintons enrolled Chelsea in Sidwell Friends, thus making a family rather than a political choice.

1108 Klein, Joe. "A Poor Excuse for Poverty Solutions." _Newsweek_, January 18, 1993, 27. Clinton administration policy on poverty could lead to a debate within the administration between "individual responsibility versus group entitlement." Clinton was seeking a synthesis between these two positions. Also criticism of Clinton cabinet selection process.

1109 Kramer, Michael. "Moving Toward Gridlock II." ("The Political Interest" column). _Time_, January 18, 1993, 29. Speculation on the difficulties Clinton would face in reducing the deficit and coordinating such efforts with Congress.

1110 Miller, Mark. "And You Thought the Campaign Was Long: Clinton Plans To Keep On Running." _Newsweek_, January 18, 1993, 25. Photo. The Clinton camp planned "to create a 'perpetual campaign' to win Clinton's program and...reelection in 1996." Such a campaign would not succeed, however, if the economy is still stagnant in 1996.

1111 Painton, Priscilla. "The Burden Of Being Bill's

Brother." <u>Time</u>, January 18, 1993, 52-54. Photo.
Profile of Bill Clinton's brother, Roger.

1112 "The Pardons." ("Comment"). <u>New Yorker</u>, January
18, 1993, 4-5. In the context of Bush granting
pardons to former members of his administration,
Clinton should work for more congressional
involvement in the foreign policy process.

1113 Post, Tom. "Bosnia Waits for Clinton."
<u>Newsweek</u>, January 18, 1993, 32. Clinton had
dwindling options regarding Bosnia.

1114 "The Quiet Man." <u>New Republic</u>, January 18,
1993, 7. Criticizes selection of Warren Christopher
as Secretary of State as well as the other nominees
on the foreign policy team--Anthony Lake and Samuel
Berger for the National Security Council and Madeline
Albright as U.S. ambassador to the United Nations,
describing them as too uniform in thought.

1115 Roberts, Steven V. and Gloria Borger. "Ready To
Rule On Day One?" <u>U.S News & World Report</u>, January
18, 1993, 28-30. On the slowness of the appointment
process. Like the campaign, the transition was run
by three or four individuals. This would cause
problems if Clinton governed that way. Also, like
Jimmy Carter, Clinton tended to micromanage decisions
and did not sufficiently delegate responsibility.
Accompanied by smaller article entitled "Brown's
Haitian Connection" by Stephen J. Hedges (p. 30)
about Commerce Secretary-designate Ron Brown.

1116 Shapiro, Bruce. "...And Who's Out." <u>Nation</u>,
January 18, 1993, 40-41. Attacks the "redbaiting" of
Johnnetta Cole, (who chaired the Clinton transition
committee on education, the humanities and labor),
but no longer was under consideration for any high
level administration appointment due to her sympathy
for the Palestinians.

1117 Taylor, John. "Plus Ca Change: Clinton's
Insiders." ("The National Interest" column). <u>New York</u>
26, 5(January 18, 1993): 12-13. Discusses Ron Brown
(nominated by Clinton as Commerce Secretary) and his
lobbying background. Also, criticized Clinton for
having lawyers predominate his cabinet.

1118 Wall, James M. "On Being 'Pro-Israel':
Diversity in the Jewish Lobby." <u>Christian Century</u>
110, 2(January 20, 1993): 43-44. On Clinton and the
"pro-Israel" lobby.

1119 "The A.G., G.E., Etc.--And Us." (Editorial).
Nation, January 25, 1993, 73. Raised questions about
the Zoë Baird nomination for attorney general
concerning whether she could lead a nonpoliticized
Justice Department. (Written before difficulties
surfaced over her nomination due to unpaid social
security taxes for child care).

1120 Alter, Jonathan. "Shooting the Moon: How Will
Clinton Measure Up To His Predecessors in the White
House?" Newsweek, January 25, 1993, 38-39.

1121 Clift, Eleanor. "Gore: Playing Second Fiddle."
Newsweek, January 25, 1993, 35. Photo.

1122 Fineman, Howard. "The New Age President;
Clinton's Style: Part Sensitive Male, Part Southern
Good Ole Boy." Newsweek, January 25, 1993, 22-23.
Photo.

1123 Klein, Joe. "And They're Off..." (Cover story).
Newsweek, January 25, 1993, 16-20. Photos.

1124 Matthews, Tom. "Warm-Up Lessons." Newsweek,
January 25, 1993, 30-31, 34. Photos.

1125 "The Power Players." Newsweek, January 25,
1993, 24-29. Photo collage.

1126 "A Talk With Clinton: The President Discusses
Education, the Economy and Foreign Policy." Newsweek,
January 25, 1993, 36-37. Photos.

Published just before the inauguration, this issue's
cover proclaims "Show Time" for the Clinton
presidency. There were great expectations of him.
Whether Clinton could fulfill his pledges to promote
change as well as how his governing/leadership style
would work in Washington was yet to be determined.

1127 Barnes, Fred. "Neoconned: Clinton and the
Hawks." New Republic, January 25, 1993, 14, 16.

1128 Steel, Ronald. "Mission Control: Beyond
Intervention." New Republic, January 25, 1993, 16-19,
Illus.

1129 Wright, Robert. "Bold Old Views: The Case For
Collective Security." New Republic, January 25, 1993,
19-23.

Appointment process for foreign policy team and

foreign policy issues facing the new administration.

1130 Barone, Michael. "The Theater of Inaugurals: Successful Presidents Have Written Their Own History on the First Day." U.S. News & World Report, January 25, 1993, 51-52.

1131 Borger, Gloria. "To Democrats: Put Up Or Shut Up." ("On Politics" column). U.S. News & World Report, January 25, 1993, 68.

1132 Budiansky, Stephen. "Rules of Engagement: Trying to Set a Doctrine for the Use of Force in the Post-Cold-War World Has Stymied the Military, Clinton's Advisers and Clinton Himself." U.S. News & World Report, January 25, 1993, 53-56.

1133 Dentzer, Susan. "Bridging the Costly Skills Gap: Job Training." U.S. News & World Report, January 25, 1993, 61-63. Photo.

1134 Duffy, Brian. "Saddam Hussein." U.S. News & World Report, January 25, 1993, 58.

1135 Friedman, Dorian. "A Reputation That Outruns Reality: Preschool." U.S. News & World Report, January 25, 1993, 63-64.

1136 Gest, Ted. "The Selling of an Alluring Concept: Crime Protection." U.S. News & World Report, January 25, 1993, 67. Photo.

1137 Glastris, Paul. "Inner-City Lending: Hits and Misses: Community Development." U.S. News & World Report, January 25, 1993, 65.

1138 Hage, David and Robert F. Black. "Pain Today, Gain Tomorrow: A New Analysis Shows How Deficit Cuts Could Aid Clinton and the Economy." U.S. News & World Report, January 25, 1993, 36, 38.

1139 Roberts, Steven V. "High Hopes: Bill Clinton Takes Office Amid a Surge of Inaugural Optimism and Popular Good Will." U.S. News & World Report, January 25, 1993, 30-34. Photos.

1140 Shapiro, Joseph P. "Do-Gooding: When It Gets Complicated: Community Work." U.S. News & World Report, January 25, 1993, 66-67.

1141 "Striking a 'Fine Balance': Clinton Wants To Pace Himself and Frets He'll Do Something To Dampen

the 'Terrific Spirit.'" <u>U.S. News & World Report</u>,
January 25, 1993, 42-43. Photo.

1142   Walsh, Kenneth T. "Now, The First Chief
Advocate: How Hillary Clinton Plans a Bold Recasting
of the Job Description For a President's Spouse."
<u>U.S. News & World Report</u>, January 25, 1993, 46-47,
50. Photos.

1143   "Welcome to the World: The Game With Three
Rules and Four Traps." <u>U.S. News & World Report</u>,
January 25, 1993, 56-57.

1144   Whitman, David. "Clinton's Grand Plans." <u>U.S.
News & World Report</u>, January 25, 1993, 60-61. Photo.

Special inaugural issue on the "Clinton Era,"
published prior to the inauguration.

1145   Blumenthal, Sidney. "Waiting for the Call."
("Letter From Washington"). <u>New Yorker</u>, January 25,
1993, 48-53. Illus. Overview of the transition
period, including assessment of appointments.

1146   Church, George J. "His Seven Most Urgent
Decisions: The New President Will Run Into Policy
Quagmires in which Almost Every Choice is a Risky
One, But He Will Have to Act Fast While He Still Has
Political Momentum." (Economy, Health Care, Bosnia,
Somalia, Military Spending, Trade, Executive Orders).
<u>Time</u>, January 25, 1993, 30-31, 33. Photo.

1147   Duffy, Michael. "Ready or Not: As Clinton Takes
Office, A Slow Start and a String of Broken Promises
Signal a Rough Ride Ahead." (Cover story). <u>Time</u>,
January 25, 1993, 26-29. Photo.

1148   Kramer, Michael. "Bash Him for the Right
Reasons." ("The Political Interest" column). <u>Time</u>,
January 25, 1993, 36. Photo.

1149   Painton, Priscilla. "Guess Who's Paying for
Dinner: In Contrast With His Folksy Campaign,
Clinton's Inauguration Will Be a Multimillion-Dollar
Corporate Sponsorfest." <u>Time</u>, January 25, 1993, 37,
40.

1150   Tobias, Andrew. "What You Can Do For Your
President." ("Money Angles" column). <u>Time</u>, January
25, 1993, 43. Illus.

Published on eve of inauguration, cover proclaims:

"Stand and Deliver: With Tough Choices at Home and a Dangerous World Abroad, Bill Clinton Takes Charge." Time's coverage of Clinton as he assumed office.

1151 Corn, David. "Beltway Bandits: From White House to Courthouse? Son of Senatorial Privilege." Nation, January 25, 1993, 80. Notes relationship between Treasury Secretary Lloyd Bentsen and White Chief of Staff Mack McLarty and the Resolution Trust Corporation and the savings and loan situation.

1152 Corn, David. "Neoconchik." (Editorial). Nation, January 25, 1993, 76. Warns against the possible nomination of Joshua Muravchik as Assistant Secretary of State for Human Rights and Humanitarian Affairs and that of fellow neoconservative Richard Schifter.

1153 "The Crying Game." (Editorial). New Republic, January 25, 1993, 7. A key to Clinton's success would be deficit reduction, involving difficult decisions and choices (such as a gas tax).

1154 Elliott, Osborn. "Decade of the Cities." ("My Turn" column). Newsweek, January 25, 1993, 12. Clinton should rebuild urban America.

1155 Kinsley, Michael. "Fortysomething." ("TRB From Washington" column). New Republic, January 25, 1993, 6. Discusses the generational change in the White House and its foreign policy implications--a younger generation president engaging in military action overseas by committing American troops.

1156 Berle, Peter A.A. "A New Era for America's Public Lands." ("The Audubon View" column). Audubon 95, 1(January/February 1993): 6. Berle called for the Clinton administration to provide "good stewardship" of the environment.

1157 "Clinton's Chance." Mother Jones 18, 1(January/February 1993): 43-61, 71, 73, 75-76. Photos. Special inaugural issue on such topics as Hillary Clinton, Al Gore, and policy toward China.

1158 Corcoran, Katherine. "Pilloried Clinton: Were the Women Who Covered Hillary Clinton During the Campaign Guilty of Sexism?" Washington Journalism Review 15, 1(January/February 1993): 27-29. Illus. Good review of press coverage of Hillary Clinton during the 1992 presidential campaign.

1159 Doerr, Edd. "Good News, So Far." ("Church and

State"). <u>Humanist</u> 53, 1 (January/February 1993):
38-39. Clinton would have a positive impact on
abortion, religious freedom, the environment, and
demography issues. Doerr, however, cautioned that it
was necessary to be vigilant of the religious right.

1160   Isaacs, John. "The Paper Chase." <u>Bulletin of
the Atomic Scientists</u> 49, 1(January/February 1993):
3-4. The tone of the transition period was set by
job seekers, various groups and interests,
speculation on presidential appointments to the new
administration, and the influx of new administration
officials and members of Congress.

1161   Ivins, Molly. "Bubba's Boy?" <u>Mother Jones</u> 18,
1(January/February 1993): 11-12. Illus. If Clinton
would be true to those who voted for him, he could be
a populist president by overhauling the banking
system, closing 1980 tax reform loopholes, and
supporting genuine campaign finance reform.

1162   Katz, Jeffrey L. "Tilt?" <u>Washington Journalism
Review</u> 15, 1(January/February 1993): 23-27. Illus.
Reviews media campaign coverage. Accompanied by
opinions from the media, including those of Larry
King, Howard Kurtz, and Cokie Roberts.

1163   Lockwood, Dunbar. "On Clinton's Calendar: Arms
Control." <u>Bulletin of the Atomic Scientists</u> 49,
1(January/February 1993): 6-8. Photo. Overview of
Clinton's arms control policies.

1164   Rosendahl, Bruce R. "Dear Mr. President." <u>Sea
Frontiers</u> 39, 1(January/February 1993): 6-7. Made an
analogy between the deficit and jobs and the
environment and the economy--both pairs come at the
expense of the other. Also offered advice to Clinton
on environmental matters.

1165   Saal, Matthew A. "Road Warriors." <u>Washington
Monthly</u> 25, 1-2(January/February 1993): 9-13.
Excellent analysis of the "turning points" in the
Clinton campaign: participating in town meetings,
Clinton's claim of being the "Comeback Kid" in New
Hampshire, his appearance on the Don Imus Show
leading up to the New York primary and the Arsenio
Hall saxophone appearance which helped Clinton make a
comeback in the polls in June, and, the bus tours.

1166   Hartley, Anthony. "The Clinton Approach:
Idealism With Prudence." <u>World Today</u> 49, 2(February
1993): 27-29. Clinton was very cautious on foreign

policy, as reflected by his appointments to foreign policy positions.

1167   Tonelson, Alan. "Clinton's World." <u>Atlantic Monthly</u> 271, 2(February 1993): 71-74.   Domestic matters must be at the heart of U.S. foreign policy.

1168   Barnes, Fred. "The Undead: White House Watch." <u>New Republic</u>, February 1, 1993, 21-22. Photo.

1169   "Clinton and Milosevic." (Editorial). <u>New Republic</u>, February 1, 1993, 9.

1170   Heilbrunn, Jacob. "Clothed Ambition: Warren Christopher, Trimmer." <u>New Republic</u>, February 1, 1993, 24, 26, 28.

1171   Judis, John. "The Great Awakening: The Religious Roots of Clinton." <u>New Republic</u>, February 1, 1993, 41, 44, 46, 48.

1172   Kinsley, Michael. "Spare Change." ("TRB From Washington" column). <u>New Republic</u>, February 1, 1993, 8.

1173   Konigsberg, Eric. "Plum Crazy: Washington Scene." <u>New Republic</u>, February 1, 1993, 16, 18.

1174   Lewis, Michael. "Econoclast: Laura Tyson's Professional Honesty." <u>New Republic</u>, February 1, 1993, 18, 20-21.

1175   Rosen, Jeffrey. "Danny and Zoë: Ms. Baird and Mr. Quayle." <u>New Republic</u>, February 1, 1993, 28-30.

1176   Weisberg, Jacob. "Springtime for Lobbyists: Sorry, Ross, They're Not in the Smithsonian." <u>New Republic</u>, February 1, 1993, 33, 36, 38, 40, 41.

1177   Wieseltier, Leon. "Covenant and Burling." ("Washington Diarist" column). <u>New Republic</u>, February 1, 1993, 77.

1178   Woodward, C. Vann. "The Bubbas: The New Democrats and Race." <u>New Republic</u>, February 1, 1993, 30, 32-33.

<u>New Republic</u>'s "Special Inauguration Issue."

1179   "Baird Facts." (Editorial). <u>Nation</u>, February 1, 1993, 113.

1180 Danto, Arthur C. "Why Not Be the Arts President? Memo to Bill--I." Nation, February 1, 1993, 116-117.

1181 Foner, Eric. "Time for a Third Reconstruction: Memo to Bill--II." Nation, February 1, 1993, 117-118, 120.

1182 Gordon, Mary. "Government For the People: Memo to Bill--III." Nation, February 1, 1993, 120, 122.

1183 "Hello, World." (Editorial). Nation, February 1, 1993, 111-112.

1184 "Honor Thy Funder." (Editorial). Nation, February 1, 1993, 112-113.

1185 Leonard, John. "Listen to the Dispossessed: Memo to Bill--IV." Nation, February 1, 1993, 124.

1186 Lifton, Robert Jay. "Beware the 'Realists': Memo to Bill--V." Nation, February 1, 1993, 126-127.

1187 "Wrong Medicine." (Editorial). Nation, February 1, 1993, 113, 128.

Nation's "Inauguration Issue."

1188 Grieder, William. "Clinton Goes Right Toward Consensus." Rolling Stone, February 4, 1993, 29-30. Little Rock economic conference and key appointments to administration economic posts indicated Clinton's economic policies were heading toward the right.

1189 "Carville, James." Current Biography 543(March 1993): 15-18. Good integration of popular sources on James Carville, a major Clinton political consultant.

1190 McKnight, Gail. "Tipper Gore: The Vice President's First Lady." Saturday Evening Post 265, 3(March/April 1993): 39-41, 77. Photos. On Tipper Gore, including background and the 1992 campaign.

1191 Winkler, Karen J. "Communitarians Move Their Ideas Outside Academic Arena." Chronicle of Higher Education 39, 33(April 21, 1993): A6-A7, A13. Includes discussion of similarities in public policy between Clinton and communitarianism--family leave, national service, and campaign reform. William A. Galston, a major theoretician of communitarianism, traced the influence of this movement on Clinton.

1192   Ladd, Everett Carll. "The 1992 Vote for
President Clinton: Another Brittle Mandate?"
Political Science Quarterly 108, 1(Spring 1993):
1-28.   Included speculation on how Clinton might do
as president and reviewed Clinton's 1992 campaign.

1193   Polett, Zach. "What We Learned in Arkansas."
Social Policy 23, 3(Spring 1993): 13-25.   Polett,
national political director of ACORN (Association of
Community Organizations for Reform Now), offered
advice on Clinton's governing style and how community
organizations could best achieve their objectives
with him.   Article also provides some good background
information on Clinton's earlier political career as
attorney general and governor.   Clinton always had
been and continues to be a "progressive reformer."

1194   Mathis, Deborah. "Advice: Don't Forget '79."
USA Today, June 9, 1993, 11A.   Based on an interview
with Rudy Moore, who served as Clinton's first chief
of staff as governor.   Clinton and his staff
attempted to make too many changes too soon, which
led to Clinton's 1980 sobering defeat.   Afterward,
Clinton adopted a more realistic approach.   Moore saw
striking similarities between Clinton's first term as
governor and Clinton as president, including too long
an agenda.   In Clinton's first term as governor,
there was an ambitious array of proposals (economic
development, tax and prison reform, energy, and
education).   While Moore expressed concern over
Clinton's well-known desire for consensus, Clinton
possessed exceptional political skills to be a good
president.   Also discusses Mack McLarty.

1195   Watson, Jack H., Jr. "The Clinton White House."
Presidential Studies Quarterly 23, 3(Summer 1993):
429-435.   Assessed Clinton's leadership and
management style based on his tenure as governor,
dealing with issues like education, health care, tax
policy, prison reform, and economic development on
both the state and national levels.

Author Index

Subject Index

Numbers refer to entries. Numbers in bold refer to dates.

About the Compiler

ALLAN METZ is Assistant Professor/Reference Librarian at Drury College in Springfield, Missouri. His primary research interests include the Clinton presidency and Latin America. He has been published in a wide variety of journals and edited books.